THE 1980 OLYMPICS HANDBOOK

A GUIDE TO THE MOSCOW OLYMPICS AND A HISTORY OF THE GAMES

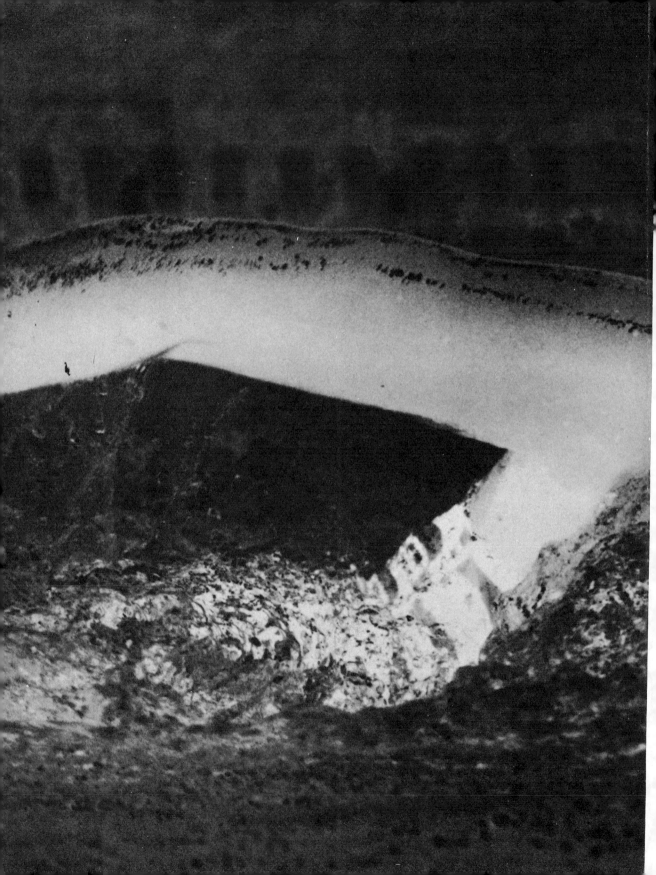

THE 1980 OLYMPICS HANDBOOK

GUIDE TO THE MOSCOW OLYMPICS AND A HISTORY OF THE GAMES

NORMAN GILLER

HOLT, RINEHART AND WINSTON
New York

Designed by Roy Williams

Published in the United States by Holt, Rinehart and
Winston, 383 Madison Avenue, New York, New York 10017.
Published simultaneously in Canada by Holt, Rinehart and
Winston of Canada, Limited.

Library of Congress Cataloging in Publication Data
Giller, Norman.
The 1980 Olympics handbook.
1. Olympic Games, Moscow, 1980. 2. Olympic games–History.
I. Title.
GV722 1980.G54   796.4`8   79-23124
ISBN Paperback: 0-03-056053-5
ISBN Hardbound: 0-03-056054-3

First edition

Printed in the United States of America
10 9 8 7 6 5 4 3 2 1

AUTHOR'S ACKNOWLEDGMENTS

In compiling this Olympic Handbook I have dipped
frequently into the waters of wisdom that have flowed in
earlier works and I hereby express due acknowledgment
and appreciation to the authors:

The Olympic Games (edited by Lord Killanin and John
Rodda, 1976); *The Olympic Games Book* (Harold
Abrahams, 1956); *The Dunlop Book of the Olympics*
(David Guiney, 1972); *Encyclopaedia of the Olympic Games*
(Erich Kamper, 1972); articles in *Track and Field News,
Athletics Weekly, The Gymnast* and *International Swimmer*;
my files of the late, lamented *World Sports* magazine, and
in particular articles by Neil Allen, then of *The Times*
and now of the London *Evening Standard*, and Alan
Hubbard now of *NOW!*; official *British Olympic
Association Reports* on past Games; files of the following
newspapers: *Daily Express* (in particular articles by
Sydney Hulls), *Daily Mail* (in particular articles by Terry
O'Connor), *The Sun* (in particular articles by Colin Hart),
London *Evening News, Sunday Times* (in particular articles
by Cliff Temple), *The New York Times, The Los Angeles
Herald Examiner* and the outstanding French sports
newspaper, *L'Equipe*.
    Most especially, I wish to place on record my
appreciation of all that I have learned over the years from
the statistical wizards, Norris McWhirter and his much
mourned brother, Ross. *The Guinness Book of Records* is
just one of their many productions that have helped make
people all over the world more knowledgeable and
enlightened.
    Finally, my thanks to Terry O'Connor, rugby and
athletics correspondent of the *Daily Mail*, who told me as
long ago as 1956 when I was boring him with Olympic facts
and figures: "Don't talk about it . . . write it." At the time,
I was Terry's teaboy. It has taken me 24 years to stop
talking and to get down to writing about the greatest sports
show on earth. I used to be equally slow making the tea!

I dedicate this book to the memory of Jim Coote, for 18
years the athletics correspondent of the *Daily Telegraph*,
whose death in an air crash in the summer of 1979 robbed
track and field sport of one of its most respected
commentators. He was President of the International
Athletics Writers' Commission and wrote excellent books,
along with John Goodbody, on the Olympics of 1972 and
1976.

Previous pages: Shirley Babashoff, Montreal, 1976.

CONTENTS

110 meters hurdles, Mexico, 1968.

MOSCOW 1980

A GUIDE TO WHOM AND WHAT TO WATCH ON TELEVISION

Moscow is all dressed up and ready to stage the 1980 Olympics on a scale in keeping with the standards of giganticism set at Munich and Montreal. For the past four years more than 100,000 Soviets have been employed directly in preparing Moscow for its largest invasion since Napoleon and his army were uninvited guests back in 1812.

A total of 99 Olympic construction projects have been completed to ensure proper facilities for the competitors and the 300,000 anticipated overseas visitors who will be converging on Moscow for the three-week span of the Games.

Some 12,000 competitors and coaches will live two to a room in the Olympic Village that occupies a 270-acre area of southwest Moscow. Eighteen apartment blocks, each 16 stories high, border three small parks that contain better training facilities than for any previous Olympiad. There are three gymnasiums, three swimming pools, a soccer field, volleyball and basketball courts and a full-scale track-and-field complex. Each apartment is strikingly designed with a kitchen, bathroom and two or three bedrooms all with extra-long beds. The food center has four 1000-seat restaurants plus a giant self-service cafeteria, and there is a well-equipped sports medicine clinic that will provide on-the-spot treatment for injuries. The Russians have remembered the mind as well as the muscle. They have built a modern cultural center that includes a 12,000-volume library, a concert hall, two movie theaters and a discotheque. Competitors will be treated to performances by the Bolshoi and Kirov ballet companies and by Russian choirs and folk dancers. Once the Olympics are over and the athletes have departed, the Village will become a housing project for 12,000 Russian citizens.

Unofficial estimates put the entire Moscow Olympic construction costs at around $400 million, less than half the totals for both Munich and Montreal. Labor overheads are much lower in Russia and thousands of Young Communist League volunteers and battalions from the Soviet army have been helping out with material and manpower. Every citizen in the Soviet Union has been made aware of the propaganda value of a successfully promoted Olympics and posters of Lenin and hammer-and-sickle flags will get greater promotion than Baron de Coubertin and the Olympic symbol.

TRACK AND FIELD
THE SPRINTS

As 1980 dawned, an Italian called *Pietro Mennea* and a young black American from Hollywood called *Evelyn Ashford* emerged as firm favorites for golden glory in the Moscow sprints.

Mennea, the idol of Rome, is no stranger to the Olympic stage. He took a bronze medal in the 200 meters in Munich in 1972 and was fourth in the 1976 final in Montreal. He has made significant improvement over the last four years as he proved in Mexico City in September 1979 when breaking Tommie Smith's 11-year-old world record in the 200 meters with a time of 19.72 sec. A week earlier he had set a new European best over 100 meters and Italian hopes are high for a 1980 Olympic double for Mennea.

But nothing is ever certain in the sprints where just a fraction of a second can separate first man from last. The United States, after two rare washouts in the Munich and Montreal sprint finals, is hoping to get back on the gold standard. Among its most consistent sprinters over the past four years have been *Houston McTear* and *James Sanford*, both of whom have shown they can produce peak power when it matters most. Sanford went to Europe in 1979 as part of his Olympic build up and impressed European track experts with his speed and style in winning the Golden Sprints title, although Mennea was conspicuous by his absence.

Left: Evelyn Ashford . . . with a golden smile that is likely to light up Moscow.

Allan Wells, the flying Scot who starts without the aid of blocks.

Alberto Juantorena (left) faces a powerful challenge in the 400 meters from versatile West German Harald Schmid.

Watch out for the rocket start of McTear if he makes it to Moscow. There would be nobody to touch him if the short sprint was over 60 meters. Also at the start watch out for *Allan Wells*, the Scottish sprinter who does not use blocks yet still managed to become the first European in six years to get the better of the menacing Mennea in the 1979 European Cup 200 meters final.

Wells himself has had to take second place several times to the long-legged Guyanan *James Gilkes*, who is formidable opposition over 100 meters but even more devastating over 200 meters when he has more time to get into his long stride. Poland has a challenger of considerable power in *Marian Woronin* but the man all of them have got to watch out for is Cuban flash *Silvio Leonard*, who delivered a warning to his rivals with an impressive sprint double in the 1979 Pan American Games in Puerto Rico.

East Germany looked to have the women's 100, 200 and 400 meters nicely sewed up until the startling emergence of Evelyn Ashford as a new world power.

Evelyn Ashford-Washington, married to a basketball player, is a mere 5ft 5in tall, weighs just 115lb and is a 23-year-old saleswoman-turned-student from Hollywood. She may have a small frame but she can generate stunning speed, as she demonstrated when winning the 100 and 200 meters in the 1979 Pan American Games. The world sat up and really took notice when she followed this double by beating East German world record

holders *Marlies Göhr* and *Marita Koch* in the 100 and 200 meters respectively in the World Cup in Montreal in August 1979.

Koch was considered unbeatable, as she has so far proved in the 400 meters, an event she is expected to win with ease in Moscow. Watch out for the farewell Olympic appearance of *Irena Szewinska*, the legendary Polish first lady of the track who hopes to be competing in her fifth Games. She won the 400 meters in Montreal in a world record time that has since been smashed out of sight by Marita Koch. It is unlikely that she can find the speed and stamina to beat the incredible East German but is such a superb competitor that she can never be written off until the tape is broken.

The men's 400 meters is not so easy to forecast. Cuban *Alberto "White Lightning" Juantorena*, magnificent winner of both the 400 and 800 meters in Montreal, has been struggling to reproduce his 1976 form following a succession of injuries. He will face powerful challenges in Moscow over 400 meters from West Germans *Franz-Peter Hofmeister* and *Harald Schmid*, and the United States will be strongly represented, with *Willie Smith* and *Tony Darden* both high in the world rankings leading up to the US Olympic trials.

Another American, *Stan Vinson*, got the taste of what it is like to win in Moscow when he was first through the tape in the Spartakiad 400 meters in the Lenin Stadium in August 1979. Watch out for *Kasheef Hassan* in the Olympic 400 meters. The man from Sudan, and Kenyans *James Atuti* and 18-year-old *Billy Konchella* will lead the powerful African challenge for the gold medal. Whoever wins in Moscow will need to be capable of running close to 44 sec. Juantereno could do it again if he regains his motivation of 1976, when he won in 44.26 sec.

---

800 AND 1500 METERS

The eyes of the world will be on great British track rivals *Steve Ovett* and *Sebastian Coe* in Moscow. In the two year build up to the Games, both have revealed that they are equipped with the speed, stamina, power and competitive drive to take on and beat the world's best over 800 and 1500 meters. But which of them is the better runner? Coe proved himself *fastest* with world record breaking runs in the 800 meters, 1500 meters and one mile during an astonishing span of 41 days in the summer of 1979. But can he match the finishing kick of the bearded Ovett, who going into 1980 had yet to find anybody who could stay with him as he unleashed his devastating bursts 200 meters from

the tape?

Ovett and Coe were so conscious of each other's ability in the 1978 European 800 meters final that they handed the race to East German *Olaf Beyer*. The two Britons were watching each other so closely that they failed to see Beyer coming up on the outside off the final bend and were unable to respond as he sprinted past them 25 meters from the tape. They have both since made considerable improvements in tactics and times and it is unlikely that Beyer can repeat his triumph in Moscow.

Alberto Juantorena will be striving to regain the 800 meters title he won in Montreal but defeat by United States two-lap expert *James Robinson* in the 1979 Pan American Games suggested the giant Cuban had lost his competitive edge. Watch out for the fast finish of *James Maina*, the African champion from Kenya who was an impressive winner of the 800 meters in the World Cup in Montreal.

Such has been the supremacy of Ovett and Coe over 1500 meters that a whole squad of talented four-lap runners was considering switching to the 5000 meters in the quest for gold in Moscow. *Eamonn Coghlan*, Ireland's American-educated miler who has proved so dominant on the US indoor circuit, started to experiment with the longer event after defeats by Ovett and Coe in Europe. *Dr Thomas Wessinghage*, a world-class 1500 meters specialist from West Germany, also considered the switch after handing African Miruts Yifter a rare defeat over 5000 meters in 1979.

The United States has produced its best 1500 meters runner since Jim Ryun in *Steve Scott* but his gold prospects looked distant when he finished a well-beaten second behind Coe, as the slim, diminutive son of an English engineer lowered the world mile record to 3 min 49 sec in Oslo in July 1979. Commonwealth champion *David Moorcroft* and Scottish champion *John Robson* have also been overshadowed in Europe by the stunning successes of Ovett and Coe. Defending Olympic champion *John Walker* started to show a welcome return to form in 1979 after hospital treatment for a recurring leg injury, and watch out for Kenyan *Mike Boit* in Moscow. He loves to run from the front and will doubtless be trying to set a blistering pace in a bid to squeeze the finishing speed out of Ovett and Coe.

The women's 1500 meters became a wide-open race when joint favorites Totka Petrova of Bulgaria and Natalya Marescu of Romania were among seven East Europeans suspended from athletics for drug abuses. Bulgarian *Nikolina Shtereva*, one of the best two-lap runners in the world, won the 800 meters for Europe in the 1979 World Cup in Montreal and is a likely gold medallist in Moscow.

Russia will be powerfully represented in both events, with *Yekaterina Poryvkina, Tatyana Providokhina* and *Giana Romanova* looming as threats to the hopes of the Bulgarians. *Essie Kelly* has emerged as a fine two lap runner for the United States but the strongest challenge could come from the vastly experienced and versatile *Greta Waitz* of Norway.

5000 and 10,000 METERS

Lasse Viren, the formidable Finn who scored a historic double in the 5000 and 10,000 meters in Munich and Montreal, has been in indifferent

Left: Sebastian Coe (left) and Steve Ovett are British rivals who could be duelling at world record pace over 800 and 1500 meters in Moscow.

Essie Kelly anchors the USA 4 × 400 meters relay team to victory in a match against the Soviet Union. But the American women will need to stretch to new peaks to beat the crack East German squad in the Olympics.

Miruts ("The Shifter") Yifter and Henry Rono (right) will be prominent in the middle and long distances, provided black Africa is not forced out of the Games by political squabbles. Craig Virgin, running at the shoulder of Yifter, is a medal prospect for the United States.

Brendan Foster: watch for his bold front-running style.

form since 1976 but this is no reason to write him off, because he thrives on the challenge of Olympic competition.

It would be a startling form upset if Viren could once again emerge as the master in two races for which Ethiopian *Miruts Yifter* came into Olympic year as favorite for a double success. "Yifter the Shifter" is a popular performer on the world's tracks, winning friends with his warm personality and influencing races with his pulverizing finishing speed. He was a bronze medallist in the 10,000 meters in Munich and missed the Montreal Games because of the withdrawal of black Africa. Yifter's finishing speed can be matched only if *Thomas Wessinghage* and *Eamonn Coghlan* elect to step up to the longer distance from the 1500 meters. Italy's European champion *Venanzio Ortis*, Switzerland's *Markus Ryffel* and East German *Hans-Jorg Kunz* will be among the leading contenders for the 5000 meters title. New Zealander *Rod Dixon* and *Suleiman Nyambui* of Tanzania are also both to be reckoned with.

Yifter could find the biggest danger in the 10,000 meters coming from another African – Kenyan *Henry Rono*, who has been one of the world's most impressive and consistent middle and long distance runners since the 1976 Games. Rono had a quiet 1979 by his standards but could be a winner in Moscow if he can reproduce the form that took him to a world 10,000 meters record. Watch for some bold front running by Britain's *Brendan Foster* and the gritty deter-

mination of his near-neighbor *Mike McLeod*. *Craig Virgin* has the ability to make his presence felt for the United States and Russia has an iron man of the track in *Aleksandr Antipov*. *Martti Vainio* showed in the 1978 European championships that he has the potential to take over from Viren as Finland's No 1 hope. Or has the old fox been saving his best for the Olympics yet again?

MARATHON AND 3000 METERS STEEPLECHASE

The hardest race to forecast and the one that always captures the public imagination is the marathon. There are plans to give extensive television coverage of this "killer" event, with cameras following the field on the 26 mile, 385 yard trek through the streets of Moscow on a route that takes the field past Red Square and finally back to the starting point of Lenin Stadium in a time – at least for the winner – that is likely to be around 2 hr 10 min.

Perhaps the best form guide is that the Spartakiad marathon, run over the Olympic course in July 1979, was won by Russian and European champion *Leonid Moseyev* in 2 hr 13 min 20 sec. But his margin of victory was hardly convincing. The second and third placed runners (*Shigeru Sou* of Japan and Russian *Viktor Zubov*) were credited with exactly the same time. Fourth placed *Sanimkul Dzumana-*

zarov, of Russia, was just a tenth of a second behind the first three in the closest finish there has ever been to a marathon. Moseyev is the obvious Olympic favorite on his home ground but a shuffling Ethiopian policeman called *Kebedz Bolsha* is being hailed in Africa as the man most likely to follow in the winning footsteps of his illustrious countrymen Abebe Bikila and Mamo Wolde. Australia could be in with a medal chance through *Dave Chettle*, and American hopes rest on *Bill Rodgers*.

Bronislaw Malinowski, Poland's silver medallist in the 3000 meters steeplechase in the 1976 Olympics, is expected to go one better in Moscow but faces stiff opposition from Italian *Mariano Scartezzini*, Russian *Anatoliy Dimov*, West German *Michael Karst* and American champion *Henry Marsh*. Malinowski's chances of winning the gold could hinge on whether the versatile *Henry Rono* elects to go for the 10,000 meters and steeplechase double. Even if he decides to miss the steeplechase, Kenya has another *Rono – Kip –* who is capable of winning the race if at the peak of his form.

THE HURDLES AND DECATHLON

The United States has two of the outstanding Olympic favorites in the 110 and 400 meters hurdles – *Renaldo Nehemiah* and *Ed Moses*. Barring accidents, there seems little doubt that they will strike gold in Moscow. Nehemiah has got high hurdling down to a fine art and the only threat to him seems to come from stylish Cuban *Alejandro Casanas* and East German *Thomas Munkelt* but neither of these fine performers is in quite the class of Nehemiah, who is capable of lowering the Olympic record of 13.24 sec.

Ed Moses, the 1976 400 meters hurdles champion, is one of the great untouchables of athletics and has set himself the astonishing target of breaking the 47 sec barrier in Moscow.

Renaldo Nehemiah just edges out East German Thomas Munkelt in a photo-finish to the World Cup high hurdles. The black American is a scorching favorite for the event in Moscow.

The time of the winner in the 1956 Olympic 400 meters *flat* final was 46.7 sec. It gives you an indication of the power of Moses. Watch for him trying to set an incredible 12-stride pattern between the hurdles. The only hurdler likely to get anywhere near him is talented West German all-rounder *Harald Schmid*.

Poland's *Grazyna Rabsztyn* has made rapid strides since finishing fifth in the final of the women's 100 meters hurdles in Montreal in 1976 and will be hard to beat in Moscow. Among her rivals will be East Germans *Johanna Klier* and *Kerstin Claus*, Russian *Tatyana Ansimova* and two fast-improving American challengers, *Deby LaPlante* and world junior record holder of 1979, *Candy Young*.

Russia is confident it can get a double gold in the all-rounder tests, the decathlon for men and the pentathlon for women. The decathlon is decided over two days of competition: first day, 100 meters, long jump, shot put, high jump, 400 meters; second day, 110 meters hurdles, discus, pole vault, javelin and 1500 meters. Points are awarded for each performance and the athlete with the overall highest number of points at the end of the competition wins. American Bruce Jenner set new standards in the 1976 Olympics with a world record 8618 points. West German *Guido Kratschmer*, silver medallist in Montreal, is favorite to succeed Jenner in Moscow but the Russians believe that European champion *Aleksandr Grebenyuk* can strike gold and so take the title of world's greatest all-rounder. British hopes rest on the wide shoulders of *Daley Thompson*, who has improved in every department since finishing 18th as a raw decathlete in the 1976 Games.

The pentathlon events are, in order: 100

Left: Grazyna Rabsztyn (right) shows the style that has made her the world's No 1 100 meters hurdler. Her rival in this picture is Russian champion Tatyana Ansimova.

meters hurdles, shot put, high jump, long jump and 800 meters. Russian *Nadyezhda Tkachenko*, fifth in the Montreal Olympics, has since proved herself the outstanding pentathlete in Europe and will be the favorite to win the gold medal on home territory. Hungarian *Magit Papp* and East German *Burglinde Pollak* are likely to be among her closest rivals.

THE JUMPING EVENTS

There are fascinating duels in prospect in all of the jumping events where the Olympic motto –

Vladimir Yaschenko (above) and Debbie Brill (below) will both be in the high jump in Moscow and should be among the medals.

citius, altius, fortius ("faster, higher, stronger") – will be truly implemented. In the men's high jump, American ace *Franklin Jacobs* will be renewing his rivalry with Europe's leading high climbers, *Aleksandr Grigoryev* (USSR), *Vladimir Yaschenko* (USSR) and *Rolf Beilschmidt* (East Germany). Poland's defending Olympic champion *Jacek Wszola* will not let his title go easily and West Germany has recently produced a gold medal prospect in 17-year-old, 6ft 7in *Dietmar Mogenburg*.

Jacobs, provided of course he qualifies in the US Olympic trials, will be slightly favored because he proved in the 1979 World Cup in Montreal that he can produce the goods when it matters most. All this crystal-ball gazing is being done before the US Olympic trials, after which the American squad is picked on a strict 1–2–3 finishing order, regardless of previous form and reputation.

Rosi Ackermann (East Germany) and *Sara Simeoni* (Italy) are likely to continue where they left off in Montreal in 1976 in the high jump. Rosi was the Olympic champion, with a Games record leap of 6ft 4in (1.93m), with Sarah just $\frac{3}{4}$in behind in second place. If they fall from their sky-scraping standards, Canadian *Debbie Brill*, the Pan American champion, will be waiting to jump into their place. *Louise Ritter* (USA) and *Nina Serbina* (USSR) have also got high hopes.

Larry Myricks has the ability to take over from his United States team-mate *Arnie Robinson* as Olympic long jump champion, and in 18-year-old *Carl Lewis* the Americans appear to have discovered another potential 29ft jumper. East German *Lutz Dombrowski*, Russian *Valeri Podluzhny* and Frenchman *Jacques Rousseau* will lead the European challenge, with Cuban *David Giralt* capable of outjumping them all if he hits peak form. Triple jump favorite *Joao Carlos de Oliveira* will be bidding to gain a gold medal double for Brazil. He only needs to maintain his 1979 form to take the hop, step and jump title in succession to the great Russian Viktor Saneyev and he has the bounce to cause an upset in the long jump pit.

Anita Stukane and *Vilma Bardauskiene* will be vying to win the women's long jump for Russia and, coming into Olympic year, they appeared to have the edge over rivals such as *Brigitte Wujak* of East Germany and *Kathy McMillan* of the United States.

One of the most spectacular and gripping of all field events is the pole vault, which is so closely contested that the competition could last nearly all day and is likely to be decided under floodlights. Among the 18ft club are

Above: Kathy McMillan hopes for a happy landing in Moscow but faces tough opposition in the long jump from the Russians.

Right: Mike Tully who could catapult his way to victory in the pole vault against a cluster of 18ft specialists.

vaulters of the caliber of *Mike Tully* (USA), *Patrick Abada* (France), *Konstantin Volkov* (USSR), *Azel Weber* (East Germany), *Vladimir Trofimenko* (USSR), *Antti Kalliomaki* (Finland), *Patrick Desruelles* (Belgium) and *Gunter Lohre* (West Germany). On 1979 form, Tully was favorite to catapult his way to victory with the Olympic record of 18ft 0½in (5.50m) looking doomed.

THE THROWING EVENTS

We now come to an area of the Olympics that causes more concern and consternation among advocates of the Olympic ideals than any other. It is common knowledge on the athletics circuit that many of the world's leading throwers take drugs to help increase their body weight and improve their performances. Gold medals are being won in the laboratory rather than in the throwing circle.

In 1973, former Olympic hammer-throw champion Hal Connolly confessed: "For eight years prior to 1972 I would have to refer to myself as a hooked athlete. Like all my competitors I was using anabolic steroids as an integral part of my training."

Connolly, gold medallist for the United States at Melbourne in 1956, later told a US Senate Committee: "I knew any number of athletes in the 1968 Olympic team who had so much scar tissue and so many puncture holes on their backsides that it was difficult to find a fresh spot to give them a new shot. I relate these incidents to emphasize my contention that the overwhelming majority of the international track and field athletes I know would take anything and do anything short of killing themselves to improve their athletic performance."

To try to beat the drug abuses, the IOC has set up a Medical Commission responsible for control at the Games, classifying the drugs that can and cannot be taken. The Commission is also responsible for carrying out sex tests on the female competitors.

But even with the strictest supervision there will still be abuses and illegal use of stimulants, as athletes try to take short cuts to Olympic glory. It is well known that a competitor can take anabolic steroids during training, discontinue their use 10 days or so before the event and report for a urine test safe in the knowledge that it will prove negative.

The following are the medal favorites in the throwing events before the Moscow Games, with East Germany having the chance of a clean sweep:

East German shot put favorites, Udo Beyer (left) and Ilona Slupianek (right).

Shot put, men: East German *Udo Beyer* has been consistently reproducing the form that won him the gold medal in Montreal. Watch out for the discus-style spin approach in the circle of Russian *Alexandr Barisnikov*, who collected the bronze medal in Montreal. Americans *Dave Laut*, *Al Feuerbach* and 18-year-old prodigy *Mike Carter* have been consistently beating 66ft but it is likely to be a put nearer 70ft that wins the gold. Women: East Germany is expected to pull off a shot put double, with European champion *Ilona Slupianek* as firm a favorite as Beyer is in the men's event. Her toughest opposition is likely to come from Czech *Helena Fibingerova* and Russian *Esfir Krachevskaya*.

Below: Wolfgang Hanisch, who could be the man with the golden arm in the javelin.

Discus, men: It looks like being a repeat of the 1976 Montreal battle between champion *Mac Wilkins* (USA) and silver medallist *Wolf-*gang Schmidt (East Germany). But both will have to be at their best to withstand the challenge of much-improved Norwegian *Knut Hjeltnes*. Legendary four-times discus champion Al Oerter has been getting wound up for an Olympic comeback but it is highly improbable that at the age of 42 he can find the distance to worry his strong, young rivals. Women: *Evelin Schlaak* of East Germany – now Frau Jahl – should retain the title she won in Montreal. Russian *Svyetlana Melnikova* and Bulgarian *Svetla Bozhkova* will push her all the way.

Javelin: The indomitable East Germans have the chance of yet another double, with *Wolfgang Hanisch* seeming set to take the men's gold and the incredibly consistent *Ruth Fuchs* almost certain to retain her Olympic title. West German *Michael Wessing*, the 1978 European champion, will be a threat to Hanisch and Romanian *Eva Raduly* appears to be the only woman with the ability to seriously challenge the supremacy of Fuchs. Britain's *Tessa Sanderson* could snatch the bronze.

Hammer: There were three main contenders for the Olympic gold medal coming into the final build-up period to the Games, Russian *Sergey Litvinov*, East German *Roland Steuk* and West German *Karl-Hans Riehm*. But they could all find that pre-Olympic form counts for nothing if 1976 champion *Yuriy Sedyh* can rise to the occasion as he did in Montreal with an Olympic record throw of 254ft 4in (77.52m).

1980 GOLD MEDAL PREDICTIONS IN THE TRACK AND FIELD EVENTS

EVENT	1976 CHAMPION	AUTHOR'S CHOICE	YOUR CHOICE	1980 CHAMPION	TIME DISTANCE
100m (M)	Haseley Crawford *TRI*	James Sanford *US*			
100m (W)	Annagret Richter *GER*	Evelyn Ashford *US*			
200m (M)	Don Quarrie *JAM*	Pietro Mennea *ITA*			
200m (W)	Barbel Eckert *GDR*	Evelyn Ashford *US*			
400m (M)	Alberto Juantereno *CUB*	Harald Schmid *GER*			
400m (W)	Irena Szewinska *POL*	Marita Koch *GDR*			
800m (M)	Alberto Juantereno *CUB*	Sebastian Coe *GB*			
800m (W)	Tatiana Kazankina *USSR*	Nikolina Shtereva *BUL*			
1500m (M)	John Walker *NZ*	Steve Ovett *GB*			
1500m (W)	Tatiana Kazankina *USSR*	Greta Waitz *NOR*			
5000m (M)	Lasse Viren *FIN*	Thomas Wessinghage *GER*			
10,000m (M)	Lasse Viren *FIN*	Miruts Yifter *ETH*			
110m hrd (M)	Guy Drut *FR*	Renaldo Nehemiah *US*			
100m hrd (W)	Johanna Schaller *GDR*	Grazyna Rabsztyn *POL*			
100m hrd (M)	Ed Moses *US*	Ed Moses *US*			
Steeplechase	Anders Garderud *SWE*	Bronislaw Malinowski *POL*			
Marathon	Waldemar Cierpinski *GDR*	Kebedz Bolsha *ETH*			
High Jump (M)	Jacek Wszola *POL*	Franklin Jacobs *US*			
High Jump (W)	Rosi Ackermann *GER*	Debbie Brill *CAN*			
Long Jump (M)	Arnie Robinson *US*	Larry Myricks *US*			
Long Jump (W)	Angela Voigt *GDR*	Anita Stukane *USSR*			
Triple Jump	Viktor Saneyev *USSR*	Joao Carlos de Oliveira *BRA*			
Pole Vault	Tadeusz Slusarski *POL*	Mike Tully *US*			
Shot Put (M)	Udo Beyer *GDR*	Udo Beyer *GDR*			
Shot Put (W)	Ivanka Christova *BUL*	Ilona Slupianek *GDR*			
Discus (M)	Mac Wilkins *US*	Wolfgang Schmidt *GDR*			
Discus (W)	Evelin Schlaak *GDR*	Evelin Schlaak (Jahl) *GDR*			
Javelin (M)	Miklos Nemeth *HUN*	Wolfgang Hanisch *GDR*			
Javelin (W)	Ruth Fuchs *GDR*	Ruth Fuchs *GDR*			
Hammer	Yuriy Sedyh *USSR*	Sergey Litvinov *USSR*			
Decathlon	Bruce Jenner *US*	Guido Kratschmer *GER*			
Pentathlon	Siegrun Siegl *GDR*	Nadyezhda Tkachenko *USSR*			

THE MAIN SPORTS CENTERS AT THE MOSCOW OLYMPICS

Lenin Stadium, now 24 years old, has been completely refurbished and given a face lift for the Olympics. A new track was laid for the 1979 Spartakiad, and though times were generally slow in the explosive events, this was considered to be a sign of low-standard competition rather than a slow track.

The newly constructed swimming arena has separate pools for swimming and diving, and 10,000 spectators can be seated in this modern building with its spectacular concave roof. The rowing canal is considered the best rowing stretch in Europe, with a main stand complex that can seat 10,000 spectators, and the cycling events will take place in the strikingly ultra-modern Velodrome Krylatskoe.

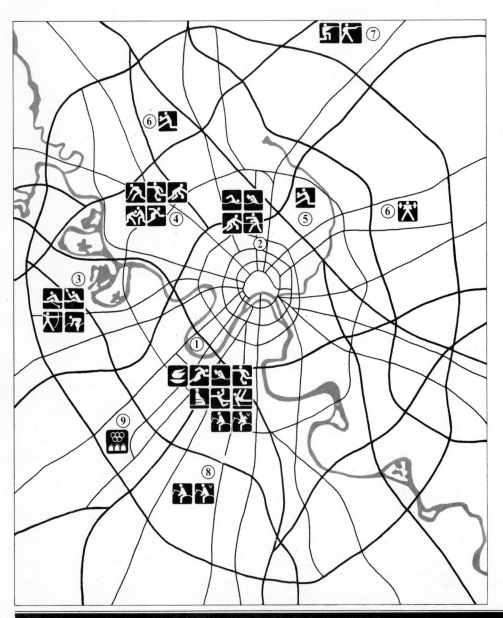

Key to map

1 Lenin Central Stadium, including the Bolshaya sports arena, the Malaya sports arena, sports palace, swimming pool and all-purpose sports hall.
2 Indoor roofed stadium and swimming pool.
3 Roofed cycling track, circular cycling course, archery fields and rowing canal.
4 Dynamo stadium, Stadium of Young Pioneers, all-purpose sports halls, football stadium, track and field indoor stadium.
5 Sokolniki Sports Palace.
6 All-purpose sports halls.
7 Dynamo shooting gallery.
8 Equestrian center.
9 Olympic village.

Opposite: Opening ceremony of the 1979 Spartakiad in Moscow's Lenin Stadium.

Two of the world's fastest sprinters – the Italian Pietro Mennea (above), and Houston McTear of the United States of America (leading, left).

East German Udo Beyer, shot put gold medallist at the 1976 Olympics and favored to win again in 1980.

Ruth Fuchs of East Germany, twice Olympic champion in the javelin event.

Britain's Daley Thompson, strong contender for a medal in the decathlon.

Cuban Alberto Juantorena after winning the 400 meters in the 1976 Olympics.

Sebastian Coe of Great Britain whose greatest rival for the 800 and 1500 meters gold medals is fellow countryman, Steve Ovett.

The famous Fosbury Flop of Dick Fosbury, American high jump gold medallist, 1968.

Left: Thomas Wessinghage (No 448) of West Germany in the 1500 meters, Montreal 1976.

Below: The legendary Polish sprinter, Irena Szewinska (left), in action at the 1972 Olympics, and East German Marita Koch who has proved unbeatable in the 400 meters.

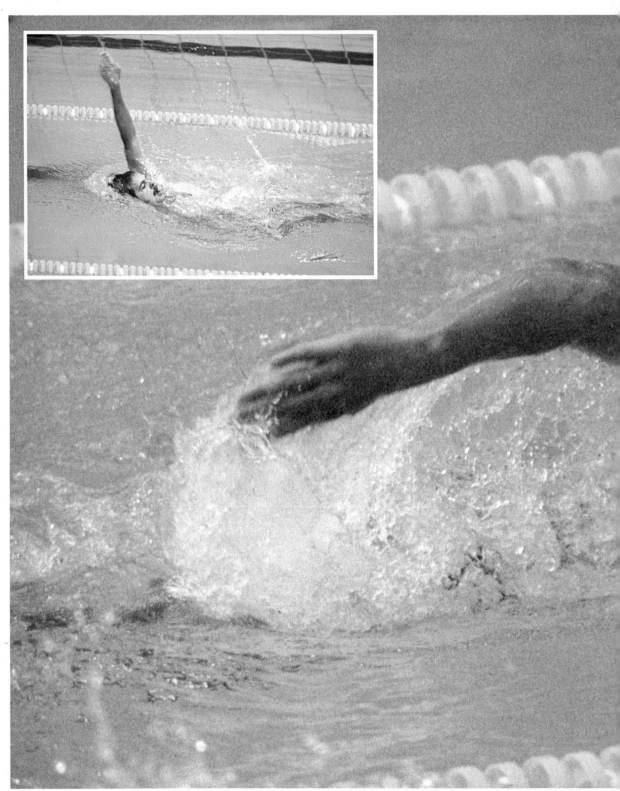

Two American swimming stars of the 1976 Olympics – John Naber (inset) and Shirley Babashoff.

Left: The French champion cyclist, Daniel Morelon, in the 100 meters sprint, 1976.

Top: Fencing match between Russian Boris Onischenko, disqualified for "bugging" his épée, and Britain's Jim Fox at the Montreal Olympics.

Above: Basketball match between Russia and Australia at the 1976 Olympics.

GYMNASTICS

Gymnastics now rivals track and field as the most popular Olympic sporting spectacular for television viewers. Its popularity is due to the poise, perfection and graceful beauty of such Olympic performers as Vera Caslavska (1968), Olga Korbut (1972) and Nadia Comaneci (1976).

The Russians believe they have discovered a new ballerina of the bars and beams who can match them all for screen charisma but possesses even greater gymnastic ability and technique.

She is *Natalya Shaposhnikova*, a schoolgirl from Voroshilovograd. Her coach is Vladislav Rastorotski, who trained the magnificent Ludmilla Turischeva to become Olympic and world champion. Ludmilla, now married to double Olympic sprint champion Valeri Borzov, is acting as advisor to Natalya and is convinced she can strike gold in Moscow.

Natalya revealed her exciting potential during the 1979 Spartakiad, the dress rehearsal for the Olympics in Moscow. She emerged as overall champion, beating world champion Elena Mukhina and unveiling an exciting program that explored new areas of dexterity and athleticism. A tiny, 4ft 9in elf of a woman, Natalya is 18 but looks 13. She has perfected a breath-taking balancing act that draws rapturous applause from the audience and high marks from the judges. Watch out for the Shaposhnikova handstand when she balances one-handed on the end of the beam, twisting her body until it becomes horizontal with the floor. She is also the first woman to introduce several difficult turns and somersaults that have

previously been attempted only by men.

Eastern Europeans and particularly the Russians are expected to dominate the women's events with performers of the caliber of *Nelli Kim* (USSR), *Nadia Comaneci* (Romania), *Elena Mukhina* (USSR), *Steffi Kraker* (East Germany) and, of course, new sensation Natalya Shaposhnikova. It is likely to be the same story in the men's events, where the Russian master *Nikolai Andrianov* has set standards followed by *Aleksandr Ditiatin* (USSR), *Zoltan Magyar* (Hungary), *Eberhard Gienger* (East Germany), *Ralph Bartel* (East Germany), *Stojanov Deltschev* (Bulgaria) and *Danut Grecu* (Romania).

Nelli Kim (above) shows the graceful style of a champion that Americans like Marcia Frederick (left) must try to match in Moscow.

Opposite: Romanian gymnast, Nadia Comaneci, in action at Montreal in 1976 when she collected two individual gold medals, a team silver and was all-round woman's champion. Her rival at the Moscow Olympics is likely to be Natalya Shaposhnikova (inset), a Russian schoolgirl who revealed her astounding talents at the 1979 Spartakiad.

33

The Japanese men will present formidable opposition against the Russians with such outstanding gymnasts as *Junichi Shimizu, Shigero Kasamatsu, Eizo Kenmotsu* and *Hiroshi Kajiyama*. There are also signs that the United States is beginning to make a breakthrough at world level, its gymnasts encouraged by the world championship wins in 1978 of *Thomas Kurt* in the floor exercises and *Marcia Frederick* on the uneven parallel bars, with *Kathy Johnson* taking a bronze in the floor exercises.

To help make your viewing of the gymnastics from Moscow more enjoyable, here are some of the main points to look for in the individual disciplines:

Floor exercises: These are performed on a soft mat which is 12m square and 4.5cm thick. The judges look for a mixture of strength, skill, balance, flair and invention, flexibility and a sense of rhythm, with competitors encouraged to project their personalities as well as their physical prowess. Typical movements to watch for are handsprings, headsprings, back handsprings, somersaults and cartwheels in the men's exercises; graceful leaps, back handsprings, chases, dives, forward and backward rolls and handstands in the women's section. The women's exercises are performed to piano accompaniment and last 90 seconds. The men's exercises are more explosive and last 70 seconds. Any static positions must be held for at least two seconds.

Vaulting horse: The leather-covered vaulting horse is a maximum 1.63m in length with a height of 1.35m for men and 1.1m for women. Take-off, with both feet together, is from a

springboard 1.2m long following a run-up approach of up to 20m. Men vault from one end of the horse while women approach it side-on. Competitors must perform a set vault and one of their own selection. They have two attempts at each, with only their best score counting each time. The judges look for poise and positive action in the obligatory vault and invention and degree of difficulty in the free vault. Women are also judged for how far they vault and are allowed to take one step after landing. A stagger on landing loses points.

Rings: This is a difficult discipline confined to the men. Two rings, 18cm in diameter, hang 2.5m above the ground. The object of the exercise is to turn and swing in as many ways as possible with little movement of the rings. There must be at least two handstands by each competitor and a static upright position with arms outstretched (the "crucifix"). It is an exercise that takes enormous strength and resolute concentration.

Parallel bars: The bars are 1.6m high and 42cm apart. They are used only by the men. Exercises consist of swinging movements that are a test of agility and strength. At least once during the exercise, both hands must leave the bars together.

Horizontal bar: An apparatus used only by the men, the bar is 2.5m high, 2.4m long and 2.8cm thick. The gymnast must swing nonstop, with turns and changes of grip. As on the

NOUANSPORT

34

continuity of movement, balance, poise, sureness, coordination, artistic interpretation and invention. Any deviation from the agreed routine in a compulsory exercise is severely penalized.

The all-round individual winner is the competitor with the highest total marks in all the exercises combined. The winning team is decided by totalling the marks of the five highest-scoring members of each team in each event.

Individual winners of separate events are decided by taking the top six in each and adding to their marks for set and voluntary exercises the score from a final additional voluntary sequence.

The Moscow gymnastics will take place in the Lenin Palace of Sports from 20 to 26 July.

Pete Korman (left) is one of the fast-improving United States team, inspired to new peak performances by the artistry of Russian all-time great Nikolai Andrianov (below).

parallel bars, both hands must at least once leave and return to the bar together. Look out for spectacular straddle dismounts.

Pommel horse: This apparatus for men only is 1.1m high with two wooden handles (pommels) 45cm apart on top. The gymnast supports himself on the pommels and must execute nonstop swings, turns and fast leg scissor movements.

Uneven parallel bars: These are parallel bars 3.5m long and 43cm apart, with one bar 2.3m high and the other 1.5m. Only the women use this apparatus, and during their routine they must swing from one bar to the other with twists and turns and smooth, supple movements. Two pauses are allowed, and if a gymnast falls off she has 30 sec in which to resume her exercise. The judges look for grace while the gymnast is suspended, changing of hand grips and invention. A sloppy dismount can cost points.

Beam: Exclusive to women, the wooden beam is 5m long, 10cm wide and 16cm deep. The flat-top surface is 1.2m above the ground. The judges look for poise and balance, turns, leaps, jumps, runs and handstands. Three pauses are allowed and the gymnast has 10 sec to resume if she falls.

The scoring: In each event four judges make independent assessments of each competitor. They score each performance out of a maximum of 10. The highest and lowest scores are discarded and the average of the remaining two is the accepted score. Each judge looks for correction of execution, difficulty of execution,

SWIMMING

This is one of the most difficult of all Olympic sports for which to make predictions because just a slight miscalculation in preparations means a swimmer can "peak" at the wrong time. But coming into the Olympic year of 1980 there was a cluster of American swimmers looming as gold medal prospects for Moscow. Shining above them all were three USA women swimmers with the ability to break the monopoly held by the East German women in the 1976 Games.

Tracy Caulkins is a versatile swimmer who made such an impact in the 1978 world championships that she was voted Sportswoman of the Year and won the coveted James E. Sullivan Memorial Trophy, the Oscar of US amateur sports. Just 17 on 11 January 1980, Tracy is an all-rounder who specializes in the 200 and 400 meters individual medley events. Her main rivals in Moscow are likely to be East Germans *Petra Schneider* and *Ulrike Tauber*, with Britain's fast-improving *Sharron Davies* an outsider in both events.

Tracy Caulkins (foreground, top right), Ulrike Tauber (below) and Cynthia Woodhead (bottom right) are among the swimmers expected to make a golden splash in the Olympic pool.

Cynthia Woodhead was 15 the day before the Pan American championships started in the summer of 1979 and celebrated her birthday by winning the 100, 200 and 400 meter freestyle events for the United States, as well as collecting two more gold medals in the relays. She is particularly impressive over 200 meters, in which she set a world record 1 min 58.43 sec on the way to victory in the Pan Am Games. If she can hit her peak at the right time in Moscow, she could clean-sweep the freestyle golds but there is certain to be pressure from East Germans *Barbara Krause, Caren Metschuck* and *Anett Kalatz.*

Mary Meagher, a 14-year-old high school girl from Louisville, Kentucky, grabbed attention in the Pan Am Games with a world record 2 min 9.77 sec for the 200 meters butterfly. This was an event in which East Germany was confident of a gold medal from its butterfly expert *Andrea Pollack* but now she knows that she faces tough opposition from Mary Meagher at both 100 and 200 meters. *Jill Sterkel* and *Lisa Buese* are also capable of world-class butterfly performances for the United States.

Australia has discovered a new "Miss Perpetual Motion" in *Tracey Wickham,* a 15-year-old schoolgirl from Queensland who will go to Moscow as the favorite for a gold in the 800 meters freestyle and a threat to Cynthia Woodhead in the shorter freestyle events. She was the only competitor to break world records at both the Commonwealth and world championships of 1978, taking the 400 and 800 meters gold medals at both of these major meets.

Russia looks unbeatable in the women's 100 and 200 meters breaststroke events, with *Lina Kaciushite* heading the challenge and quite capable of taking both gold medals. *Margaret Kelly* could be prominent for Britain.

The 100 and 200 meters backstroke finals could be carbon-copy races featuring American *Linda Jezek* against East German *Cornelia Polit,* with Australian specialists *Lisa Forrest* and *Deborah Forster* pushing them to peak performances.

America's men are unlikely to be quite so dominating in Moscow as they were in Montreal, when they won 12 of the 13 swimming gold medals, but they will once again have leading challengers in all the events.

Jim Montgomery, David McCagg, Rowdy Gaines and *Bill Forrester* are likely to spearhead the US assault on the 100 and 200 meters freestyle titles and sprint relay. *Brian Goodell* has been America's most consistent world-class performer over the 400 and 1500 meters distances, in both of which he won gold medals in the Montreal Olympics. But Russia has produced an outstanding prospect in *Vladimir Salnikov,* who could strike double gold if he can maintain his 1979 form. Another Russian, *Sergey Kopliakov,* is a dangerman in the 100 and 200 meters freestyle events. *Bob Jackson,* sixth in the Montreal 100 meters backstroke final, has made the sort of improvement that justifies him being installed as favorite for the gold medal in Moscow, with his American team-mate *Peter Rocca* hoping to go one better than his 1976 silver medal in the 200 meters backstroke. Both Jackson and Rocca can expect tough opposition from Russian record

holder in both events, *Viktor Kuznetsov,* and also from Aussie *Mark Kerry.*

Jesse Vassallo, a 17-year-old Puerto Rican-born American, emerged as the world's top 200 and 400 meters medley specialist during 1979, and looks capable of avenging his defeat in the 1978 world championship by Canadian *Graham Smith.* But both Vassallo and Smith will have to be at their best to hold off the challenge of Russians *Sergey Fesenko* and *Aleksandr Sidorenko.*

Steve Lundquist was America's leading breaststroke swimmer of 1979 but coming into

Mary Meagher, a butterfly specialist hoping to strike gold for the United States.

Margaret Kelly, Britain's outstanding breaststroke expert who will lead the Commonwealth challenge.

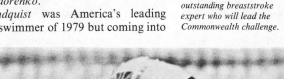

Olympic swimming championships is likely to be the emergence of Russia as a world power in the pool, particularly in the men's events. It will have happened more by design than accident. They planned with Moscow in mind as far back as 1975, when they had a nation-wide search for talented teenage swimmers who could be specially prepared for the 1980 Games. The Russians have been equally thorough in all the sports featured in the Olympics, as they set out to prove they are the world's No 1 sports nation.

THE SWIMMING STROKES

Freestyle: Any stroke may be used in a freestyle event but it is almost unheard of for a modern Olympic competitor to use anything but the front crawl, which is the fastest stroke. The swimmer kicks his legs up and down in short movements as he propels himself through the

Sergey Fesenko, a leader of the Russian revolution in the swimming pool that is bringing the Soviets into the reckoning for gold medals.

Right: The start of the women's 200 meters back stroke in the 1976 Olympics, which was won by East German Ulrike Richter (third from top).

Olympic year, he knew he had to improve on his best in the 100 and 200 meters events if he were to beat West Germans *Gerald Mörken* and *Walter Kusch*, and Russians *Alexandr Fedorowski, Robertas Schulpa, Timur Podmarev* and *Vladimir Tarasov.*

Joe Bottom, silver medallist in the 100 meters butterfly in Montreal, looked in 1979 as if he could go one better in Moscow, but he will have to battle to beat the likes of Sweden's *Petar Arvidsson*, East German *Roger Pyttel* and Canadian *Dan Thompson. Philip Hubble* could power into a medal-winning position for Great Britain. He will also be a challenger for the 200 meters butterfly gold, an event in which Russian *Sergey Fesenko* and American *Craig Beardsley* are joint favorites, with another Russian – *Mikhail Gorelik* – ready to pounce if either of them is below peak form.

The most significant thing about the 1980

water using alternate overarm pulling strokes. There are many different leg kicks, from two beats to one pull with each arm, up to six beats. Watch the top front crawl swimmers and see how long it is before they take their first breath. They often sprint 25 meters before turning their head sideways to breathe.

Backstroke: This is like the front crawl but performed while lying on the back, the arms windmilling alternately. Some swimmers use a leg kick but many of the leading performers make little leg movement, concentrating on the pull of their arms to power them through the water. It is the only event in which swimmers start in the water.

Breaststroke: This is the stroke that causes more controversy than any other because of the different interpretations of the rules. The body should be kept "perfectly on the breast" and both shoulders have to be in line with the water surface. All four limbs have to move simultaneously in the same horizontal plane, the hands going forward together and brought back on or under the surface of the water. Part of the head must be visible above the water level except at the start and when turning. Swimming under the water is now banned.

Butterfly: The second fastest and most exhausting of all the strokes. It was derived from the breaststroke when performers started using an over-the-water arm recovery. Both arms pull together and are lifted over the surface together. The swimmers use a dolphin leg movement, with both shoulders having to be in line with the water surface.

Medley: This is an event for the most versatile of swimmers. The swimmer does four "legs," one in each of the accepted styles and in the same order: butterfly, backstroke, breast stroke and freestyle. In a medley relay, each member of the team swims one leg in the following stroke order: backstroke, breaststroke, butterfly and freestyle.

In contrast to track and field, all qualifications for the swimming semi-finals and finals go to the competitors with the fastest times in the heats, and are not based on their placings. In the final, the swimmer with the fastest qualifying time is allocated lane No 4. The second fastest goes into lane No 5 and the other qualifiers, in descending order, occupy lanes 3, 6, 2, 7, 1 and 8.

The controlling officials are a referee, a starter, placing-judges at each corner of the pool checking that turns are made correctly and the order in which the contestants finish, a timekeeper for each lane and two stroke judges who patrol the poolside making sure stroke rules are properly followed.

DIVING

For the first time for four Olympics there will be a new men's highboard diving champion, now that Italy's triple gold medallist Klaus Dibiasi has retired. *Greg Louganis*, American winner of the silver medal in Montreal, is favored to succeed him as champion and should confirm his superiority over East German *Falk Hoffmann* and Russian *Vladimir Aleinik*, who were second and third to him in the 1978 world championships.

The main danger to these three world leaders is likely to come from East German *Dieter Waskow* and Mexican champion *Carlos Giron*, both of whom showed an improvement in technique and application during 1979.

Louganis will be going for a double in the

Franco Cagnotto shows the style that won him a silver medal in the men's springboard competition in the 1976 Montreal Olympics.

highboard and springboard, but reigning Olympic champion *Phil Boggs* is expected to retain his title. He slipped from his usual stunning standards during 1979 because his concentration was on his final examinations at Michigan Law School but the Olympics will be getting his full attention. Among his rivals will be *Falk Hoffmann*, Italian *Franco Cagnotto*, Cuban *Roland Ruiz*, Russian *Alexander Kosenkov* and Great Britain's 20-year-old *Chris Snode*, who is at college in the United States.

There is the likelihood of a golden double in the women's diving for Russian *Irina Kalinina*, who won both the springboard and highboard titles in the world championships in 1978. In the springboard she will get pressure from Russian *Tatiana Podmarjova*, Americans *Cynthia Potter* and *Carrie Finneran*, Canada's *Janet Nutter* and Australian *Valerie McFarlane*. Her highboard rivals will include Russian *Lena Gorina*, East German *Martina Jasckke*, American *Barbara Weinstein* and *Janet Ely*, now Mrs Thorburn, the former world champion who is hoping to compete in her third Olympics for the United States.

The springboard is 3 meters above the surface of the water and the diver can adjust the degree of springiness. The highboard is 10 meters above the water. All dives from the highboard are voluntary and each contestant must give written notification of the dives he or she is going to make. If a dive is performed in any position other than the one announced, a maximum of only two points can be scored. On the springboard the men and women must do five compulsory dives from the following groups:

● Forward. The diver starts facing the water and turns over forwards.
● Backward. Starts with back to the water, turns over backwards.
● Reverse. Starts facing the water, turns over backwards.
● Inward. Starts back to the water, turns over forwards.
● Twist. Starts facing either direction and twists body in the air from half twist to three times.
● Armstand (highboard only). Starts from a handstand.

During a dive, a contestant can make from $\frac{1}{2}$ to $3\frac{1}{2}$ somersaults. Making $\frac{1}{2}$, $1\frac{1}{2}$, $2\frac{1}{2}$ or $3\frac{1}{2}$ somersaults culminates in a head-first entry into the water. Most divers prefer the $\frac{1}{2}$ somersaults to single, double or triple somersaults, which end in feet-first entries that are more difficult to control.

There are 73 internationally recognized dives, classified by type and the body's position

in the air, which can be *straight* (not bent at the hips or knees), *pike* (bent at least 90 degrees at the hips but with the legs straight), *tuck* (a crouching position with knees together and hands clasping the lower legs) and *free* (any position but applying only to difficult multi-twist dives).

The recognized dives are various permutations of types, somersaults and body positions, which are each given a point value of from 1.2 to 3, according to the degree of difficulty. The seven judges can each award up to a maximum 10 points per dive, in half points. Two points are deducted for a false start and a second false start counts as a scoreless failure.

All judges must make a simultaneous assessment. The highest and lowest scores are disregarded and the remaining five are added together and the total then multiplied by the point value of the dive.

The recognized scoring formula is: complete failure, 0 points; unsatisfactory, 0.5–2; deficient, 2.5–4.5; satisfactory, 5–6; good, 6.5–8; excellent, 8.5–10.

Each dive is marked on quality, with the judges looking for grace, steadiness, smoothness, control, correct carriage, confidence and a vertical or near-vertical entry into the water.

OTHER SPORTS

Here are some likely highlights from other Olympic sports to watch out for in Moscow:

● Cuban heavyweight boxer *Teofilo Stevenson* going for his third successive gold medal. If he achieves it, he will equal the three-in-a-row record set by Hungarian southpaw Laszlo Papp from 1948 to 1956.

● *Vasili Alexeev*, 37-year-old Russian superheavyweight weightlifter, bidding for his third successive gold medal. He has already "lifted" 82 world records and has won eight world titles, and few dispute his claim to the unofficial title of world's strongest human.

● *Danny Nightingale*, a member of Britain's gold medal winning team in the modern pentathlon in Montreal, trying to win the individual title in Moscow. He became one of the favorites by winning the Spartakiad title over the Games course in Moscow in 1979. The modern pentathlon is a series of five events: riding, fencing, pistol shooting, swimming and cross-country. There are three members in each team and the

Teofilo Stevenson (opposite below) will be trying to punch his way to a third successive heavyweight boxing gold medal.

Danny Nightingale (opposite above) will lead Britain's team in their defense of the modern pentathlon title.

competition is spread over five days. The competition ends with an exhausting run over a 4 kilometer course including a 60–100 meters climb. Three points are added or subtracted for every second inside or outside the standard finishing time of 14 min 15 sec.

● The United States shooting for its ninth out of a possible 10 Olympic basketball gold medals, with Russia – the only other winners, albeit hotly disputed when beating the Americans in the final dramatic seconds in 1972 – determined to break the USA domination.

●The United States volleyball team endeavoring to break the Japanese/Russian monopoly on the women's title. They stunned two Soviet teams to defeat during the 1979 Spartakiad and would cause one of the shocks of the Games if they could strike gold in Moscow.

XXII SUMMER OLYMPIC GAMES
TABLE OF EVENTS

19 JULY 1980 TO 3 AUGUST 1980

	19	20	21	22	23	24	25	26	27	28	29	30	31	1	2	3
OPENING	●															
Track & Field						●	●	●	●	●		●	●	●		
Rowing		●	●	●	●	●	●	●	●							
Basketball		●	●	●	●	●	●	●	●	●	●	●				
Boxing		●	●	●	●	●	●	●	●	●	●				●	
Canoeing												●	●	●	●	
Cycling		●		●	●	●	●	●		●						
Fencing				●	●	●	●	●	●	●	●	●				
Football	●	●	●	●	●	●		●		●				●	●	
Gymnastics		●	●	●	●	●	●									
Weightlifting		●	●	●	●		●	●	●	●	●					
Handball		●	●	●	●	●	●	●	●	●	●	●				
Hockey		●	●	●	●	●	●	●	●	●	●	●	●	●		
Judo									●	●	●	●	●	●	●	●
Wrestling Freestyle									●	●	●	●	●			
Wrestling Greco-Roman		●	●	●	●	●										
Swimming		●	●	●	●	●	●	●	●	●						
Mod. Pentathlon		●	●	●	●	●										
Equestrian					●	●	●	●	●		●	●	●	●	●	
Shooting		●	●	●	●	●	●	●								
Archery												●	●	●	●	
Yachting			●	●	●	●				●	●	●				
Volleyball		●	●	●	●	●	●	●	●	●	●	●	●	●		
CLOSING																●

41

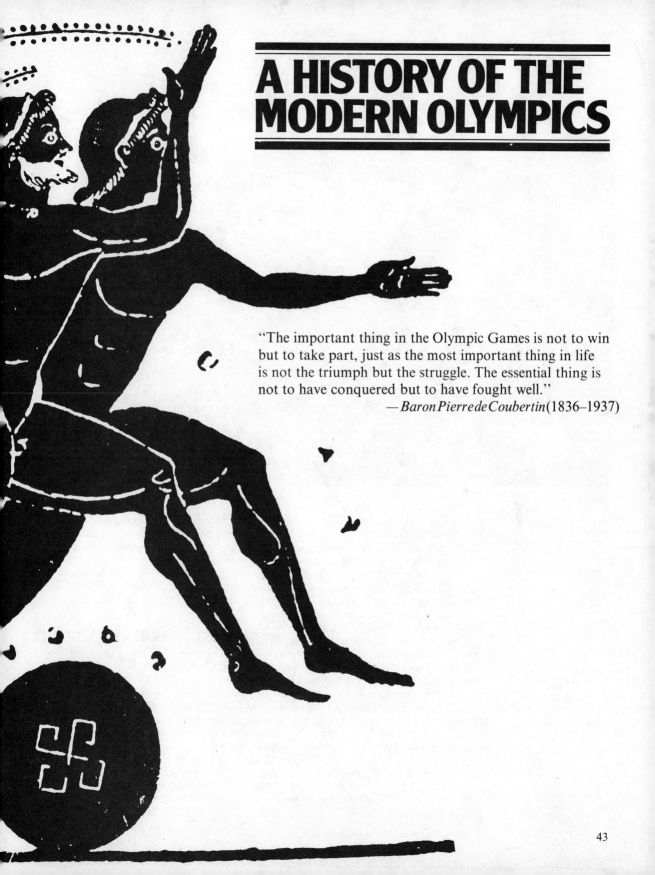

A HISTORY OF THE MODERN OLYMPICS

"The important thing in the Olympic Games is not to win but to take part, just as the most important thing in life is not the triumph but the struggle. The essential thing is not to have conquered but to have fought well."

— *Baron Pierre de Coubertin* (1836–1937)

ATHENS 1896

This picture captures the atmosphere and excitement generated by the revival of the Olympic Games, as Spyridon Louis wins the marathon for Greece.

*6 April on the new Gregorian calendar, which had not yet been adopted by Greece.

44

It was just after three o'clock in the afternoon on Monday, 25 March,* when King George of Greece rose from his seat in the reconstructed Panathenaic Stadion of Herodis and made a short, historic declaration: "I hereby proclaim the opening of the First International Olympic Games in Athens."

The opening ceremony, witnessed by a capacity crowd of more than 70,000 and overlooked by many thousands more spectators from vantage points in the surrounding hills, was followed by an anthem specially composed for the occasion. Then a strident bugle call signalled the first event, the heats of the 100 meters.

After an interval of nearly 1500 years since the last of the Hellenic Olympics in the fourth century A.D., the Olympic Games had begun again. The persistent enthusiasm of Baron Pierre de Coubertin for a revival of the Olympics had triumphed over all obstacles and an opposition which had at times been mountainous. The dream of the idealistic French nobleman had become reality.

Here in the following pages we are concerned with the personalities and performances that have made the Olympics the greatest sports show on earth. But without the perception, the vision and above all the determination of Baron de Coubertin the modern Games would never have got off the ground.

BARON PIERRE DE COUBERTIN
THE MAN WHO REVIVED THE OLYMPIC GAMES

Born into a French aristocratic family on 1 January 1863, Baron de Coubertin dropped out of the French military academy at St Cyr to study political science and education. In his youth he had discovered the virtue of sport, enjoying the comradeship and sportsmanship of his rivals while competing at fencing, rowing and boxing. He made a close study of the way sport and education were combined by Thomas Arnold, the headmaster of Rugby School in

England, who created the classic pattern of English public school education. It was after a pilgrimage to Thomas Arnold's tomb at Rugby that the Baron started to make public his then controversial views that mental and physical development should be linked. During a conference on English education in 1887, he extended his theories to embrace the revival of the Olympics: "It is not easy, if indeed easiness is a good thing, to get children enthusiastic about Alexander or Caesar. They need something more alive, more real. Olympic dust is what excites their emulation best and most naturally."

His idea of reviving the Olympics met a wall of indifference, skepticism and, in some cases, hostility. But the Baron was not to be denied and travelled around the world gathering and garnering support for his plan. He even had to overcome the opposition of the Greek government to staging the 1896 Games in Athens. They were on the brink of bankruptcy and refused to help finance the competition. But de Coubertin's idea had fired the imagination of the Greek people and Crown Prince Constantine headed a 12-man fund-raising committee. Thanks largely to a donation of a million drachmas (then worth about $80,000/£40,000) from a Greek philanthropist called Georgios Averoff and the sale of special commemorative stamps and medals, enough money was raised to build the necessary stadia and to make the Baron's dream come true. De Coubertin was President of the International Olympic Committee from 1896 to 1925 and was made Honorary President on his retirement. After his death in Geneva on 2 September 1937, his heart was interred at Olympia in a marble monument commemorating the father of the modern Olympics.

De Coubertin spread his Olympic gospel to 13 nations at a special congress in Paris in 1894 and another 21 nations pledged their support for a unanimously passed resolution that *"in order to maintain and promote physical culture, and particularly to bring about a friendly intercourse between the nations, sports competitions should be held every fourth year on the lines of the Greek Olympic Games and every nation should be invited to participate."*

For the rebirth of the Olympics at Athens in 1896, the 2000-year-old ruins of the Panathenaic Stadion of Herodis were reconstructed in marble under the supervision of architect Anastasios Metaxas. The 400-meter running track had two long straights and tight bends that could not be negotiated at high speed. There were 311 competitors representing 13 nations: Australia (1), Austria (4), Bulgaria (1), Chile (1), Denmark (4), Germany (19), France (19), Greece (230), Great Britain (8), Hungary (8), Sweden (1), Switzerland (1), United States (14).

Most of the athletes came to Athens at their own expense to take part in a program that consisted of nine sports: athletics, cycling, fencing, gymnastics, lawn tennis, shooting, swimming, weightlifting and wrestling. Every competitor was presented with a commemorative medal, and each champion and runner-up received a medal, a diploma and a crown of olive branches (for the winner) and a laurel crown (for second place). There was no presentation made to third-placed competitors. The crowning with olive branches was a ritual revived from the ancient Games when the Greeks believed that the recipient would be blessed with the vitality of the sacred olive tree.

The first modern Olympic champion to be crowned by King George of Greece was an American athlete by the name of James B. Connolly.

JAMES B. CONNOLLY
HE DROPPED OUT OF HARVARD FOR OLYMPIC GLORY

James Bernard Connolly was one of 11 track and field athletes in the 14-strong American team that had arrived at Athens by cross-Atlantic tramp steamer just one day before the opening ceremony. They thought they had given themselves 11 days to acclimatize and train but they had timed their arrival by the Gregorian calendar. Their Greek hosts were so overjoyed to see them that they insisted on giving them a huge welcoming banquet on their first night in Athens. It was an overfed and hungover United States team that reported for training the next morning.

But when the bugle call came for action on the track and field, the American athletes reacted as eagerly as if it were the signal for a cavalry charge. They won all three heats in the opening 100 meters event and then James Connolly triple-jumped to the first championship of the modern Olympics. He hopped, hopped again and then jumped to a winning distance of 44ft 11¾in (13.71m). Under today's rules he would have been disqualified because the correct sequence is a hop, *step* and jump. There is no record of how the Dean of Harvard University reacted when he heard the news of Connolly's triumph. He had refused a request from Connolly for leave of absence so that he could travel to Athens to compete in the Games. The headstrong student shrugged his shoulders

45

and dropped out of Harvard. (He later became a celebrated war correspondent.) Not for the last time, studies had come second to the lure of the Olympics.

Connolly added another medal to his collection when he finished second in the high jump, and he also finished third in the long jump behind two team-mates. The American athletes dominated the track and field events in dazzling fashion. They won nine of the 12 athletic competitions, with Robert Garrett emerging as the first great all-rounder of the modern Olympics.

ROBERT GARRETT
SO THIS IS WHAT A DISCUS LOOKS LIKE!

A student at Princeton University, shot-put specialist Robert Garrett had heard of a discus but had never actually seen one. While studying the Olympic program before leaving for Athens, he noticed that the discus was one of the field events. He asked a colleague what a discus looked like and was told that the dimensions were one inch in thickness and 12 inches in width. Garrett ordered a special disc to be made exactly that size. When it arrived at Princeton it looked like a giant pancake and

Spyridon Louis loaded with awards after his victory in the first Olympic marathon.

weighed nearly 20 pounds. Garrett had a couple of test throws and then decided to leave the discus to the Greeks.

It was not until he arrived in Athens that he saw a real discus for the first time. He was delighted to find it was much smaller and lighter than the home-made implement he had been heaving around at Princeton. After some practice throws, he decided to enter the discus event so that he could get accustomed to the stadium atmosphere in preparation for the shot put. Garrett was as stunned as the two stylish Greek favorites when with his final throw of the competition he won the Olympic title with a distance of 95ft 7¾in (29.15m). He then went on to win the shot put and to place second in the long jump and third in the high jump, both events being won by his countryman Ellery Clark.

Garrett was noted for his generosity as well as his strength. From a wealthy family, he paid for three fellow Princeton students to make the trip to Athens as members of the American team. Five others came from the Boston Athletic Association. It was not an officially selected United States team. As with several of the visiting teams, the selection process seemed to be quite simple: if you can get to Athens, you're in!

The newly-laid track quickly cut up and was not conducive to fast times. American sprinter Tom Burke added to his victory in the 100 meters (12.00 sec) by easily winning the 400 meters in 54.2 sec, a time he bettered by nearly six seconds a few weeks later. The Greek spectators sportingly applauded this procession of American triumphs but were longing to cheer a home victory. They had to wait until the final athletics event, the marathon.

SPYRIDON LOUIS
THE FIRST OLYMPIC MARATHON WINNER

Ever since the idea of the Athens Games had first been mooted, it had become a matter of national pride that Greece should provide the winner of the inaugural running of the marathon. This was to be the highlight of the Games, the brainchild of Frenchman Michel Bréal – a student of Greek mythology who suggested that a long-distance race should be staged from Marathon to Athens. Bréal based his idea on the legend that in 490 B.C. the Greeks had won a battle at Marathon against invading Persian forces. Pheidippides, a Greek soldier and Olympic champion runner, was dispatched on foot to carry the news of the victory to the people of Athens. He ran the 25 miles to the capital and had only enough breath on arrival to exclaim, "Rejoice, we conquer," before dropping dead in the town center. The imaginative plan of introducing a marathon race over the route Pheidippides had taken appealed to the Greeks, who made a nationwide search for competitors. They found 21 after a series of eliminating races. Among them was a former Greek shepherd, Spyridon Louis, who after army service had become a post office messenger. He used to build up his stamina by running alongside his mules while delivering letters and barrels of water to outlying districts on the Marathon to Athens route. All types of inducements were offered to inspire the Greek entrants to try to win, a prompting policy that would have appalled Baron de Coubertin, who hated commercialism of any sort and who was a strict advocate of the amateur code. Among the victory bribes being offered was one of a million drachmas plus the hand of his daughter in marriage by Georgios Averoff, the chief benefactor of the Games. There were also offers of a lifetime's free supply of clothes, wine, chocolate, bread, shaves and haircuts, and gifts of cattle, sheep and jewelry. All for any Greek who could win the Olympic marathon.

There were four foreign competitors in the field of 25 starters: Frenchman Albin Lermusiaux, Hungarian Gyula Kellner, American Arthur Blake – second in the 1500 meters – and Australian Edwin Flack, who was attempting an ambitious treble after winning both the 800 and 1500 meters on the track.

The first ever Olympic marathon was started by a pistol shot from the bridge of Marathon at 2:00 P.M. Accompanying the runners on horseback were Greek soldiers to clear the path ahead of the thousands of spectators lining the marathon route. Bringing up the rear in horse-drawn carts were a team of doctors and nurses.

The Frenchman, Lermusiaux, set off at a suicidal pace and with less than a third of the race run was nearly a mile ahead of the rest of the field, led by Flack and Blake. After being prematurely crowned as the winner by spectators, Lermusiaux collapsed in exhaustion, with more than an hour's running between him and the finish in Athens. Flack and Blake, both choked by the dust being kicked up by the escort of soldiers on their horses, also dropped out, leaving the jogging, fresh-looking Louis out on his own for the last three miles.

As Louis entered the stadium to a tumultuous roar from the crowd, Prince George and Crown Prince Constantine raced from the Royal Box to join him on the final lap to the finishing tape.

Three marathon competitors have a training run before the start of the gruelling race. There were just four overseas runners in a field of 25.

Louis became a Greek hero on the same scale as Pheidippides but he lived to enjoy it and was showered with gifts that made him comfortably well off for the rest of his life. The one offer he turned down was marriage to Miss Averoff. He was already a married man with two children.

Greek runners filled five of the first six places, with the Hungarian Kellner being awarded a special bronze medal as the first (and only) foreigner to finish the race. He came in fourth but was promoted to third after the Greek who finished just ahead of him had been disqualified for taking a lift in a horse-drawn carriage.

The excitement of the marathon took the attention away from the final field event of the Games, with Americans William Hoyt and Alfred Tyler filling first and second places in the pole vault. There was a standing ovation for Hoyt when he hoisted himself over the bar at 10ft 10in (3.30m) for victory.

Beyond the running track there were some astonishing things going on, particularly in the cycling events.

PAUL MASSON
FIRST OF THE TRIPLE OLYMPIC CHAMPIONS

France dominated the cycling at the specially erected Velodrome, with Paul Masson becoming the first triple champion of the Olympics. A sprint cyclist of formidable strength and speed, he won all three short races. The 100-kilometer race was surprisingly staged inside the Velodrome and Frenchman Leon Flamaud had to make 300 dizzy circuits of the track before winning in a little over three hours. Only one other competitor finished the race.

The Greeks found another marathon hero when Konstantinidis won the 87-kilometer cycle race from Athens to Marathon and back but his victory was not without incident. He wrecked two bikes *en route* and finished the race on a bicycle borrowed from a startled spectator who had just witnessed the sight of him crashing at full speed into a wall.

The only medals for America outside the athletics stadium were won by brothers John and Sumner Paine. They pulled off the first family double of the Olympics, John winning the 25-meter military revolver shooting and Sumner taking first place in the 30-meter event.

There was no more surprising or surprised Olympic champion than the young Irish lawyer Pius Boland, who won the lawn tennis singles and partnered Germany's Fritz Thraun to victory in the doubles. Boland just happened to be on holiday in Athens and entered what he thought was only a local tennis tournament on the spur of the moment. In an interview some years later, Boland admitted that he was not aware that he had become an Olympic champion.

Rough seas caused the cancellation of the rowing and the sailing programs but the swimming went ahead as scheduled – in the open sea at Phaleron. There were waves of over 10 feet and the water was freezing. Three competitors had to be rescued from drowning and dual Olympic champion Alfred (Guttman) Hajos of Hungary was quoted as saying: "My will to live completely overcame my desire to win."

Hajos, who changed his name by deed poll from Guttman, later won a silver medal in the architectural section of the 1924 Olympic art competition and is the only man to have won Olympic honors in the sports and cultural fields. He was awarded a special diploma for his services to the Olympic movement after the 1952 Helsinki Games.

Sir George Stuart Robertson was one of Britain's leading academics, with a Double First from Oxford, where he was elected a Fellow. But his first love away from his studies was athletics and he was a leading exponent of the hammer throw. Sir George travelled to Athens to compete in the hammer throw only to find the event was not included in the Olympic program. So that his journey was not entirely wasted, he took part in the shot and discus, finishing fourth and sixth respectively, and also competed in the lawn tennis championship. He did not return home empty handed. King George presented him with a special gold medal for writing and reciting a Greek ode in praise of the Games.

Sir George shared lodgings with Australian Edwin Flack and English hurdler Grantley Goulding. He persuaded the butler of the British Ambassador to accompany Flack on the marathon run as a pace-making cyclist. The butler rode alongside Flack, resplendent in bowler hat and pin-stripe trousers.

Grantley Goulding won a medal for Britain when he finished second behind American Tom Curtis in the 100 meters hurdles. There were only two competitors, the rest of the qualifiers withdrawing because of the looseness of the track. Goulding thus became the only athlete in Olympic history to finish last and still win a medal.

At this distance, much of what went on in Athens seems farcical and quite primitive but the Olympic flame had been relit and continues to burn, thanks to the organizers of these first revived Games at Athens. It was such a successful 10-day festival of sport that King George requested that Athens should become the permanent home of the Olympics but Baron de Coubertin ruled that this would rob the Games of a truly international flavor. He wanted all countries of the world to share in the celebration of the Games. The next temporary home for them was Paris in 1900.

OLYMPIC FUN AND GAMES

Britain's Launceston Elliott won the one-handed weightlifting competition with a lift of 156½lb. An attendant was unable to shift the weight with the use of two hands and looked on in embarrassment as Prince George picked it up with little trouble and tossed it to one side. The Prince was considered one of the strongest men in Greece and many of his countrymen believed he would have won the competition had he entered.

The second Olympiad was a disastrous affair, poorly organized and totally over-shadowed by the great Paris International Exhibition of 1900. Baron de Coubertin had what in theory seemed the bright idea of staging the Games in conjunction with the Exhibition but it led to the Olympics being reduced to little more than a novelty side-show.

De Coubertin's plans for the promotion and projection of the Games were sabotaged by his colleagues in the Union of French Athletic Associations (USFSA). They were blindly opposed to the principles of the Olympics and stubbornly refused to support the Baron, who finally resigned as USFSA secretary-general. After a long series of squabbles he managed to get the Games under way but without the grand presentation that he had at first envisaged. He later admitted: "It is a miracle that the Olympic movement survived this celebration."

A total of 1319 competitors from 22 nations took part in the Games but as they were spread out over five months (20 May to 28 October) there was confusion and, from the point of view of the public, great indifference as to who had won what and where. Olympic events took place at 15 different venues in and around Paris and were referred to in what little promotional publicity they were given as being part of the "International Meeting of Physical Exercises and Sport." It was not until 1912 that a roll of honor for the Paris Games was officially drawn

up by the International Olympic Committee and medals struck for the winners. Prizes presented to them immediately after their events included books, umbrellas and souvenirs of Paris. But amid all the chaos and confusion, the show did go on and the most successful of all Olympic athletes made his Games debut.

RAY C. EWRY
THE JUMP SPECIALIST WHO WON 10 GOLD MEDALS

Born at Lafayette, Indiana, on 14 October 1873, Ray C. Ewry was partially paralyzed by polio as a boy, and a doctor advised him that jumping from a standing position would help restore strength to his withered limbs. Little did he know it but the doctor had launched one of the most incredible of all Olympic careers. Ewry's therapy became his sport and he made a specialty of the standing jump while attending Purdue University.

A beanpole of an athlete at 6ft 3in and 152lb, Ewry made his Olympic debut in Paris on 16 July 1900, and in one afternoon won the standing high jump, standing long jump and standing triple jump. He set a world record of 5ft 5in (1.65m) in the high jump and finished third in the running high jump. In the 1904 Games in St Louis, Ewry successfully defended all three titles, stretching his own world record for the

Ray Ewry in action in the standing long jump in the 1908 Games, when he took his gold medal collection to an all-time record of 10.

standing long jump to 11ft 4⅛in (3.45m).

The greatest influence on his career was his wife, who, according to legend, used to nag constantly at her husband to keep in training. She travelled to Athens in 1906 as the team cook for the United States athletes competing in the unofficial Olympics and was at the side of the jumping pit encouraging her husband as he won the standing long jump and the standing high jump. He won both titles again at the London Olympics in 1908 at the age of 34. It took his gold medal collection to an unrivalled 10, eight of them in official Olympics. His extraordinary achievements can never be surpassed because the standing jumps were dropped from the Olympic program after 1912.

To add to his list of honors, Ewry was 15 times an American champion during a career that spanned 17 years. But he was not the most successful member of the United States athletics team competing on the grass track at Croix-Catelan in the Bois de Boulogne.

ALVIN KRAENZLEIN
A FOUR-TIME OLYMPIC CHAMPION

Alvin Kraenzlein, a pioneer of the modern technique of hurdling, was the outstanding all-rounder at the Paris Games. He won the 60 meters dash, 110 and 200 meters hurdles and the long jump, and remains the only athlete to have won four individual events in track and field at a single Olympics.

Kraenzlein won the long jump by just one centimeter from his great American rival Myer Prinstein, who missed the final because, along with many of the competitors, he refused to compete on a Sunday. Earlier in the year he had taken the world long jump record from Kraenzlein and led the qualifying competition for the Olympics final with a leap of 23ft 6½in (7.175m). But the championship went to Kraenzlein with a Sunday jump of 23ft 6¾in (7.185m). Prinstein was reported to have been so furious about his defeat that he attacked Kraenzlein with his fists and they had to be separated by team-mates. There was consolation for Prinstein when he won the hop, step and jump, beating defending champion James Connolly into second place. In the 1904 Games in St Louis, Prinstein won both the long jump and the hop, step and jump.

The decision to hold several finals on a Sunday caused a mass walk out of competitors. Irving Baxter, a descendant from Sioux Indians, benefitted when he won the pole vault to add to his high jump title. After a protest from two of his never-on-Sunday team-mates, it was agreed to re-stage the event. This time Baxter

finished third and Dan Orton was declared the champion with a new Olympic record vault of 11ft 3¾in (3.4m). Charles Dvorak, the first athlete to use a bamboo pole and the champion in St Louis in 1904, finished second. But the French officials caused further confusion by later ruling that the original Sunday result would stand. So Baxter, three times runner-up to Ewry in the standing jumps, was restored as champion.

Baxter, Kraenzlein and John Walter Tewksbury (winner of the 200 meters and the 400 meters hurdles) were room-mates at the University of Pennsylvania. Between them they won 14 medals in Paris. Americans captured 17 of the 23 track and field titles, with Frank Jarvis becoming the first man to break the 11.00 sec barrier in the 100 meters with a world record 10.8 sec in the heats. Another American, Arthur Newton, *thought* he had won the marathon.

MICHEL THEATO
A MARATHON CHAMPION WHO KNEW THE SHORT CUTS

Michel Theato, a Parisian baker's roundsman, knew all the ins-and-outs and short cuts of the back streets of Paris and it was strongly suspected that he had used some of them on his way to victory in the 25-mile marathon.

American Arthur Newton was convinced he had won the race. He claimed that he had taken the lead just after the halfway stage and that nobody had overtaken him from then until the finish line. Newton, who had proved himself one of the world's greatest distance runners during the previous two years, could not believe it when he was told he had come in sixth, more than 30 minutes behind Theato.

Another American, Dick Grant, later brought an unsuccessful lawsuit against the International Olympic Committee. He alleged that a cyclist had knocked him down as he was making a challenge for the lead. The race was poorly signposted and there was no marshalling of the crowds of sightseers. Twelve of the 19 starters gave up in a mixture of despair and exhaustion. It was 12 years later that Theato was officially confirmed as the winner.

The United States was stopped from making a clean sweep in the track and field events by British strength in the middle-distance races and some powerful discus throwing by Hungarian Rudolf Bauer. Almost from force of habit, the French bandsmen struck up the American National Anthem when Bauer climbed onto the victory rostrum. Bauer pointed out the error and new music sheets were hurriedly passed to the musicians. The victory ceremony was started again, this time with the band playing the Austrian anthem!

Alfred Tysoe (800 meters) and Charles Bennett (1500 meters) were winners for Great Britain in events weakened by American withdrawals because of the Sunday racing. Bennett then led Britain to victory in the team 5000 meters with a world record of 15 min 29.2 sec and his team-mate John Rimmer won the exhausting 4000 meters steeplechase. It took a combined team of Swedes and Danes to get the better of the Americans in the tug of war final.

Much to the disgust of Baron de Coubertin, the organizers managed to mix some professional athletics in with the amateur. Irish-American Mike Sweeney, considered a professional because he had accepted money to coach at a New York school, won both the high jump and long jump with better performances than in the official Games. Norman Pritchard, an American Indian hurdler, won the handicap 400 meters despite giving a four meter start to Olympic champion John Walter Tewksbury. The prize for each professional winner was 250 francs.

The swimming championships were held in the River Seine at Asnières in a current that swept the competitors yards off course. Farther down the river, anglers took part in the first and last Olympic fishing contest. Australian Freddie Lane won the 200 meters freestyle swimming title and then added a second championship by coming in first in a 200 meters obstacle race in which he had to clamber through three barrels on the way to the finish. A sign of how the current affected the swimmers is that he swam the obstacle race faster than the freestyle event. Britain's John Jarvis won the 1000 meters and 4000 meters freestyle race, and Frenchman M. de Vaudeville took the gold medal in the 60 meters underwater event, a race from which several competitors withdrew after looking at the muddy waters of the Seine.

For the first time, there was a woman among the Olympic champions.

CHARLOTTE COOPER
THE FIRST WOMAN OLYMPIC CHAMPION

Charlotte "Chattie" Cooper was an established British lawn tennis star when she went to Paris to challenge for Olympic titles. She had won three Wimbledon championships (1895–96–98) and was noted for her speed and agility about the court despite the long skirts that women players wore at the turn of the century. She beat French favorite Hélène Prevost 6–1, 6–4 in the singles final and then partnered the elder of the famous Doherty brothers, Reginald, to win the mixed doubles Olympic title. Charlotte added two more Wimbledon championships to her collection (1901 and 1908) before retiring.

OLYMPIC FUN AND GAMES

American Robert Garrett, defending the discus title he had won in Athens, had a disastrous time in Paris. The competitors had to throw the discus in a straight line between an avenue of trees, taking care to miss the single large tree that was directly in line with the throwing circle. Garrett kept bouncing the discus off the trees and was unplaced. In the shot put, he improved on his winning Athens performance by four feet but was still beaten into third place by his hefty team-mates Richard Sheldon and Josiah McCracken. The hammer-throwing competition took three times longer than expected because officials had to keep untangling the hammer wires from the branches of the surrounding trees. Irish-American strongman John Flanagan won the first of his three successive Olympic hammer-throwing titles.

President Theodore Roosevelt was called in as arbitrator when St Louis and Chicago clashed over which of the cities should stage the third Olympiad. The President sided with St Louis, which wanted to promote the Games along with a World Fair in celebration of the hundredth anniversary of the acquisition of Louisiana from Napoleon for $15 million. For the second – and last – time the Olympics became a side-show to a larger event.

These Games were little more than a glorified American championship. Of the 617 officially registered competitors, 525 were Americans and another 41 came from Canada. The other 51 entrants came from 10 different nations.

All sports events staged during the World Fair were publicized as being part of the Olympics but as these included inter-schools competitions, exhibition basketball, YMCA championships and open handicap events, many of the winners naturally did not find their way into the official Olympic records.

The track and field championships, held at the Washington University sports and recreation center from 29 August to 3 September, captured most public interest. They were particularly significant for the emergence of the first great Olympic sprinter.

ARCHIE HAHN
TRIPLE GOLD FOR "THE MILWAUKEE METEOR"

There have been several cases of sprint doubles in the Olympics but Archie Hahn – nicknamed "The Milwaukee Meteor" – is the only champion to have won three individual sprint gold medals at a single Olympiad. There was a 60-meter dash included along with the now traditional 100 and 200 meters at St Louis, and Hahn won all three.

Born in Dodgeville, Wisconsin, in 1880, Hahn set a remarkable record in the 200 meters that was an Olympic best for 28 years. Taking full advantage of running on a straight course and not having to negotiate a bend, he clocked 21.6 sec to complete his sprint triple. The race got off to an extraordinary start. After three false starts, the other three finalists were each ordered to start one full meter back behind the line. It was alleged that the cool Hahn had caused the false starts by pulling the old sprinter's trick of making a pretense of moving off immediately after the "get set" instruction from the starter. Hahn confirmed his superiority two years later by winning the 100 meters in the unofficial Olympics in Athens.

There were three more triple gold medal

winners in the track and field events, all of them Americans. Ray C. Ewry retained his three standing jump titles, Harry Hillman won the 200 meters hurdles, the 400 meters hurdles and the 400 meters flat race, and James D. Lightbody finished first in the 800 and 1500 meters and the 2500 meters steeplechase.

Lightbody, a Scottish-American from Chicago, had only recently switched to middle-distance running after making a reputation for himself as a sprinter. He also came second in the team 4000 meters while representing Chicago Athletic Club. In the 1500 meters final he beat W. F. Verner and L. C. Verner into second and third places respectively. They were the first brothers to win medals in Olympic track and field.

The versatile Hillman was at first credited with a world record 53.00 sec after winning the 400 meters hurdles. It was Hillman himself who had to advise embarrassed officials that a record was not possible because the hurdles had been only 2ft 6in high instead of the regulation 3ft. There were 13 starters in the 400 meters flat race final, Hillman winning a jostling match off the bend to go on to victory in an Olympic record time of 49.2 sec. George Poage finished third, the first black athlete to win an Olympic medal.

The outstanding athlete of the St Louis Olympics did not even get his name in the record books.

THOMAS KIELY
THE LONGEST DAY OF A GREAT ALL-ROUNDER

Based with the Irish-American Club of New York, Thomas Kiely won the Olympic "all-rounder championship," which was the fore-runner of the decathlon. In one exhausting day, the athletes had to compete in the 100 yards, 880 yards walk, 120 yards hurdles, shot put, high jump, pole vault, hammer, long jump, 56lb weight and a one-mile race! Kiely won four of the events on his way to the title of top all-rounder of the Games but it was not until 1954 that his name was at last entered in the official Olympic records.

Along with Irishman Kiely, there was only one other non-American winner in the track and field championships. French-Canadian policeman Emile Desmarteau from Montreal hitch-hiked to St Louis, where he broke the American stranglehold on the strongman events by winning the 56lb weight competition. He heaved the weight 34ft 4in (10.46m) to beat the legendary Irish-American John "Whaleman" Flanagan, the triple hammer champion.

The giant Ralph W. Rose, 6ft 5in tall and a bulky 235lb, was just 20 when he won his first Olympic gold medal in the shot put at St Louis. He retained the title in London in 1908 and won the two-handed shot at Stockholm in 1912. Born in Louisville, Kentucky, in 1884, he set four world records in the shot between 1907 and 1909 and was unbeaten in the event for 19 years. He also set a world record in the hammer throw and took the silver medal in the discus at St Louis, where he threw exactly the same distance as the eventual winner Martin Sheridan. Another of the army of American powermen, Sheridan won the shot and discus in the 1906 Interim Olympics in Athens and retained his discus title in London in 1908.

Once again, it was the marathon that provided the biggest drama and controversy of the Games.

THOMAS HICKS
THE MARATHON WINNER WHO FOLLOWED A JOKER

Thomas Hicks, born in Birmingham, England, but representing the United States, won the St Louis marathon but not until after a hoaxer had been hailed as the champion. Fred Lorz had dropped out of the race after nine miles because of a severe cramp and gratefully accepted a lift to the stadium. The automobile in which he was travelling broke down and so Lorz completed the last four miles on foot. When he came trotting into the stadium way ahead of marathon leader Thomas Hicks the crowd rose to acclaim Lorz, thinking he was the winner of the exhausting race. Lorz did nothing to disillusion them and allowed himself to be carried in triumph to the VIP area of the stadium, where he was introduced to Alice Roosevelt, the daughter of the President. He was about to be presented with the gold medal when officials who had been accompanying Hicks stopped the presentation and exposed Lorz as an impostor. It was later announced that Lorz had been banned from athletics for life but his explanation that he had only been having a joke that got out of hand was accepted. He won the American marathon championship the following year without any motorized assistance.

Judging by today's strictly applied rules of the road in marathon running, Hicks himself would have been disqualified. He was in a state of near collapse for the last third of the race and was kept going by the administration of strychnine tablets, raw eggs and brandy. At one stage

Martin Sheridan, one of the army of American powermen. He dominated the discus in 1904 and 1908.

two spectators supported him as he weaved around on rubber legs. He finished the 40 kilometer race at walking pace and collapsed unconscious after crossing the finish line. It was only after he was discharged from hospital that he was awarded his medal. He never ran the marathon again. The race was run in blistering heat, with temperatures a scorching 90 degrees in the shade. Seventeen of the 31 runners failed to complete the course.

There was more controversy and confusion on the cycling track.

MARCUS HURLEY
FOUR GOLDS ON TWO WHEELS

Totally ignorant of the strict Olympic rules on amateurism, the cycling organizers in St Louis invited professionals to compete along with the amateurs. After long argument and angry protests, the professionals walked out and held a meeting of their own on another track. American Marcus Hurley was unbeatable in the short races, winning the quarter-mile, one-third of a mile, the half-mile and the mile. He is the only cyclist ever to have won four gold medals in one Olympiad but is not included in the official record books because his events were not over recognized Olympic distances.

Zoltan von Halmay interrupted the American monopoly in the swimming pool, which was an asymmetrical lake with the judges working from rafts. But the Hungarian swimmer had to win the 50 yards freestyle event twice before getting his gold. Most observers thought he had beaten

American Scott Leary in a tight finish to the final. After a bitter argument between the judges during which fists were thrown, von Halmay agreed to a re-staging of the race. This time he beat Leary by over a yard in 28 seconds. He also won the 100 yards event.

Boxing was part of the Olympic program for the first time in 1904 but only Americans entered and several of the boxers competed in more than one weight division. O. L. Kirk won both the bantam and featherweight titles, the flyweight champion George Finnegan was runner-up in the bantamweight class, H. J. Spangler was a gold medallist at lightweight and a silver medallist at welterweight, and middleweight winner Charles Mayer was runner-up at heavyweight.

The Cubans sent a strong team but were prominent only in the fencing, where Ramon Fonst won the foil and épée events to add to the gold medal he had won in the épée in Paris in 1900. He collected a fourth gold medal at St Louis when he helped Cuba beat a combined team that included two Americans and one of his own countrymen.

Among sports that came under the Olympic banner for the first and only time were golf (won by leading American amateur George S. Lyon) and Indian club swinging. American Edward Hennig was the gold medallist in the Indian club, and 47 years later was American champion at his sport for the umpteenth time.

The Games were turned into a parody of the Olympics for two days when ethnic groups were invited to take part in sports for which they were not properly prepared. There was, for instance, a pygmy in the shot put and Zulu natives were persuaded to take part in bow and arrow contests. All the competitors were in St Louis working on exhibition stands and in side-shows at the World Fair. The organizers thought that by getting them involved in the Olympics it would give the Games an international flavor but instead it lifted the Olympics into the area of farce.

Baron de Coubertin did not attend the Games in St Louis. When told of how they had been allowed to become a circus for two days during what was billed as the "Ethnographical Olympics," he was reported to have said: "This outrageous charade will lose its appeal when black men, red men and yellow men learn to run, jump and throw, and leave the white men behind them."

OLYMPIC FUN AND GAMES

Felix Carvajal, a postman from Cuba, raised his boat fare to the United States by giving running exhibitions in the center of Havana and then taking a begging bowl around the gathered crowds. During the boat trip, he lost all his money in a dice game and had to hitch his way from New Orleans to St Louis, where he was entered in the marathon. He turned up for the start wearing walking shoes, long trousers and a long-sleeved shirt. American discus thrower Martin Sheridan felt sorry for him because everybody was laughing and borrowed a pair of shears and trimmed his sleeves and trouser legs so that he at least looked an athlete. Carvajal, running his first ever marathon, was giving a good account of himself and was in with a victory chance until he found a fruit orchard and started stuffing himself with apples and peaches. He then started chatting with spectators before returning to the race in which he finished a creditable fifth. Two South African competitors were chased three-quarters of a mile off course during the marathon by a ferocious dog.

A thens staged an interim Games in 1906 but they were not given official status by the International Olympic Committee, which had awarded the fourth Olympiad to Rome. With less than two years to the 1908 Games the Italians decided that because of the devastation caused by the eruption of the volcano Vesuvius they could not cope with the organization, and London took over at short notice. It was 19 November 1906 when London was officially asked to become the next home for the Olympics. The Games opened on 13 July 1908 at the White City, where a new stadium had been built to house the athletics, swimming, cycling, fencing, gymnastics and wrestling.

Thanks to the organizational flair of Lord Desborough and the industry of the British Olympic Committee, the Games were the most successful to date and set the pattern for future Olympiads. They were, however, soured by some highly debatable and possibly chauvinistic decisions by the British judges in the athletics arena, with the powerful American team being particularly alienated.

Heading the United States Olympic officials were the outspoken James Sullivan (the Sullivan Award continues to be made to outstanding American athletes) and the legendary American football coach Amos Alonzo Stagg. Both made bitter protests about what they considered anti-American attitudes and Sullivan reported on his arrival back in the States: "They [the officials] were unfair to the Americans, they were unfair to every athlete except the British but their real aim was to beat the Americans. Their conduct was cruel and unsportsmanlike and absolutely unfair."

Relationships between the British and American athletic associations were temporarily broken off and feelings ran so high that angry officials in London produced a book titled *Replies to Criticisms of the Olympic Games*. It was above all the final of the 400 meters that triggered the hostility.

WYNDHAM HALSWELLE
THE LONELINESS OF THE SHORT-DISTANCE RUNNER

One of the saddest sights of any Olympics was that of Wyndham Halswelle running alone around the White City track to take the gold medal in a ridiculous mockery of a 400 meters final. This was the sensational sequel to a race that caused so much controversy it nearly led to a walkout by the entire American team.

Halswelle, a London Scot who was serving as a regular soldier and held the rank of lieutenant

in the British Army, was one of four qualifiers for the final. He had set an Olympic record time of 48.4 sec in the semi-final, and British victory hopes were high as he lined up against a powerful trio of Americans, J. C. Carpenter, W. C. Robbins and black sprinter J. P. Taylor, who had been the pre-Games favorite. The race was not run in lanes, or strings as they were then called, and there was no staggered start. Carpenter lined up on the inside, with Halswelle alongside and Robbins and Taylor outside him. There was something of a free-for-all after 50 meters with Robbins cutting across Halswelle to run at Carpenter's shoulder on the inside.

As they entered the long home straight on the horseshoe-shaped third of a mile track, Halswelle made his bid for the lead but Carpenter took a diagonal course for the finish line and made the British champion chop his stride. Straw-hatted British officials watching from the center of the track shouted out in protest and one of them stepped forward and snapped the tape before Carpenter could cross the line in first place. There was uproar, with the Americans threatening a mass withdrawal of their team. The United States camp was already seething over what they considered biased decisions against them, and the tug-of-war team had refused to take any further part in their event. They claimed they had been unfairly beaten by a British tug-of-war team wearing heavy boots that the Americans insisted were illegal.

Wyndham Halswelle, the British 400 meters runner who was literally out on his own.

Olympic officials studied the footprints of the runners in the 400 meters and ruled that Carpenter had deliberately forced Halswelle wide. They disqualified the American and ordered the race to be re-run two days later. Robbins and Taylor pulled out in protest and Halswelle ran a solo race in exactly 50 seconds, the only athlete ever to win an Olympic gold medal with a walk-over. But even this was not the biggest sensation of the Games.

DORANDO PIETRI
COLLAPSE OF THE MARATHON MAN

It was scorching hot at 2:30 P.M. on Friday, 24 July 1908, when 54 competitors set out from Windsor Castle on a 26-mile marathon run to the White City. Once they reached the stadium they would have just another 385 yards to negotiate around the track to cross the finish line in front of the royal box, where Queen Alexandra was waiting to greet the winner. Thus it was that the marathon distance became standardized throughout the world at 26 miles 385 yards. Those extra 385 yards were the undoing of Dorando Pietri, a slim little candy-maker from Capri in Italy.

Dorando, a comical looking figure in his white vest and red knickerbockers, overtook South African favorite Charles Hefferon with two miles to go and was comfortably in the lead when he reached the stadium. But the sweltering conditions that had already forced 29 of the runners out of the race suddenly took their toll on the Italian and he slowed to what looked like a drunken walk as he came on to the track in front of a roaring, capacity crowd. He turned right instead of left, tottered and crumpled slowly to the ground like a puppet that has

had its strings cut away. Doctors and track officials crowded anxiously around him as he was helped to his feet and pointed in the right direction for the finishing tape. Four times Dorando collapsed and each time willing hands helped him up. Finally, with the crowd urging and willing the near-unconscious Italian on, he staggered across the line, supported on both sides by officials. Soon after, the American No 1 John Hayes, who had paced himself intelligently, became the second man to enter the stadium and he finished with an impressive sprint and under his own steam. There were efforts made to award the race to Dorando but after an American protest he was – inevitably under the rules – disqualified and Hayes was declared the Olympic champion. But it was the little candyman from Capri who had captured the hearts of the British public and Queen

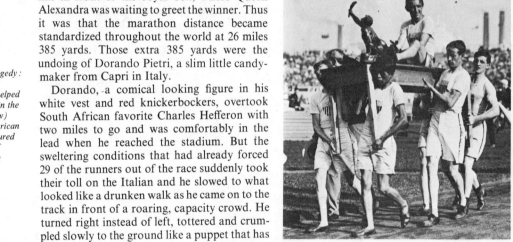

Olympic triumph and tragedy: Dorando Pietri was disqualified after being helped across the finishing line in the London marathon (below) and victory went to American John Hayes, who is pictured being carried on a lap of honor by his team-mates (right).

Alexandra was so moved by his performance that she presented him with a special gold cup. Dorando became one of the immortals of Olympic history, while the winner, Hayes, a New York department store clerk, was virtually forgotten outside the United States. The United States team dominated the track and field events and Hayes was but one of the 16 American gold medal winners.

JOHN J. FLANAGAN
HAMMERING THE OPPOSITION

Born in Limerick, Ireland, in 1868, John J. Flanagan did more than anybody to make the hammer throw an event to be taken seriously. He was Olympic hammer champion in 1900, 1904 and again in 1908, and in London – at the age of 40 – broke his own Olympic record with a throw of 170ft 4¼in (51.92m). An immensely powerful man, he won a silver medal in the 56lb weight in 1904 and at the same Games finished fourth in the discus.

Flanagan set new world records in the hammer no fewer than 16 times, improving his best from 145ft 10½in (44.47m) in 1895 while in Ireland to 184ft 4in (56.20m) in 1909, by which time he was an American citizen. Until the emergence of four-times champion Al Oerter, Flanagan was the only Olympian to win three successive gold medals in a standard track and field event. Flanagan inspired an army of Irish field event experts and for many years Irishmen dominated the strongman events. All three medal winners in the hammer event in London were Irish-born but were representing other countries. Silver medallist Matt McGrath was competing for the United States and bronze medallist Con Walsh wore a Canadian vest.

Sweden's Erik Lemming halted an American monopoly of the throwing events in the London Games by winning the orthodox and freestyle javelin titles. He was a versatile athlete, finishing fourth in the pole vault and fifth in the high jump in the Paris Olympics in 1900. But the javelin was his speciality event and he broke the world record he first set in 1899 at the age of 19 nine times. He retained his orthodox javelin championship in the 1912 Olympics and came fourth in the two-handed throw. Lemming is one of the few Olympic athletes who have twice won gold medals with world record performances. Finland's Ville Ritola achieved this notable double in the 3000 meters steeplechase and 10,000 meters in 1924, and Ethiopian marathon runner Abebe Bikila bettered the world best time for his event when winning gold medals in 1960 and 1964.

America's Melvin Sheppard was in world record breaking form on his way to three gold medals on the track in London in 1908.

MELVIN SHEPPARD
THE RUNNER WHO LIKED TO LEAD ALL THE WAY

A powerful runner from New Jersey, Melvin Sheppard was one of the first athletes at top level to prove that you could lead from gun to tape. He had no time for cautious tactics and

Melvin Sheppard beats Britain's Harold Wilson to the tape in the 1500 meters final on his way to a golden double in the 1908 Games.

High jumper Harry Porter and pole vaulter Edward Cooke touch golden heights for the United States.

believed in trying to burn off the opposition with a "killer" pace. This bold method brought him not only a gold medal in the 800 meters in London but also a new world record of 1 min 52.8 sec. He also won the 1500 meters with some impressive front-running and ran a leg in the

1600 meters medley relay for the winning United States quartet.

Sheppard tried his from-the-front tactics again in the 800 meters in Stockholm in 1912 but was overhauled in a tight finish by his 19-year-old countryman Ted Meredith, who – thanks to Sheppard's pacemaking – set new world records for 800 meters and 880 yards. Sheppard again helped the United States win the relay to take his personal gold medal haul to four.

Forest Smithson was rated fourth best of the Americans who reached the 110 meters hurdles final but he was a great competitor and streaked to victory in a world record 15.00 sec. For the third successive Olympics Americans were first, second and third in this event – a triple triumph that was repeated again in Stockholm in 1912.

America won *two* gold medals in the pole vault. Edward Cooke and Alfred Gilbert both cleared 12ft 2in (3.71m), and because the athletics program was running late, owing to the marathon dramas, it was decided to call it a tie rather than have a jump-off in the darkened stadium.

J. P. Taylor became the first black gold medallist when he ran a leg in the United States medley relay team. He was clocked at 49.8 sec in his 400 meters stage of the relay. Tragically, this talented athlete was dead from typhoid before the year was out.

The London Games were staged on a larger scale than ever before with the number of sports increased to 21, including for the first time a winter sport in the form of ice-skating. Taking second place in prominence to the track and field events were the swimming championships, which were staged in a pool set in the middle of the athletics arena. Britain had a triple gold medal winner.

HENRY TAYLOR
MAKING A SPLASH AT THE WHITE CITY

An orphan from Chadderton in Lancashire, England, Henry Taylor was raised by an elder brother and learned to swim in the shipping canals near his Oldham home. He competed in three Olympiads during a long and successful career that saw him win 15 English championships in distances ranging from 440 yards to five miles.

The peak of his career came in July 1908, when he won three Olympic medals in the 100 meter pool specially erected in the center of White City Stadium. He set world records on his way to victory in the 400 meters freestyle

(5 min 36.8 sec) and 1500 meters freestyle (22 min 48.4 sec) and anchored Britain to victory in the 4 × 200 meters relay. Taylor later competed in the 1912 and 1920 Olympics, winning a bronze medal at each of them in the 4 × 200 meters relay.

Hungary's outstanding sprint swimmer Zoltan von Halmay was surprisingly overhauled by Taylor on the final leg of the 4 × 200 meters relay in the 1908 Games. Only at the end of the race did spectators realize the courage von Halmay had shown to finish the event at all, let alone getting Hungary home in second place. He got a cramp on the last length and twice sank, forcing himself to keep going by sheer willpower. After beating America to the silver medal by a touch, he sank for a third time and was unconscious when lifted out of the water. It was several anxious hours before he recovered. He also got a silver medal in the 100 meters freestyle behind American Charlie Daniels, who set a new world record of 65.6 sec on his way to victory.

Britain's Dick Gunn became the oldest boxer to win an Olympic championship when he beat countryman C. W. Morris in the featherweight division. Gunn was making a comeback at the age of 38, having retired after winning the British amateur championship three successive times between 1894 and 1896. There was a poor overseas entry for the boxing with Britain having a virtual clean sweep. J. W. T. Douglas was the middleweight champion and later went on to captain England at Test cricket. He was nicknamed "Johnny Won't Hit Today" Douglas because of his defensive batting.

There was a lot of activity away from the main stadium, even as far away as Scotland. The yachting events of 1908 were divided between Ryde in the Isle of Wight and the Bonny Firth of Clyde in Scotland. Again British entries made a clean sweep, as they did in lawn tennis, rowing, racquets and polo.

Among the yachting medal winners was the Duchess of Westminster, the sister-in-law of Jenny Jerome, who was the mother of Winston Churchill. The Duchess entered her 8-meter yacht, Sorais, at Ryde and sailed the 16-mile course on three successive days with a four-man crew. The 31-year-old Duchess collected a silver medal.

The Duke of Westminster was also in Olympic action in the rare sport for the Games of motorboat racing. There were just seven boats racing for three gold medals. The Duke looked certain to win the unrestricted class in his powerful 40-foot Wolseley-Siddeley when he ran onto a sand bank and out of the race.

For the first time in the Olympics, there was a father and daughter medal double. Britain's W. Dodd won the men's archery gold and his daughter, Miss N. Dodd, took the silver in the women's archery.

Despite the acrimony between Great Britain and the United States, it was agreed that the British had set new standards for staging the Games. The pattern had been set for future Olympiads.

The 1908 wrestling championships were held on a raised canvas mat in the middle of the track and field arena at the White City Stadium, London.

OLYMPIC FUN AND GAMES

Asked how he had prepared for the 200 meters final in the track and field, which he won in style, Canadian sprinter Robert Kerr revealed: "I went out last night and got nicely drunk and danced until the early hours of this morning." Kerr felt he had been beaten in the 100 meters final because he had overtrained. So he went out on the town instead.

The Danish women's team gives a demonstration of Olympic gymnastics 1912 style.

JIM THORPE
THE DOUBLE CHAMPION WHO WAS ORDERED TO RETURN HIS MEDALS

Jim Thorpe, a full-blooded Sac Indian from Carlisle, Pennsylvania, won both the pentathlon and the decathlon in Stockholm but his name will not be found in the Olympic record books. Thorpe, whose tribal name was Wa-Tho-Huck, meaning Bright Path, was an extraordinary all-round athlete. Legend has it that he once represented his Carlisle Indian school on his own in an athletics match against a team from Lafayette College and won eight events. His strongest events were high jumping and high hurdling, and apart from winning the pentathlon and decathlon in Sweden, he also finished fourth in the individual high jump and seventh in the long jump.

Six months after his phenomenal performances in the Games, the United States Olympic Committee informed the IOC that they were ordering Thorpe to return his gold medals because they had evidence that he had played professional baseball. Thorpe's name was removed from the official records, with the runners-up being declared as substitute champions. It is true that Thorpe played in minor professional baseball for a few dollars expenses when little more than a schoolboy but he had the sympathy of everybody outside – and a lot of people inside – the Olympic movement for what seemed harsh punishment.

The world of professional sport welcomed Thorpe with open arms and he added to his record of renown with his feats on the American football field. In a poll organized in the United States in 1950 Thorpe was voted the Athlete of the Half-Century. Following his death in 1953, the Indians commemorated their idol by erecting a monument in his memory.

There was one challenger to Thorpe for the title of oustanding athlete of the 1912 Games – the Finn Hannes Kolehmainen.

HANNES KOLEHMAINEN
FATHER OF THE GREAT FLYING FINNS

"Hannes the Mighty" Kolehmainen started the tradition of great Finnish middle and long distance running by winning three gold medals at Stockholm. He was the most famous and talented of three athletic brothers: there was Tatu, who competed with him in the 1912 Games, and William, who was an outstanding professional runner, competing in marathon

The 1912 Games in Stockholm set new peaks in Olympic promotion, participation and performance. They were superbly organized by the Swedes, who provided top-quality facilities for more than 3000 competitors from 18 nations. Olympic records tumbled in almost every event and there was none of the bitterness and chauvinism that threatened to disrupt the London Games.

These were truly a modern Olympics, with an electrical timing device, a photo-finish camera and a public-address system introduced for the first time. The Swedes erected a magnificent new athletics stadium and also a 100-meter pool for the swimming and diving events. The cinder running track was designed and laid by famous British groundsman Charles Perry, who had also laid the track for the 1896 Games in Athens.

These Games popularized gymnastics as a major sport, with 13 nations entering teams totalling more than 1000 men and women competitors. Troupes of Scandinavians gave exhibitions of elegant gymnastic movements and there were five days of competition staged in the athletics stadium before knowledgeable and appreciative near-capacity crowds. Italy won the men's team gold medal and their star performer Alberto Braglia retained the individual title he had won in London. Since the 1908 Games he had been working in a circus as an acrobat and trapeze artist and it was debatable whether he still qualified as an amateur.

The Olympic International Committee was fierce in its interpretation of the amateur code and its strict rulings led to one of the saddest stories in the history of the Games.

2 hr 30 min. He continued running into his mid-thirties, retiring after setting world records at 25,000 meters and 30,000 meters in 1922.

The United States was again the dominant force in the track and field events, taking 16 gold medals (two of which were later taken away from the luckless Jim Thorpe). The Americans were understandably confident of winning the 800 meters, with six of the eight finalists, but were themselves stunned by the outcome of the race.

TED MEREDITH
THE WORLD RECORD-BREAKING SCHOOLBOY

James "Ted" Meredith was still at school in Philadelphia when he won selection in the United States team for the Olympic 800 meters. American officials thought he had surpassed himself by reaching the final with a best-ever run of 1 min 54.4 sec in the heats. Defending champion Mel Sheppard decided he would make a world record bid in the final, and special arrangements were also made to record the time at 880 yards, which was 4.67 meters past the 800-meter finishing line. The 19-year-old Meredith was asked whether he would act as a pace-maker, which he readily agreed to. But after 200 meters Sheppard decided the pace was not fast enough and took the lead with one of his typical long bursts for the tape. Meredith clung gamely to the champion's heels and then in the finishing stretch powered past the tiring Sheppard to set world records for 800 meters (1 min 51.9 sec) and 880 yards (1 min 52.5 sec). Sheppard in second place also finished inside the old world records.

It was a disappointing Games for Sheppard in defense of the two titles he had won in London. He also reached the 1500 meters final but was unplaced in an astonishing race where the favorites were three Americans: Abel Kiviat, the world record holder; John Paul Jones, who held the world one-mile record; and Norman Taber, who was destined to set a new mile record. Little attention was given to two Britons in the 14-man final: Arnold Strode-Jackson, an Oxford University student, and Philip Noel-Baker from Cambridge University. This was the last Games at which individual entries were accepted, and both British students had made their own way to Stockholm and wore the colors of their respective and rival universities. The trio of Americans were so concerned with watching each other in the finishing stretch that they did not see the long-

events on both sides of the Atlantic. But it was Hannes (an abbreviation of Johannes) who became regarded as the father of Finnish running.

He won three key events in Stockholm, the 10,000 meters, the 5000 meters and the 8000 meters cross-country race. His effortless, economical style was the despair of his hard-worked opponents as they watched him race easily to two Olympic records and a world record in the 3000 meters team race (in which he received a silver medal because his team-mates were unable to give him sufficient support). Including heats, Kolehmainen ran a total of more than 25 miles in the Stockholm Games and was first through the tape in every race he entered. Frenchman Jean Bouin, world record holder for the greatest distance run in an hour, was the only athlete to give him any real opposition but the Finn timed his home-stretch run to perfection to win a thrilling 5000 meters race after Bouin had set a sizzling pace.

Kolehmainen went to live in the United States in 1913, where he won five national championships and created a whole string of new American track and road records. He returned home to Finland in time to compete in the 1920 Games in Antwerp, where he won the marathon in 2 hr 32 min 35.8 sec. The course was later found to be 600 yards farther than the official marathon distance so he was robbed of the chance of being one of the first men inside

The Olympic rowers of 1912 had to share the water with tugs and steamers. For the Moscow Games there is an exclusive rowing canal that is considered the best stretch of rowing water in Europe.

striding Strode-Jackson come up on the outside to snatch victory by one-tenth of a second from Kiviat, who beat Taber by a stride for the silver medal. Philip Noel-Baker finished sixth but gained valuable experience that enabled him to take the silver medal in the same event at Antwerp in 1920.

Both Strode-Jackson and Noel-Baker, life-long friends, went on to gain distinction off the track. Strode-Jackson showed immense courage during action in the First World War. He was wounded four times and was awarded the Distinguished Service Order and three bars. His colleague from Cambridge University became the Right Honourable Philip Noel-Baker, Privy Councillor, the winner of the 1959 Nobel Peace Prize. But even these two great Olympians could not match the staying power of American sprinter Ralph Craig.

RALPH CRAIG
EIGHT FALSE STARTS FAIL TO DAMPEN HIS OLYMPIC SPIRIT

Born in Detroit, Michigan, in 1889, Ralph Craig made a reputation for himself as a sprinter while studying at the University of Michigan. He won three inter-collegiate sprint titles and twice equalled the world 220 yards record. His cool competitive nature served him well in Stockholm in the final of the 100 meters. There were eight false starts, and after one of them Craig and most of the other runners completed the full course before they were recalled. Tempers were getting snappy down on the

starting line but Craig gave total concentration to the race, and when the field got away at the ninth time of asking, he bulleted into action to win in 10.8 sec with his countrymen Alvah Meyer and Dave Lippincott in second and third places. In the 200 meters final, Craig produced a storming finish to defeat his team-mate Lippincott on the line in 21.7 sec with Britain's Willie Applegarth in third place.

Craig was overwhelmed by the camaraderie and spirit of the Games and vowed that one day he would again take part in the Olympics. But his chances seemed lost when war wiped the scheduled 1916 Games off the calendar. The determined Craig tried 20 different sports as he strove for another Olympic selection. Finally, at the age of 59 and by then a wealthy industrial engineer, he was back on the Olympic roster when he captained the United States yachting team in the 1948 Games in London, 36 years after his double gold medal success in Stockholm.

Danish fencer Ivan Osiier had an even longer-running love affair with the Olympics. He competed in seven Olympiads between 1908 and 1948, deliberately missing the 1936 Games as an anti-Nazi gesture. Osiier won one medal, a silver in the épée in 1912.

Hammer-thrower Matt McGrath, one of the Irish-American power men, was another durable competitor. He won the 1912 hammer at the age of 36, increasing the Olympic record with each of his six throws and finishing with a gold medal winning distance of 179ft 7in (54.74m), a Games best that endured for 24 years. McGrath was still competing at the age of 58.

Pat McDonald – another of "The Mighty Macs" in the American team – heaved the 16lb shot over 50ft only once in a career that lasted more than a quarter of a century. But he did it when it mattered, winning the gold medal with a put of 50ft 4in (15.34m) to beat his team-mate Ralph Rose with his very last attempt. McDonald also won the 56lb weight event at Antwerp in 1920 and was American champion in the shot put as late as 1933. The giant Rose, weighing 250lb and eating two pounds of steak and six raw eggs for breakfast every day, won the two-handed shot.

South Africans Ken McArthur and Charles Gitsham scored a one-two in a marathon that was overshadowed by the tragic death of Portuguese entrant Lazaro. He collapsed in the closing stages of the race and was taken to a hospital where he died the following day.

Beyond the track, it was the swimming events that captured public imagination. There were 313 competitors from 18 countries and the standards were high, with a popular character from Hawaii receiving the biggest ovation from the sporting Swedish spectators.

DUKE KAHANAMOKU
THE CHEERFUL CHAMPION FROM HONOLULU

Duke Paoa Kahanamoku was born in the Royal Palace in Honolulu in 1890, three years before the end of the Hawaiian monarchy. Duke was not a title but a name, given to him because Queen Victoria's son, the Duke of Edinburgh, happened to be visiting the island when he was born. He became a powerful swimmer by spending all his spare time swimming and surfing in the Pacific Ocean. An expert at surfing, he introduced the sport around the world after his long competitive career was over. He and Johnny Weissmuller, whose careers overlapped, shared the distinction of being the only men to win the 100 meters free-style title at two successive Olympics. Both of them also later started film-acting careers, with Kahanamoku usually cast in the role of a Hawaiian king. The bronzed man from Honolulu had a lot of charm and charisma and always had a wide smile on his face. Controversy surrounded both his 100 meters victories but he did not let the incidents upset his cheerful composure.

He easily won his two 100 meters heats in the salt-water pool in Stockholm but because of a mix-up over starting times he missed the semi-finals. This triggered one of the few arguments of the friendly 1912 Games, and after protests from the American Olympic Committee it was decided that Kahanamoku and two team-mates who also missed the semi-finals could swim in a special 100 meters race. Provided they bettered the time of the slowest qualifiers from the semi-finals, they would be allowed into the final. The Hawaiian was so anxious to make it into the final that he spurted through the water to a new world record 62.4 sec. He confirmed his superiority the next day by taking the gold medal, beating the Australian ace, Cecil Healy, by more than a second.

Kahanamoku smashed the world record again when retaining the title in Antwerp in 1920. His new record of 60.4 sec was allowed to stand even though the race had to be re-swum because of a protest from an Australian competitor who had been obstructed by an American swimmer. The Duke – as he was known to Olympic followers throughout the world – smiled and shrugged and went out and won the race for a second time. He won another gold medal in the 4 × 200 meters freestyle relay to go with the silver he had won in the same event in 1912. Johnny Weissmuller prevented him completing a hat-trick of title wins in the 100 meters when he beat him into second place in the 1924 final in Paris.

Weissmuller and Kahanamoku found fame in other spheres after their swimming careers were over but not to the extent of a competitor in the modern pentathlon. A young army cadet from West Point, G. S. Patton, finished fifth and was awarded a special Olympic Diploma for being the highest placed of the non-Swedish entrants. Young Patton, so neutral observers reported, might have fared even better had he not insisted on shooting with a Colt revolver rather than the conventional target pistol. He later became known throughout the world as General George Patton, who led an historic armored advance through western Europe during World War II. Another American entrant in the pentathlon – and the decathlon – who was to become better known in the future was Avery Brundage, President of the International Olympic Committee from 1952 until 1972.

OLYMPIC FUN AND GAMES

Greco-Roman middleweight wrestler Max Klein of Russia beat Finland's Alfred Asikainen in a bout that lasted more than 10 hours. They were said to be good friends at the end of the contest! Klein was too exhausted to take part in the final. The light-heavyweight final between Finland's Ivar Bohling and Anders Ahlgren of Sweden was declared a draw after nine hours and both men were presented with silver medals.

ANTWERP
1920

The guns had barely been silenced in "the war to end all wars" when Baron de Coubertin summoned the International Olympic Committee to Switzerland for a meeting to decide the next venue for the Games. Antwerp was selected as a tribute to the gallantry of the Belgian people during four years of enemy occupation and some of the bloodiest fighting in the history of mankind.

Thankful for something to put their minds to after the nightmare of war, the organizers of the Belgian Games worked wonders to get the shell-shattered city of Antwerp dressed up and properly prepared for the VII Olympiad (the VI Berlin Games scheduled for 1916 inevitably had to be cancelled). In under 18 months following the armistice, the Belgians had built a main sports stadium and provided superb facilities for the swimmers, cyclists, fencers and all the other competitors in the 22 sports to be featured.

None of the defeated Central Powers – Austria, Bulgaria, Germany, Hungary or Turkey – was invited and Russia chose not to compete. But 29 countries sent teams, including Finland, which was newly independent from Russia. And it was Finland that produced the greatest athlete of the Games, perhaps of the century.

PAAVO NURMI
"THE PHANTOM FINN" WITH THE FLYING FEET

Born in Turku, Finland, in 1897, Paavo Johannes Nurmi revolutionized middle and long distance running. Inspired by the feats of his idol Hannes Kolehmainen, Nurmi set new standards and peaks not only for performances on the track and road but also for training. He was like a time machine, running with a stopwatch in his hand as he paced himself to a long procession of new world records. During a running career that stretched more than 20 years, he set 22 world records for distances between 1500 meters and 20 kilometers and won six individual Olympic gold medals and three team-event gold medals, a story of supremacy unrivalled on the track.

Nurmi had a natural passion for running from the age of nine but it was not until he started to combine speed work with his stamina training that he began to make a breakthrough as a major force in world athletics. He started his exhausting but productive training technique while serving as a young soldier in 1919. Selected for the 1920 Games, he was launched on a career that made him one of the most

phenomenally successful Olympians of all time.

But "The Phantom Finn," as he became dubbed, had to be content with a silver medal in his first Olympic final. He was beaten into second place in the 5000 meters by the powerful French runner Joseph Guillemot, who had the unusual distinction of having his heart on the right side of his body. Nurmi gained revenge over the Frenchman in the 10,000 meters and then led the Finnish team to victory in the 8000 meters cross-country race.

Right: Paavo Nurmi caught in a rare Olympic moment when he was actually standing still after winning the 5000 meters at Antwerp.

64

It was in the Paris Games four years later that Nurmi produced his most astonishing running. He was unbeaten between the two Olympics and set world records at 1500 meters and 5000 meters within an hour of each other during a warm-up meeting a month before the 1924 Games. He was unbeatable in Paris. Over a period of six consecutive days, Nurmi ran in seven races and won them all. Stopwatch in hand, he won his heats of the 5000 and 1500 meters on two successive days, and then within a time span of just 90 minutes on the third day he was first in both finals and with an Olympic record in each of them. The day after this incredible double, Nurmi led the Finnish team home in the heat of the 3000 meters team race and just 24 hours later won the 10,000 meters cross-country event in blazing hot conditions that forced 24 of the 39 starters to retire. He completed his gold rush on the sixth day by leading the Finnish team to victory in the 3000 meters team race, breaking the tape in a time just 1.4 sec outside his own world record.

In the final two months of the season, Nurmi broke six more world records and then crossed the Atlantic to the United States for a series of 68 races, of which he won 66. He was past his peak by the time of the 1928 Olympics in Amsterdam but was still good enough to win the 10,000 meters in a new Games record. His Finnish compatriot Ville Ritola beat him into second place in the 5000 meters, and he had to be content with the third silver medal of his career when yet another of the flying Finns, Toivo Loukola, beat him in the 3000 meters steeplechase.

"Paavo the Peerless" was, at the age of 35, getting himself in tune for a marathon challenge in the 1932 Olympics when he was charged with infringing the amateur code. The International Amateur Athletics Federation found him guilty and banned him from all international athletics but Nurmi was allowed to continue to run in domestic competitions in Finland, where he won the national 1500 meters title at the age of 36.

And there was just one more Olympic appearance from this track master. In 1952, when the Games were in Helsinki, Finland paid their greatest athlete the honor of inviting him to carry the Olympic torch into the stadium. Joining him for the traditional ceremony of lighting the Olympic flame was the man who had fired his early ambitions, Hannes Kolehmainen.

It was in Antwerp that Nurmi made his Olympic debut and Kolehmainen his Olympic farewell. "Hannes the Mighty" bowed out with victory in the marathon as Finland staged the first challenge to United States supremacy in Olympic track and field. Eero Lehtonen emerged as the best all-rounder at the Antwerp Games, with victory in the pentathlon (long jump, javelin, discus, 200 meters, 1500 meters) and he successfully defended his title in Paris four years later. Finnish throwers took the first three places in the javelin and placed first and second in the shot and discus.

Nurmi may have been the greatest runner at Antwerp but he was not the fastest.

CHARLEY PADDOCK
FIRST OF "THE WORLD'S FASTEST HUMANS"

Charley Paddock, a powerful, well-muscled Texan, was the first of several sprinters to be labelled by the media "The World's Fastest Human." Between 1921 and 1924 he equalled the world 100 yards record of 9.6 sec five times. During his career he set new world-best times for every distance from 50 yards to 300 meters. He was not only the swiftest but also the most spectacular of all the sprinters in the 1920s. To the delight of photographers and the despair of his opponents, he developed a flying-leap finish to his races, going through the tape with arms outstretched and airborne like a long jumper at the peak of his effort.

Paddock had a high knee-lift, which gave him the appearance of running almost in a sitting position. At Antwerp, he won the 100 meters in 10.8 sec, finished second to compatriot Allan Woodring in the 200 meters and helped the United States team win the sprint relay.

There were American protests that the 100 meters should have been re-run because one of their finalists, Loren Murchison, was standing up when the starter fired his pistol. There was consolation for Murchison when he joined Paddock, Morris Kirksey and Jackson Scholz to win the 4 × 100 meters relay.

By skyscraping American standards, 1920 was a disappointing Olympics for the United States team. Many of the track and field athletes had their concentration disturbed by a pre-Games row. With world triple jump record holder Dan Aherne as their spokesman, they protested to the American Olympic Committee about their cramped conditions on the ocean liner that was serving as their quarters during the Games. Several of them walked off the ship to find their own accommodation and were promptly suspended by the Committee. Other team members then threatened to withdraw but after long and sometimes bitter negotiations the ship "mutiny" was squashed and all suspended athletes were reinstated.

American-trained athletes nevertheless won six out of six medals in the 110 and 400 meters hurdles. But the low hurdles gold medal went to Canada because Dartmouth College student Earl Thomson was representing the country of his birth.

With the shot put, discus, javelin, triple and broad jumps going to the Scandinavians, it was left to 37-year-old Patrick (Paddy) Ryan to save American faces with victory in the hammer. He continued the Irish-American monopoly with the ball and chain. This was the fifth time the event had been on the Olympic program and the fifth time that an Irish-born American had won. John Flanagan (1900–04–08), Matt McGrath (1912) and Ryan were all born within a 30-mile radius of one another in southern Ireland.

Richard Landon (high jump) and Frank Foss (pole vault) boosted the United States gold haul but their hopes in the 800 and 1500 meters on the track were dashed by a 31-year-old British veteran.

ALBERT HILL
"THE SLEEPER" WAKES UP FOR A DOUBLE GOLD

Albert Hill wide awake as he breaks the tape on his way to a golden double in the 800 and 1500 meters.

Railwayman Albert Hill was jokingly referred to as "The Sleeper" by his British team-mates in Antwerp. While most Olympic competitors were strung up with nerves, Hill could barely

keep awake between races. He had a tough timetable of five races in four days and he won them all on his way to a magnificent gold medal double in the 800 meters and 1500 meters.

His routine on each day of competition was to have a light, early lunch and then sleep for three hours. He was certainly wide awake on the track in the 800 meters final, beating American ace Earl Eby by just one meter in 1 min 53.4 sec. Joie Ray, eight times United States champion, was favorite for the 1500 meters but clever tactical running clinched both the gold and silver medals for Britain. Philip Noel-Baker set just the right pace to suit his team-mate Hill, who unleashed a powerful finishing burst to win in 4 min 1.8 sec.

Hill, born in Tooting, Surrey, in 1889, also won a silver medal in the 3000 meters team race. It was the peak of a long track career that had shown great promise as early as 1910 when he won the British four-mile championship. Following service in the British Army for the full four years of World War I, he returned to athletics but many people thought it was too late for him to achieve his ambition of winning an Olympic title. After setting a British mile record in 1921, he turned professional and continued to serve athletics for many years as a respected coach. Among his pupils was Sydney Wooderson, one of the greatest of all British milers who in 1937 set a world mile record of 4 min 6.4 sec.

British-born Bevil Rudd, brought up in South Africa and then educated at Oxford University as a Rhodes Scholar, threatened to stop his good friend Hill from winning the 800 meters in Antwerp. He was leading as they swept into the final stretch but twisted an ankle on the uneven track and had to be content with third place and a bronze medal. Rudd, who had won the Military Cross while serving as a major in the Royal Tank Corps, recovered from his injury in time to win the 400 meters final in 49.6 sec and completed his full set of Olympic medals three days later by anchoring the South African team to second place in the 4 × 400 meters relay. Beyond the track, a 72-year-old medal winner was stealing the headlines.

OSCAR SWAHN
THE OLDEST GUN IN THE WEST

Born in Tanum, Sweden, in 1847, the astonishing Oscar Swahn was a dead-eye shot with a rifle in more than 60 years of top competition. He competed in the Games of 1908, 1912 and 1920, winning three gold medals, one silver and two bronze – all of them in the running dee-

single shot and double shot competitions. Aged 72 at Antwerp, he was the oldest of all Olympic competitors. He qualified to represent Sweden in Paris in 1924 but was taken ill shortly before the Games. His son Alfred was also a crack shot and won three gold medals, one silver and one bronze in four Olympiads. Together, the shooting Swahns hold the record for a family haul of Olympic medals.

There was also a family double in the swimming pool at Antwerp. Pua and Warren Kealoha, from the island of Hawaii and representing the United States, became the first brothers to win swimming gold medals at the same Games. Pua won his gold in the 4 × 200 meters freestyle relay and also took the silver in the 100 meters freestyle, won by the great Hawaiian Duke Kahanamoku. Warren struck gold in the 100 meters backstroke to continue the success story of Hawaiians in the water. There were eight of the happy islanders in the American team and only one failed to reach a final.

The diving proved a triumph for youth. Aileen Riggin, a 14-year-old American schoolgirl, took the gold medal in the women's springboard event and 13-year-old Swede Nils Skoglund was the silver medallist in the men's plain high-diving competition. It was virtually an American monopoly in the Olympic pool. United States swimmers and divers won 11 of the 15 events, with Norman Ross finishing first in the 400 and 1500 meters freestyle and Ethelda Bleibtrey emerging as the golden girl of the Games with victory in the 100 and 300 meters freestyle and a share in the United States win in the 4 × 100 meters relay.

A crowd riot shattered the peace of the pool after the water polo final in which a British swimmer completed a remarkable triple.

PAUL RADMILOVIC
THE KING OF THE WATER POLO POOL

The son of a Greek father and Irish mother and born in Wales – with his background Paul Radmilovic had to be something special, and indeed he had few peers in the swimming pool. Even though his Olympic career was interrupted by the war, he managed to represent Britain in five Olympiads, and his four gold medals are still a record for any UK competitor.

In the 1908 Games in London, Raddy – as he was known to his team-mates – was a member of Britain's winning 4 × 200 meters relay team and also collected a gold medal in water polo. He was captain of the British team that completed a hat-trick of water polo suc-

cesses in Stockholm and Antwerp, was a member of the team that was unplaced in Paris in 1924 and at the age of 42 helped Britain to fourth place in the water polo competition at the Amsterdam Games in 1928.

Born in Cardiff in 1886, Radmilovic was a top-class soccer player and a scratch golfer but he was happiest when in the water. He was the Welsh 100 yards freestyle champion 15 times between 1901 and 1922, and as late as 1929 set a Welsh record in the 440 yards freestyle. Raddy was also a redoubtable long-distance swimmer and won the English 5-mile River Thames race three times, in 1907 and then in 1925 and 1926.

But water polo was his first love and he was both angry and disappointed over the Belgian reaction to Britain's triumph in the Olympic final in Antwerp in 1920. The British team scored a disputed victory over Belgium in a bitterly contested final; protesting Belgian supporters attacked the UK players, who had to fight their way to the dressing-room. They had to have an armed guard escort back to their hotel and it was several days before the medal presentation could take place, following a publicly broadcast apology from the Belgian Olympic Committee.

Tempers were also lost on the soccer pitch. Belgium was leading Czechoslovakia 2–0 after 37 minutes of a brutal and bruising first half when the referee ordered a Czech player off for striking an opponent. His team-mates walked off with him in protest and the match was abandoned, with Belgium declared champion and the Czechs disqualified.

It was the fencing event that produced the most successful of all competitors in the Antwerp Games. Nedo Nadi, a 27-year-old Italian, has been described as the finest fencer of the century.

Bevil Rudd, the war hero who won a full set of Olympic medals for his adopted country of South Africa. The Rhodes Scholar was awarded the Military Cross for bravery while serving as a major in the Royal Tank Corps during World War I.

NEDO NADI
NOBODY CAN FOIL HIM AS HE WINS FIVE GOLD MEDALS

Taught the fencing arts in his father's gymnasium while still at school, Nedo Nadi started his international career at the age of 17 and won the gold medal in the foil in the Stockholm Games without suffering a single defeat.

His performances in Antwerp were considered near to perfection. He won the individual foil and saber titles and was undefeated as he led Italy to three victories in the team events. Nadi's haul of five gold medals in a single Olympiad remains a record in fencing. His brother, Aldo, was also a member of the strong Italian team. A supreme stylist with perfect balance, timing and rapid reflexes, Nadi turned professional and became a fencing teacher in Buenos Aires. He had his amateur status reinstated on his return to Rome and in 1935 became President of the Italian Fencing Federation, a post he held until his death in 1940.

American boxer Eddie Eagan, an intellectual educated at the Universities of Yale and Oxford, was another Antwerp Olympic champion who went on to an administrative role in his sport. He won the light-heavyweight gold medal and 12 years later was back in Olympic action, this time as a member of the United States team that won the four-man bobsleigh title. Thus Eagan became the only man in Olympic history to win gold medals at both the summer and winter celebrations of the Games. He was later appointed head of the New York Boxing Commission.

There were arguments and disputes throughout the boxing tournament in Antwerp but New York Italian Frankie De Genaro was unarguably the most accomplished of the flyweight contestants. He won the gold medal and went on to win the world professional flyweight championship eight years later.

The United States provided another supreme champion in Philadelphian rower John B. Kelly, who later became even more famous for his offspring. His film star daughter, Grace Kelly, became Princess Grace of Monaco, and his son, Jack, was an oarsman in four Olympiads and later aspired to President of the Amateur Athletic Union of America. John B. Kelly built up immense arm and shoulder strength as a bricklayer in Philadelphia and between 1919 and 1920 won 126 consecutive rowing races. He remains the only man to have won two Olympic sculling titles on the same day. After narrowly beating Britain's Jack Beresford in the single sculls final, he was back in powerful action just 30 minutes later to partner his cousin Paul Costello to victory in the double sculls. Kelly and Costello, a great double act, repeated their success at Paris in 1924. Costello made it a personal hat-trick in 1928, but this time with Charles McIlvaine as his partner.

Jack Beresford was the greatest of all British oarsmen. He competed in five consecutive Games from 1920 to 1936, winning gold medals in 1924 (single sculls), 1932 (coxless fours) and 1936 (double sculls). Beresford was also a silver medallist in the single sculls in 1920 and as a member of the British eights crew in 1928. It was an astonishing record of consistency for a man who rarely weighed more than 160lb.

The Antwerp Games also featured one of the most consistent sportswomen of all time in Suzanne Lenglen. This legendary French lawn tennis player won the women's singles, partnered Max Decugis to victory in the mixed doubles and was a losing finalist in the women's doubles. She won the Wimbledon singles championship six times between 1919 and 1926.

Probably the biggest shock of the Games was the victory of the United States over France in the Rugby Union final. People who dismissed it as a fluke were made to eat their words four years later when the Americans again emerged as the winners.

But the greatest winners of all were the Belgian organizers of the Games who had proved that even "the war to end all wars" could not break the Olympic spirit.

OLYMPIC FUN AND GAMES

American sprinter Morris Kirksey, one of the gold-medal winning US relay team, finished the Games in a prison cell. He had returned to his dressing-room to pick up some running shoes, only to find it locked, and was arrested as a suspected thief as he tried to climb through a window!

Opposite: Paavo Nurmi (above) beats his great Finnish rival Ville Ritola by a stride in a thrilling finish to the 5000 meters in Paris. Ritola (below) won four gold medals but had to live in the shadow of the fabulous Nurmi.

The 1924 Games were staged in Paris at the request of Baron de Coubertin, who wanted his homeland to show that the farcical 1900 Paris Olympics did not typify French organizational ability. The Games looked doomed for a late switch of venue when the Seine overflowed its banks in 1923 and caused serious flood damage in Paris, but despite this and financial difficulties the French Olympic Committee battled on and finally produced an Olympiad in which even the perfectionist de Coubertin could take great pride and satisfaction.

It was for these Games that the Olympic motto was coined by a French schoolmaster: *citius, altius, fortius* ("faster, higher, stronger"). The motto met with instant response from the athletes and swimmers. Six new world records were set in track and field events and another 15 Olympic records were equalled or broken. In the swimming pool there were two new world records and 10 new Olympic marks.

More than 3000 competitors took part in the Games from 44 nations. The United States was again the most successful, winning 49 gold medals. But it was the Finnish track and field team that caused the greatest stir, with Paavo Nurmi leading the way with an extraordinary exhibition of controlled running. His performances (as described in the previous chapter) overshadowed some remarkable running by his compatriot Ville Ritola.

VILLE RITOLA
THE MAN WHO RAN IN THE SHADOWS OF THE GREAT NURMI

Not many people can recall Ville Ritola. He suffered through being a contemporary of the legendary Paavo Nurmi and in any other era would have been hailed as an outstanding Olympian. Nurmi was so dominant at the Paris Games that Ritola was regarded as "just another" of the small but talented Finnish team despite his impressive haul of four gold and two silver medals.

Born in Finland in 1896. Ritola had emigrated to the United States, where he quickly established himself as a runner of great potential by winning an American cross-country championship. Representing the Finnish-American Athletic Club, he won the AAU 10 miles track title in 1922 and 1923 and also became American steeplechase champion. Encouraged by these performances he returned to Finland early in 1924 to challenge for a place in the Olympic squad. Six weeks before the

Games he caused a sensation by breaking Nurmi's world record in the 10,000 meters, and the Finnish selectors made him their first string in this event, leaving Nurmi to concentrate on the shorter distances.

Ritola duly won the 10,000 meters gold medal in Paris, slicing more than 12 seconds off his own world record with a time of 30 min 23.2 sec. "Paavo the Peerless" was peeved to have been left out of the race, and to prove his point he set out on a training run over the same distance while Ritola was winning his title. Nurmi was timed on his training spin at 29 min 58 sec.

Two days later Ritola became Olympic 3000 meters steeplechase champion in a new world best time of 9 min 33.6 sec. But he could not get out of Nurmi's shadow. He tried to run the legs off his team-mate in the 5000 meters final, which was staged just an hour after Nurmi had won the 1500 meters final. Ritola thought his fast pace would burn off Nurmi's finishing power but he was beaten to the tape by a fifth of a second as the master surged past him in the home stretch.

Nurmi confirmed his superiority over Ritola by beating him into second place in the team 3000 meters and the 10,000 meters cross-country that was run in exhausting conditions with the temperature hitting 113 degrees.

Their intense rivalry continued over the next four years, with Nurmi beating Ritola in five out of six indoor track events in the United States. Ritola was unbeatable provided Nurmi

69

was not in the field. He set indoor world records in America over five miles and three miles and won 14 AAU titles on the outdoor track.

The two flying Finns were battling against each other again in the 1928 Amsterdam Games. Nurmi won the 10,000 meters with Ritola second but the places were reversed in the 5000 meters. They had just about exhausted each other when they clashed in the 3000 meters steeplechase. Ritola failed to finish and Nurmi came in second after falling at the water jump. The race was won by another Finn, Toivo Loukola.

Between them, Nurmi and Ritola amassed a total of 20 Olympic medals. Nurmi won 12 and Ritola had eight to show for a career that brought him great personal satisfaction but not the public recognition that his exploits deserved.

The Finns also took the marathon through Albin Stenroos and Eero Lehtonen retained his pentathlon title. Jonni Myyrä, a trend-setter in the great tradition of Finnish javelin throwers, won his second successive gold medal in his specialty event.

Only the United States, with 12 gold medals, did better than Finland in the track and field events at the Colombes Stadium in Paris. One of their squad set a new world record in the long jump but had to be content with a bronze medal.

ROBERT LeGENDRE
A WORLD RECORD BUT NO GOLD MEDAL

Robert LeGendre considered himself America's best long jumper but failed to win selection in his favorite event. He went to Paris as a competitor in the pentathlon. William DeHart Hubbard won the long jump for America with a leap of 24ft 5in (7.44m). But this was nowhere near as impressive as LeGendre's performance the previous day in the pentathlon long jump section of the five-event test for all-rounders. He catapulted himself to a new world record distance of 25ft 5in (7.76m). It was not listed as an Olympic record because it was set outside the individual event. LeGendre had to be content with a bronze medal in third place in the pentathlon, the last time that this competition was on the men's Olympic program.

Harold Osborn, a powerful all-rounder from Butler, Illinois, pulled off a remarkable double when he won both the decathlon and the high jump. He set a world best points haul in the decathlon and created a new high jump Olympic record of 6ft 6in (1.98m), a mark that survived until the 1936 Games. The winner of 18 US

titles in six different events, he was still competing at the age of 37 when he set a new world standing high jump record of 5ft 6in (1.68m).

Clarence Houser was another double gold medallist in athletics for the United States. He was the first discus thrower to perfect the skill of rotating at speed before propelling the discus from the circle. His technique brought him discus gold medals in 1924 and 1928 and a world record of 158ft 1¾in (48.20m) in 1926. In 1924 he also won the shot, the last man to win both these events in the Olympics.

Fred Tootell continued America's monopoly in the hammer throw but was the first American-born winner of the title. The previous winners since the 1900 Games had been wearing the United States badge but had all been born in Ireland. Matt McGrath, 46-year-old veteran, was runner-up to Tootell but his Olympic record of 179ft 7in (54.74m) – set in 1912 – survived and was in fact not beaten until 1936.

Dan Kinsey won the 110 meters hurdles for America and his team-mate Morgan Taylor won the 400 meters hurdles in what would have been a world record time but for toppling one of the barriers. Under the then existing rules, this cost him the record. Jackson Scholz edged out world record holder Charley Paddock in the 200 meters but neither of them could catch Britain's stylish sprinter Harold Abrahams in the 100 meters. He equalled the Olympic 100 meters record of 10.6 sec three times on his way to victory in the final.

The 100 meters heats were held on a Sunday, which led in a roundabout way to one of the most unexpected Olympic title victories of the 1924 Games.

ERIC LIDDELL
THE NEVER-ON-SUNDAY GOLD MEDAL WINNER

The Reverend Eric Liddell was Britain's champion and record holder over 100 yards but declined to take part in the Olympic 100 meters, held on a Sunday, because of his religious principles. The never-on-Sunday sprinter elected instead to compete in the 200 meters (he took the bronze medal) and, surprisingly, the 400 meters, in which he had never broken 49 seconds. A determined character who played in seven Rugby international matches for Scotland, Liddell set a personal best of 48.2 sec in winning his 400 meters semi-final. But he was not expected to be a serious danger to American favorite Horatio Fitch, who had set a new Olympic record in winning his semi-final in 47.8 sec.

Liddell was drawn in the outside lane in the final and decided to adopt make-or-break tactics. He came hurtling out of his blocks as if he was competing in a 100 meters race and sped through the first 200 meters in 22.2 sec. None of his opponents could live with this scorching pace and he was four meters ahead of silver medallist Fitch as he broke the tape in a new world record of 47.6 sec.

Born to Scottish parents in China in 1902 and educated at Edinburgh University, Liddell returned to China as a missionary in 1925. He died in a Japanese prisoner-of-war camp in 1943.

Britain produced a third gold medallist on the track when Douglas Lowe, a Manchester-born Cambridge University graduate, won the 800 meters with a superbly timed finish to beat Switzerland's Paul Martin by a fifth of a second in 1 min 52.4 sec. Four years later in Amsterdam, Lowe retained the Olympic title in an Olympic record time of 1 min 51.8 sec.

The United States, as expected, won both the 4 × 100 meters and the 4 × 400 meters relays, setting world records in both events. And in the swimming pool, too, the Americans won both relays. But it was the individual swimming of Johnny Weissmuller that took the eye.

JOHNNY WEISSMULLER
RECORDS ALL THE WAY FOR HOLLYWOOD'S TARZAN

It was on the screen as the best-known of the Hollywood Tarzans that Johnny Weissmuller was famous in the 1930s. But his early fame came in the swimming pool. He won 52 US titles, had 28 world records ratified and was the first man to break the one-minute barrier in the 100 meters (59.6 sec in 1922) and the first to beat five minutes for the 440 yards freestyle (4 min 57 sec in 1923). His world record of 51 sec for 100 yards freestyle lasted for 17 years, and at the age of 36 – when a professional and already established as a film star – he trimmed his personal best for 100 yards down to 48.5 sec.

Weissmuller had taken up swimming to give himself strength and stamina as a child when he was fragile and suffering from what doctors feared was a heart ailment. He grew to a muscular 6ft 3in and developed a new crawl technique under the guidance of his coach Bill Bachrach at Illinois Athletic Club.

He began his Olympic career in Paris by breaking the 60 second barrier in the 100 meters freestyle to beat defending champion Duke

Johnny Weissmuller, a far cry from Tarzan as he relaxes in the Olympic pool after winning the 400 meters freestyle final.

Kahanamoku by the enormous margin of 2.4 sec. Sweden's Arne Borg tried hard to stay with him in the 400 meters freestyle but Weissmuller kicked away in the final length to win in 5 min 4.2 sec. Third was Australian Andrew "Boy" Charlton, who at 16 was a match for most of the men. Charlton showed his full power in the 1500 meters final, winning in a world record 20 min 6.6 sec, with the previous record holder Arne Borg more than half a minute back in second place.

Weissmuller's third gold medal came in the 4 × 200 meters relay and he revealed his versatility by collecting a bronze as a member of the United States water polo team.

Four years later in Amsterdam, Weissmuller retained his 100 meters title and gained a fifth gold medal in the relay. This was a record gold medals haul in swimming until Don Schollander (1964) and then Mark Spitz (1972) came along.

Weissmuller had just about run out of records to beat after the Amsterdam Games and toured the world as a professional, receiving what was then a lucrative contract of $500 a week to sponsor swimwear. His film career began in 1932 with *Tarzan, the Ape Man* and he became the screen's first talking Tarzan. He led a full life off the screen and out of the water and married five times. He still has a lot of support from swimming experts who consider him the greatest swimmer of all time.

The United States won all but three of the titles in the swimming and diving events in Paris, with Andrew Charlton (1500 meters), his fellow Australian Richmond Eve (plain high diving) and Britain's Lucy Morton (200 meters breaststroke) breaking the monopoly. In six of the events, Americans took all three medals. Aileen Riggin set a unique record when she won the silver medal in the springboard championship (the event she won at the age of 14 in Antwerp) and came third in the 100 meters backstroke. She is the only Olympic competitor to win medals in swimming and diving events.

There was another incredible double in the men's diving. Albert White, a member of the all-conquering Stanford University diving team, became the first diver to win the springboard and highboard gold medals at the same Games. He never once lost a lowboard diving competition throughout his career in the United States.

Martha Norelius, whose father had been an Olympic swimmer for Sweden before emigrating to the United States, was an impressive winner of the 400 meters freestyle. She became the first woman to win an Olympic medal for the same event at successive Games when retaining her title in 1928. Coached by her

father and then by New York swimming specialist Louis de B. Handley, she won 16 US titles and held 19 world records, all in freestyle events from 200 meters to a mile. She married Canadian oarsman Joseph Wright, who won a silver medal in the double sculls at Amsterdam in 1928. The AAU suspended her in 1929 for giving an exhibition swim during a professional gala. She turned professional and won the $10,000 first prize in the 10-mile Wrigley marathon in Toronto.

Another member of that 1924 USA swimming team who went on to greater fame was Gertrude Ederle, who collected bronze medals in the 100 meters and 400 meters freestyle events. She was clearly better suited to distance swimming as she proved on 6 August 1926, when she became the first woman to swim across the English Channel. But none of these great swimmers had quite the bite in their performances as a British boxer called Harry Mallin.

HARRY MALLIN
THE CHAMPION BOXER WHO HAD TEETHING TROUBLES

Defending the Olympic middleweight championship he had won in 1920, British boxer Harry Mallin was involved in an extraordinary incident in the quarter-finals against Frenchman Roger Brousse. In the final round when seemingly ahead on points, Mallin was bitten on the chest by Brousse. Mallin attempted to protest to the referee but because of language difficulties could not make himself understood. Brousse was awarded a controversial points decision but following a complaint from a Swedish official who had seen Mallin get bitten, the boxing committee held an inquiry. They studied the tell-tale teeth marks on Mallin's chest and reversed the decision, disqualifying Brousse. Mallin, a London policeman, went on to retain his title by outpointing his countryman John Elliott in the final. British champion from 1919 to 1923, Mallin went through his career of more than 200 amateur contests without a single defeat.

Harry Mitchell won the light-heavyweight title to give the United Kingdom two successes in the boxing, the same gold medal tally as the American boxing squad. The two United States champions, flyweight Fidel LaBarba and featherweight Jackie Fields, both later became world professional title winners.

Fields was left out of the original US squad until his close friend and sparring partner, Joe Sallas, started a campaign to get him selected.

Sallas, a featherweight like Fields, threatened to withdraw from the team if Fields was not picked and organized a petition to get his friend on the ship bound for France. Under the weight of public opinion and the protests from Sallas, the selectors conceded and Fields made the trip. Both he and Sallas qualified for the featherweight final and it was Fields who emerged as the gold medal winner after a fierce and close contest. Five years later Fields became world welterweight professional champion.

France, heavily represented in most events, was the third most successful nation behind the United States and Finland, with 13 gold medals. Its best moments were on the cycling track and in the fencing championships. Lucien Michard won the cycling sprint gold medal and went on to become the world professional champion. The road race was the most emphatically won in the history of the Olympics, with Armand Blanchonnet crossing the finishing line more than 10 minutes ahead of his nearest rival. French pride was restored in the fencing following its complete failure against the Italians in Antwerp four years earlier. Roger Ducret was the individual hero, taking three golds and two silvers.

Lawn tennis was included in the Olympics for the last time, with Helen Wills from California taking the women's singles title and sharing a doubles triumph with Hazell Wightman (who donated the Wightman Cup). The United States made a clean sweep on the tennis courts and Helen Wills (Moody) took over from Suzanne Lenglen as the queen of the world's courts over the next 10 years.

There was a father-and-son double in the yachting. August Ringvald, Sr, and August Ringvald, Jr, were first in the eight meters class, a repeat of their triumph in Antwerp in 1920.

Helen Wills having a smashing time on her way to an Olympic doubles victory with Hazell Wightman, famous for donating the Wightman Cup.

American rifleman Morris Fisher was another champion who successfully defended his championship in Paris. He first became a crack marksman at competitive level while serving in the US Marines and won three gold medals at Antwerp and two in Paris. His gold medal victories came in the individual and team free rifle and military rifle events.

After the Paris Games, Baron de Coubertin resigned as President of the International Olympic Committee because he felt he should make way for a younger man. Thanks largely to his efforts the Olympic movement was by then a strong and flourishing world-wide organization. He had lit the flame of the modern Olympics and he handed on the torch confident the flame would not go out.

OLYMPIC FUN AND GAMES

The Spaniard Ricardo Zamora, known throughout the soccer world as "The Great Zamora," was considered an unbeatable goalkeeper. An eccentric genius, he boasted that no opponent would get the ball past him in the 1924 Olympic soccer championship. He was right. Spain was knocked out by Italy in a first round match when the Spanish captain turned the ball past Zamora into his own net in the last minute. It was the only goal of the game and "The Great Zamora" sank to his knees and wept.

AMSTERDAM 1928

In this age of equality and women's liberation, it seems remarkable that it was not until 1928 that women were allowed to compete in the major Olympic sport of track and field athletics. It was with some reluctance that the International Olympic Committee agreed to a women's program limited to just five events: 100 meters, 800 meters, 4 × 100 meters relay, high jump and discus.

Even this modest venture into competition among the fair sex triggered in Amsterdam a lot of criticism from people who considered athletics not suitable for girls. They were given fuel for their arguments when at the end of the 800 meters several of the runners collapsed with exhaustion. It was clear that they had not been properly trained for the two lap event – some of the competitors were running the distance for the first time in their lives. The critics of women's athletics refused to put it down to lack of training but insisted that "girls are just not built to run such 'killer' distances . . ." and there was such an uproar over the distressed condition of some of the 800 meter runners that the event was removed from the Olympic program for 36 years.

Canada emerged as the most successful nation in the women's events. They won the high jump, the sprint relay and took a silver and a bronze medal in the 100 meters behind American Elizabeth Robinson. Ethel Catherwood not only won the high jump with a world

record 5ft 2⅝in (1.59m) but was also admired as the prettiest woman at the Games. She brought grace and beauty to the track and field and her presence won a lot of supporters for women's athletics.

World records were set in all five of the women's events, with the 800 meters being won in 2 min 16.8 sec by Lina Radke, one of a powerful 300-strong team entered by Germany, which was back in the Olympic fold for the first time since the First World War.

The Amsterdam Games were truly international. More than 3500 competitors represented 46 nations and the gold medals were shared between contestants from 28 different countries. The United States again led the way with 22 gold medals but they had a disappointing time on the track, winning only the relays and the 400 meters. This was somewhat embarrassing to their team manager, who had said prior to the Games: "This is the best prepared squad ever sent overseas by the United States." These words were spoken by General Douglas MacArthur, who in later competition of a more severe kind was rarely wrong with his prognostications.

America's one individual track success was scored by Ray Barbuti, who was better known for his feats as a football player in Syracuse. Canadian James Ball was favorite for the 400 meters but was overtaken in the last strides by Barbuti as Ball committed the cardinal sin for an athlete of looking back over his shoulder as he approached the tape.

For the only time in Olympic history, the United States failed to win a single medal in either of the two sprints, and it was an ex-waiter from Canada who provided the fastest service on the track.

PERCY WILLIAMS
HE HITCH-HIKED TO OLYMPIC GLORY

A student at Vancouver College, 20-year-old Percy Williams hitch-hiked across Canada to compete in the Canadian Olympic trials in the 100 meters and 200 meters. To pay for his accommodation while living in Toronto, Williams worked as a waiter in a restaurant. He won both his trial races in Toronto but few people outside Canada realized his great potential.

Williams had a cool temperament to go with his sprinting ability and in the final of the Amsterdam 100 meters never let three false starts upset his concentration. The field got away at the fourth time of asking and Williams was off the quickest and sliced through the tape

Ethel Catherwood, the darling of the Games in Amsterdam, and Lina Radke (below right, on the inside) on her way to victory in the controversial 800 meters.

in 10.8 sec, with Britain's Jack London second and Germany's Georg Lammers third. In the 200 meters final Williams unleashed a tremendous burst of speed over the last 50 meters to win in 21.8 sec, again with a British sprinter (Walter Rangeley) and German (Helmuth Kornig) in second and third places. Just to prove his victories were no fluke, Williams won the Empire Games 100 yards title in 9.9 sec in 1930 and in the same year set a world record of 10.3 sec for 100 meters.

There was some consolation for the dejected American sprinters when Frank Wykoff, James Quinn, Charlie Borah and Henry Russell worked smoothly together to win the 4 × 100 meters relay final in an Olympic record equalling time of 41.00 sec. Ray Barbuti collected a second gold medal for himself when he anchored the American 4 × 400 meters relay squad to victory.

It was the flying Finns who were again dominant on the track. They were first and third in the 1500 meters (Harri Larva and Eino Purje), first and second in both the 5000 and 10,000 meters (Nurmi and Ritola taking a gold and silver each) and filled all three first places in the 3000 meters steeplechase (Toivo Loukola, Nurmi and Ove Andersen). It was a remarkable performance for Nurmi to finish second in the steeplechase. He had never competed in the event before the Games and he fell at several barriers, including the water jump, when he lost the watch he always carried in his left hand.

Douglas Lowe repeated his 1924 triumph in the 800 meters but it was his British team-mate – Lord Burghley – who attracted world-wide interest with his performance in the 400 meters hurdles.

LORD BURGHLEY
A GOLD MEDAL FOR THE ARISTOCRATIC HURDLER

Lord Burghley, son and heir of the Marquess of Exeter, first emerged as an athlete of great promise when winning the 120 yards high hurdles and 220 yards low hurdles for Cambridge University in their annual match against arch rivals Oxford in 1925. He repeated this double triumph in 1926 and 1927 and also scored a hat-trick of victories in the British AAA national championships over the 440 yards course. He was at his peak for the 1928 Games but was not expected to beat the American ace Morgan Taylor, who had been 400 meters hurdles champion in Paris in 1924 and started out in defense of his title by setting a new Olympic record of 53.4 sec in the semi-finals.

Lord Burghley, who had failed to survive the first round of the 110 meters hurdles in the Paris Games, was quietly impressive in reaching the final in Amsterdam but few outside the British camp considered him strong enough to win the gold medal.

In the final, American No 2 Frank Cuhel was drawn on the inside lane with defending champion Taylor in lane three. Lord Burghley was on the outside stagger, unable to see how his rivals were progressing. "His Hurdling Lordship" – as he was dubbed by the press – set off at what seemed a suicidal pace and had opened a big lead by the halfway mark. But inevitably he began to tire as the effects of his sprint start dragged at his leg muscles in what has always been considered the "man killer" event of the track. Cuhel and Taylor gradually began to chop back Lord Burghley's lead but he managed to pick up his pace again after clearing the last hurdle to cross the finishing line the winner in a new Olympic record time of 53.4 sec. Cuhel just edged out Taylor for second place, both of them timed at 53.6 sec.

Lord Burghley entered politics after the Olympics and became a Member of Parliament but he took time off from his duties at the House of Commons to defend his Olympic title in Los Angeles in 1932. He set a new British record of 52.3 sec in the final but this was good enough only for fourth place in a race won by his former Cambridge University colleague Bob Tisdall of Ireland. Yet he returned home from Los Angeles with a silver medal after helping the British 4 × 400 meters relay squad finish second behind the United States.

A triple gold medallist at the Empire Games in 1930, Lord Burghley later became the 6th

Lord Burghley, aristocratic winner of the 400 meters hurdles in Amsterdam. He later became a Member of Parliament and served for many years as a prominent member of the International Olympic Committee.

Pat O'Callaghan unleashing his winning throw in the 1928 Olympic hammer competition.

PAT O'CALLAGHAN
FROM NOVICE TO CHAMPION IN 12 MONTHS

It was not until the summer of 1927 that a young Irish doctor called Pat O'Callaghan threw the hammer in serious competition. He won a domestic throwing contest with an effort of 136ft 1in (41.47m). Twelve months later he became Olympic hammer throw champion with a distance of 168ft 7in (51.39m) to continue the Irish monopoly in this event for the strongmen of the athletics world. Defending his title in Los Angeles in 1932, O'Callaghan was trailing the veteran Finn Ville Porhola (the 1920 Olympic shot put champion) by just three inches. He then proved his great competitive spirit by pulling out a winning effort of 176ft 11in (53.92m) with his final throw.

O'Callaghan was a magnificent all-rounder, as he revealed in 1931 when winning six Irish championships: the hammer, shot put, 56lb weight (for both distance and height), discus and high jump. His greatest performance did not even make the record books. He hurled the hammer 195ft 5in (59.56m) in 1937, six feet farther than the 24-year-old world record set by Irish-American Patrick Ryan. But it was later discovered that the hammer was six ounces overweight and the throwing circle six inches too small, so the record was not ratified.

O'Callaghan's gold medal in Amsterdam was the first won for the Irish Free State as an independent country. There were also first track and field medals for Japan and Haiti.

The triple jump became a Japanese speciality after Mikio Oda had hopped, stepped and jumped to a gold medal winning distance of 49ft 10¾in (15.21m). Thirty-six years later, Oda – the first Asian gold medallist – was a member of the organizing committee for the Tokyo Olympics, and his historic performance in Amsterdam was commemorated in 1964 by a flagpole bearing the Olympic flag at a height of exactly 49ft 10¾in.

Haiti had just one solitary competitor in Amsterdam: long jumper Silvio Cator. He won the only medal Haiti has ever collected in the Olympics when he came second in the long jump behind American Edward Hamm, who won with a leap of 25ft 4½in (7.73m). Cator subsequently became the first man to break the 26ft barrier in the long jump.

The United States swimmers were again in dominant mood in the Olympic pool, taking 10 of the 15 gold medals. Once again it was Stanford University that produced the outstanding diving champion.

Marquess of Exeter and continued to serve athletics as President of the International Amateur Athletic Federation and the British AAA and as a member of the International Olympic Committee. When David Hemery won the 400 meters hurdles gold medal for Britain at the 1968 Olympics in Mexico, it was Lord Burghley who presented him with his gold medal.

The United States redeemed itself for its disappointing performances on the track by taking 13 medals out of the 24 to be won in the field events, including five golds. Americans won the high jump (Robert W. King), long jump (Edward Hamm), pole vault (Sabin W. Carr), shot (John Kuck) and discus (Clarence Houser).

Finnish athletes finished first and second in the decathlon (Paavo Yrjola and Akilles Jaervinen) but it was an Irish doctor who produced one of the most remarkable victories of the Amsterdam Olympics.

PETE DESJARDINS
SHEER PERFECTION ON THE SPRINGBOARD

Born in St Pierre, Canada, in 1907, Pete Desjardins became an American citizen after moving to Miami Beach with his family while still a young boy. Stanford University spotted his potential as a diver and was glad to enroll him as an economics student. He got his degree in economics and also perfected his diving technique under the guidance of the Stanford University coaches who had already put both Clarence Pinkston and Albert White on the path to Olympic glory in the diving events. Desjardins was runner-up to dual champion White in the springboard competition in the Paris Games when still at school. The valuable experience paid dividends four years later when he won both the springboard and high-diving titles.

Only 5ft 3in tall, Desjardins was noted for his technique and smooth entry into the water. The judges were so impressed by one of his springboard dives in Amsterdam that they gave him the maximum 10 points, a rarity at any level of competition. It has never been achieved by any other diver in the Olympics. Desjardins turned professional in the early 1930s and toured the world giving diving exhibitions. He became known as "The Little Bronze Statue from Florida" and was so popular in Europe that his diving displays drew sell-out crowds wherever he performed.

The Amsterdam Games marked the diving debut in Olympic competition of Dorothy Poynton, a 13-year-old schoolgirl from Salt Lake City who learned her diving technique in Los Angeles. She was a springboard silver medallist behind American team-mate Helen Meany. Four years later she won the gold medal in the highboard event, a title she retained in 1936 in her married name of Mrs Hill. A woman of great beauty, she later ran her own aquatic club in California.

She was not the only successful schoolgirl member of the United States swimming team in 1928. Albina Osipowich, barely 14, won the 100 meters freestyle and also had a share in the 4×100 meters relay triumph. She is the youngest ever double gold medallist.

Japanese Yoshiyuki Tsuruta interrupted the American golden splash in the pool when he obliterated the Olympic record in the 200 meters breaststroke, winning the title in 2 min 48.8 sec, which was more than seven seconds inside the previous best. Four years later Tsuruta trimmed another 3.4 sec off the record when retaining his title, the only swimmer ever to have scored a double victory in Olympic breaststroke events.

Intense rivals Arne Borg of Sweden and Andrew "Boy" Charlton of Australia were so busy watching each other in the final of the 400 meters freestyle that they failed to see unrated Argentinian Alberto Zorilla come through in the outside lane to beat them both to the gold medal.

There was another success for Argentina in the soccer. Their skillful team reached the final where they met South American rival Uruguay. They drew the first match 1–1 after extra time and the Uruguayans won a rugged and sometimes ill-tempered replay the next morning by two goals to one.

The Dutch fans flocked to the hockey stadium hoping to see the Netherlands win the hockey championship final but victory went to an Indian team boosted by one of the greatest players of all time.

DHYAN CHAND
A WINNER OF THREE GOLDS ON THE HOCKEY FIELD

The game of field hockey was introduced to the Indian sub-continent by British servicemen early in the twentieth century. It immediately caught on with the Indians, who adopted the game as a national sport. In no time at all, the pupils were giving hockey lessons to their teachers. Dhyan Chand, a captain in the Indian Army, made his Olympic debut as center-forward with the Indian team in Amsterdam in 1928 and over the next 20 years was to become the most famous of all hockey players.

The start of India's domination on the hockey field as they master host nation Holland in the 1928 final.

He and his skillful colleague Richard Allan were the stars of an Indian team that beat the Netherlands 3–0 in the 1928 final. It was the start of an unbreakable domination by the Indians on the Olympic hockey field. Chand, who had astonishing skill and control with the stick, was the main goal-scorer and along with team-mate Allan won three gold medals. Proof of India's superiority is that in winning the Olympic title in 1928, 1932 and again in 1936, they scored an aggregate of 102 goals and conceded only three.

Chand, captain of the team in Berlin in 1936, continued playing until his mid-forties and finally retired from international hockey after leading India on an unbeaten tour of East Africa in 1947–48. During a tour of New Zealand in 1935 he amassed an astonishing total of 201 goals out of an aggregate 584.

India was Olympic champion again in 1948, 1952 and 1956, with Randhir Gentle winning three gold medals to equal the pre-war feat of Chand and Allan. Their stranglehold on the title was finally broken in 1960 when they were narrowly beaten 1–0 in the Rome final by Pakistan.

With gymnastics gaining in popularity, there was a lot of attention focused on two outstanding pre-war bar and mat masters who were in opposition in Amsterdam. Switzerland's hero Georges Miez added to the bronze medal he had won in Paris by taking golds in the combined exercises (individual and team) and on the horizontal bar, plus a silver on the pommel horse. His floor exercises brought him a silver medal in Los Angeles, and in Berlin in 1936 he won a gold in the same event and was a silver medallist with the Swiss team in the combined exercises.

Miez won more world and Olympic championships than any other Swiss sportsman. For many years, his closest rival was Yugoslav Leon Stukelj. He won gold medals in the combined exercises and on the horizontal bar in 1924 and on the rings in 1928. Two bronze medals were added to his collection in 1928 in the team and individual combined exercises, and at the age of 38 he won a silver medal on the rings in 1936. A lawyer by profession, he competed at top international level for 20 years.

French fencer Lucien Gaudin was another long-playing Olympian. He was one of the world's master fencers from 1904 until 1930 but it was not until he was 42 and competing in Amsterdam that he won his two individual gold medals in the foil and épée. He collected two team golds in 1924 and a team silver in 1920 and another in 1928.

A fencer with a similar name, Giulio Gaudini, won a team gold and an individual bronze medal for Italy in 1928. His total medals collection from four Olympics (1924–36) was three gold, four silver and two bronze.

The Wyld brothers of Great Britain created a family record on the cycling track. Harry, Percy and Frank – with Frank Southall as the fourth member of the team – were bronze medallists in the 4000 meters pursuit event. It was the first time that three brothers had won Olympic medals in the same Olympic event.

Dutchman Charles Ferdinand Pahud de Mortanges gave his home supporters plenty to cheer in the show jumping. As a winner of two consecutive individual gold medals in Olympic three-day events, he set an equestrian record which still stands. A lieutenant (who later became a general) in the Dutch Hussars, he rode in four Olympiads. He won the individual three-day event gold medal in 1928 and retained his title in 1932. He was a team gold medal winner in 1924 and again in 1928 and collected a silver in the team three-day event in 1932. His two individual gold medal successes came on a palomino called Marcroix which – at the age of 17 – was also his mount in 1936 when he was unplaced.

Despite poor weather, the IXth Olympiad was well supported by the public, and General MacArthur summed up the feelings of everybody present at the Amsterdam Games when he reported on his return to America: "These were a model for all future Olympics."

OLYMPIC FUN AND GAMES

Cupid was in action with the arrival of women athletes. Soon after the Games, Canadian high jumper Ethel Catherwood – the pretty Olympic champion – married America's former Olympic high jump and decathlon champion Harold Osborn.

Many Americans were left in a state of shock after the Wall Street crash of 1929 and the Los Angeles Games provided just the diversion they needed to help lift them out of their depression. The Organizing Committee, under the inspiring leadership of an Olympic devotee called William May Garland, performed wonders to promote the most efficiently staged Games to date. Over a million people watched as 16 world records were broken and two equalled, and the Olympic record book had to be rewritten for 33 events.

A 100,000-seat stadium was erected for the Games and for the first time a special Olympic village was constructed. The 1300 men participating in the Games were housed in the village, which consisted of neat, two-roomed Mexican-style villas. The 200 women competitors stayed in the large and luxurious Chapman Park Hotel on Wilshire Boulevard.

Many nations were concerned about the cost of sending teams to the American West Coast but the Organizing Committee subsidized their expenses and arranged reduced steamship and railroad fares. The result of this imaginative gesture was that 34 nations were represented in Los Angeles where, as usual, the main interest was centered on the track and field events. The United States naturally had the strongest representation and won 11 of the 23 men's titles, with the women capturing five of the six gold medals in their events. They could also claim at least a share in the sixth gold medal, won by Polish sprinter Stanislawa Walasiewicz,

The impressive opening ceremony at the 1932 Olympics in Los Angeles. It set the standard for subsequent Games.

who had lived in the USA since the age of two. She was known in her new country as Stella Walsh and won 40 US sprint titles under that name. But she elected to run for Poland in Los Angeles and won the 100 meters with a world and Olympic record of 11.9 sec.

The queen of the 1932 Games was a gifted all-rounder from Texas.

MILDRED DIDRIKSON
SHE WAS KNOWN AS "BABE THE UNBEATABLE"

It is little wonder that in 1950 in an *Associated Press* poll, an all-rounder by the name of Mildred Zaharias was voted the greatest woman athlete of the half-century. Not only did she win two gold medals and one silver at the Los Angeles Games but during her phenomenal career she also hit three baseball home runs in one game, made an incredible 313ft (95.4m) throw from the centerfield to the plate, was twice selected for the All-American basketball team, was an expert at diving, lacrosse and billiards and was considered one of the greatest women golfers of all time.

Born in 1914 in Port Arthur, Texas, of Norwegian parents, she first came to world prominence as a 16-year-old schoolgirl called Mildred Didrikson when she set a women's world record for the javelin with a throw of 133ft 3¼in (40.6m). Shortly before the Olympics in 1932, she won the American national team athletics championship on her own. The team that finished second had 22 competitors. In the space of just two and a half hours, she won five events and placed in three more.

Nicknamed "Babe," she was the darling of the crowd at the Olympics and gave them plenty to cheer by winning the 80 meters hurdles final in a world record 11.7 sec. She also set a world record when winning the javelin (143ft 4in; 43.68m) and was robbed of a possible third gold medal by a disputed disqualification in the high jump. She and her American team-mate Jean Shiley tied at the world record height of 5ft 5¼in (1.67m). To decide the winner, the bar was lowered to 5ft 5in (1.65m) for a jump off. Shiley went clear and then Miss Didrikson cleared the bar. The judges then announced they were disqualifying Babe because they considered her dive-and-roll technique illegal. She had the consolation of being allowed to receive a silver medal.

Banned from amateur athletics four months after the Games for using her name to promote automobile sales, Babe toured in a vaudeville act in which she gave exhibitions of her all-round sports skill and played the harmonica! In 1934 she switched to professional golf with astonishing success, winning all the major titles including the women's world championship for four successive years from 1948. By then married to wrestler-showman George Zaharias, a 285lb man-mountain known as "The Crying Greek from Cripple Creek," she continued to tour the world as a golfer until a few months before her death from cancer in 1956.

In the men's track and field events there was only one double gold medallist.

EDDIE TOLAN
THE FIRST BLACK SPRINT CHAMPION

Nicknamed "The Midnight Express," Eddie Tolan was the first of a long procession of black sprinters to win an Olympic gold medal. He won both the 100 and 200 meters in Los Angeles but it was not until judges had studied film of the shorter event that he was confirmed as the winner.

Born in Denver, Colorado, in 1908, Tolan was near-sighted and used to run with his spectacles taped to his head. The world was alerted to his potential in 1929 when he streaked to a new world record 9.5 sec in the 100 yards on the Evanston, Illinois, track. For the next three years, he was clearly America's No 1 sprinter but in the 1932 American championships was beaten into second place in both the 100 and 220 yards by fellow black speed merchant Ralph Metcalfe.

A few weeks later at the Olympics, Tolan got his revenge against Metcalfe in the 100 meters but only by a matter of inches. Both were timed at a world record equalling 10.3 sec. There was no doubting Tolan's supremacy over 200 meters. He won by two meters in an Olympic record 21.2 sec, with another American, George Simpson (fourth in the 100 meters), just beating Metcalfe for second place.

America's astonishing strength in depth in sprinting was revealed when they won the 4 × 100 meters relay without need of the services of their top trio, Tolan, Metcalfe and Simpson. Their quartet of Bob Kiesel, Emmett Toppino, Hector Dyer and Frank Wykoff won the final by 10 meters in a world record 40.0 sec.

The US 4 × 400 meters relay team was also in world record shattering mood, beating runner-up Great Britain by three seconds in the final in 3 min 8.2 sec. The anchor leg was run by Bill Carr, who had won the individual 400 meters in a new world record 46.2 sec. He beat arch rival Ben Eastman, who had to be content with a silver medal even though he was also inside the old world record. There was tragedy for Carr before the year was out when he broke both legs in an automobile accident, and he never ran competitively again.

For the one and only time in the Olympics, three men's track gold medals went to bespectacled athletes. As well as the two by Tolan, Britain's Tommy Hampson was another "glassy-eyed" winner in the 800 meters.

TOMMY HAMPSON
HE BROKE THE "IMPOSSIBLE" BARRIER

The son of a keen middle-distance runner, Tommy Hampson could barely make the Oxford University team while a freshman. But in the space of three years he rose from being "just another" two-lap runner to the fastest 800 meters performer in the world. His best time in 1929 was 1 min 56.0 sec but he showed improvement the following year by winning the first of three successive British AAA championships, defeating the French world record holder Sera Martin in 1 min 53.2 sec. A month later he was first in the 880 yards final in the British Empire Games in a personal best 1 min 52.4 sec. But victory in the Los Angeles Games looked beyond him because the field for the final included six crack athletes who had clocked faster times than him over two laps. It was such a powerful line-up that experts predicted a winning time close to what had been considered the impossible time barrier of 1 min 50 sec.

Black Canadian Phil Edwards led at the bell in a fast 52.3 sec. Top Europeans Sera Martin and Otto Peltzer and the trio of powerful Americans were on his heels, with Hampson running comfortably in joint fifth place. A master of pace judgment, Hampson went through the bell in 54.8 sec. He knew the men in front of him were setting a suicidal tempo. Slowly they came back to him as he maintained his powerful but economical stride. Only the Scottish-Canadian Alex Wilson was ahead of him as they came off the final bend. Wilson threw his hands aloft as he approached the tape thinking victory was his but Hampson, the afternoon sun glinting on his glasses, suddenly found another gear and went past him on the outside to win by half a yard in a world record barrier-breaking time of 1 min 49.8 sec. The English schoolmaster had run the second lap in 54.9 sec, just one-tenth of a second slower than the first. His winning time was at first given as 1 min 49.7 sec but was later rounded up to 1 min 49.8 sec. This was the fourth successive victory in the Olympic 800 meters by a British competitor.

Five days later, Hampson ran the second leg for the British 4 × 400 meters relay team that took the silver medal behind the USA. For Canadian Alex Wilson it was a Games of mixed fortune. He collected a bronze medal in the 400 meters and a silver in the 800, in which he had the consolation of becoming the second man to break the "impossible" 1 min 50 sec barrier.

The Finnish domination in the middle and long distances was finally broken and one of their two gold medals on the track was hotly disputed. They failed to get a runner in the first three in the 1500 meters, with Italian Luigi Beccali producing a sprint finish to beat Britain's Jerry Cornes in an Olympic record 3 min 51.2 sec. Canada's Phil Edwards was third, a repeat of his performance in the 800 meters final. He completed a hat-trick of bronze medals in Berlin four years later when finishing third in the 1500 meters final.

Finland kept the 5000 meters title but not without shouted protests from the crowd over the final-straight tactics of winner Lauri Lehtinen. He took an almost zig-zag path to the tape to prevent underrated American Ralph Hill from passing him in the final 50 meters. Lehtinen crossed the line just a stride ahead of the impeded Hill and with the spectators jeering and booing. But before these friendly Games could be scarred, the announcer Bill Henry restored peace and cordiality by saying over the loudspeakers: "Please remember that these people are our guests!"

There was another jolt for the Finns when Poland's Janusz Kusocinski ran off with the 10,000 meters title in an Olympic record 30 min 11.4 sec. Chasing him in second place was another of the great family of flying Finns, who was going to have to work overtime to win a gold medal in the 3000 meters steeplechase.

VOLMARI ISO-HOLLO
THE CHAMPION WHO HAD TO RUN AN EXTRA LAP

Not quite in the class of the peerless Paavo Nurmi on the flat, Volmari Iso-Hollo specialized in the steeplechase. The day after finishing second in the 10,000 meters final in Los Angeles, he set an Olympic record of 9 min 14.6 sec in his heat of the 3000 meters steeplechase. He would almost certainly have bettered that time in the final but for an extraordinary mix-up by the trackside officials, who managed

Volmari Iso-Hollo (right) is congratulated after his victory in the 3000 meters steeplechase in which he had to run an extra lap because of a judge's error.

to miscount the number of laps. At the time that Iso-Hollo – way out on his own in front – should have been crossing the finish line the bell was rung to signal the start of the final lap. Iso-Hollo ran an extra lap and still managed to win by a comfortable margin over Britain's Tom Evenson, who was lying third behind American Joe McCluskey at what should have been the finish line. Evenson moved past the tiring McCluskey on the unexpected extra lap and came home in second place. When the mix-up over the laps was revealed, Evenson pleaded with McCluskey to take the silver medal to which he was entitled but the sporting American refused. "I am more than happy with my bronze medal," he said.

Paavo Nurmi was the pre-Games favorite for the marathon but just prior to the opening ceremony it was announced that the grand master of distance running had been banned because of alleged professionalism. Nurmi was a sad spectator as he watched the tightest finish in the history of the punishing race. Just 65 seconds covered the first four runners, with Argentina's Juan Zabala beating Britain's Sam Ferris by just 100 yards for the gold medal in 2 hr 31 min 36 sec.

There was another close finish in the 110 meters hurdles, with American George Saling beating his team-mate Percy Beard. The judges gave third place to another American hurdler, Jack Keller. But film of the race clearly showed that Britain's Don Finlay had crossed the line ahead of him. In an act that epitomized the sportsmanship of the 1932 American team, Keller hunted Finlay down in the Olympic village and presented him with his bronze medal.

Lord Burghley was hoping to win a gold medal for Britain in the 400 meters hurdles, the title he had won in Amsterdam four years earlier, but there was an Irishman with other ideas.

BOB TISDALL
CHEERS FOR THE CHAMPAGNE CHAMPION

Born in Ceylon of Irish parents in 1907, Bob Tisdall was educated at Cambridge University, where Lord Burghley had perfected his hurdling technique. A fine all-round athlete, Tisdall scored seven victories in three representative matches for Cambridge against its old rival Oxford. In his last year at college – 1931 – he achieved an unprecedented four wins in one afternoon. He took the 120 yards hurdles, shot put, long jump and 440 yards.

It was after a victory over Lord Burghley in a 220 yards hurdles race that Tisdall decided to concentrate on the 400 meters hurdles in Los Angeles, even though he had had little experience at the event. He wrote to the Irish Olympic selectors and asked to be considered for their team. They selected him for the decathlon and also, a little reluctantly after an unimpressive time trial, for the 400 meters hurdles. Tisdall decided to give the Games all his concentration. He gave up his job and lived for the four months before the Games with his wife in a converted railway carriage in an orchard in Sussex, southern England. There were no hurdles available for him to practice his specialty event and so he concentrated on building up his stamina with cross-country runs over the rolling Sussex Downs. When he arrived in Los Angeles, he had run over the 400 meters hurdles course only three times in competitive races.

He won his heat in a modest 54.8 sec and then surprised himself as well as his rivals by winning his semi-final in an Olympic record equalling 52.8 sec. Tisdall celebrated his victory with several glasses of champagne. He thought it would help him relax and not get too tense before the final.

Tisdall had led on the first day of the decathlon but then fell away to eighth place. All his hopes now rested on the 400 meters hurdles. He ran like a man inspired from the moment the starter's pistol signalled the start of the final. Chased by Lord Burghley, 1924 Olympic champion Morgan Taylor and race favorite Glenn Hardin, Tisdall led from the first hurdle and was never headed. Hardin was closing fast on him in the finishing straight but the Irishman held on to win in 51.7 sec. This would have been a world record but he knocked down the last hurdle. (The rules then required a hurdler to leave all 10 barriers standing for a record run to be ratified.) American Glenn Hardin, the champion in Berlin four years later, was credited with a world record of 51.9 sec in second place.

There were wild scenes of delight among the many Irish-Americans in the crowd just 10 minutes later when Dr Pat O'Callaghan retained his hammer championship with his final throw to give Ireland a double gold.

America's long monopoly in the high jump was finally broken by Canadian Duncan MacNaughton, a student at the University of Southern California. He had tried to get into the USA team trials but was turned down. Canada at first refused to put him in their team because they did not know enough about his form. But he convinced them that he was good enough and proved it where and when it mattered by producing a winning jump of 6ft 5½in (1.97m).

Finland scored a one-two-three in the javelin, with Matti Jaervinen leading the way with an Olympic record throw of 238ft 6½in (72.71m). The Japanese gave even the all-powerful Americans a tough time in the jumping events. Chuhei Nambu won the triple jump with an Olympic record of 51ft 7in (15.72m) and also took the bronze medal in the long jump with 24ft 5½in (7.44m). Kenkichi Oshima was a bronze medallist in the triple jump and in the pole vault Shuhei Nishida pushed America's Bill Miller to a world record 14ft 1⅞in (4.32m). Nishida was second just a fraction of an inch behind. Both Nishida and Nambu were medallists again in Berlin. However, it was in the water where the Japanese progress was the most impressive.

KUSUO KITAMURA
SCHOOLBOY MAKES A GOLDEN SPLASH FOR JAPAN

The Japanese swimmers were as dominant in the Olympic pool as the American athletes were on the track. Kusuo Kitamura was a remarkable winner of the 1500 meters freestyle in an Olympic record time of 19 min 12.4 sec, a Games best that was not beaten for 20 years. At the time of his victory Kitamura was a 14-year-old schoolboy and remains the youngest swimming gold medallist in the history of men's Olympic competition. Just a year older, Yasuji Miyazaki was a double gold medallist in the 100 meters freestyle and the 4 × 200 meters relay. On his way to victory in a heat of the 100 meters, Miyazaki broke the

renowned Johnny Weissmuller's Olympic record with a time of 58.0 sec.

All three medals in the 100 meters backstroke went to Japanese swimmers and Yoshiyuki Tsuruta retained his championship in the 200 meters breaststroke. Japan's tally of medals in the pool was 11 out of a possible 16 and all of the three permitted competitors got through to the final of every men's race.

American divers restored some prestige by taking all 12 diving medals and the USA women swimmers won four of the five events in their program. Helene Madison won the 100 meters freestyle, the 400 meters freestyle in world record time and collected a third gold in the winning relay team. The only non-American gold medallist among the women was Australian Clare Dennis, who set a world record of 3 min 6.3 sec in the 200 meters breaststroke. There was romance in the pool when, during the Games, America's Olympic diving champions Mike Galitzen and Georgia Coleman announced their engagement.

Away from the track and the pool, it was the wrestlers who produced headline-hitting performances.

Bob Tisdall shows the hurdling technique that carried him to golden glory in Los Angeles. He celebrated his victory with champagne.

IVAR JOHANSSON
THE SWEDISH GRAPPLER WHO GOT A HOLD ON THREE GOLDS

One of the most versatile wrestlers in Olympic history, Sweden's Ivar Johansson had the distinction in Los Angeles of winning gold medals in different styles of wrestling and at two different weights. He won the freestyle middleweight title and then competed in the Greco-Roman category and won the welterweight gold medal. He was elected Sweden's Sportsman of the Year. Four years later in Berlin he collected a third Olympic gold medal by winning the Greco-Roman middleweight title. This championship had been won in Amsterdam and again in Los Angeles by Finland's Vaino Kokkinen, famed for his merciless nelson and power-house push-overs.

Another outstanding Finn in action in Los Angeles was Kustaa Pihlajamaki. He won the featherweight freestyle, a title he successfully defended in Berlin four years later. His Olympic career had started in 1924 with a gold medal in the freestyle bantamweight division and in 1928 he took the silver at featherweight. Two of his brothers were outstanding wrestlers and his cousin, Hermanni Pihlajamaki, was an Olympic medallist in the freestyle category.

Sweden's Johan Richthoff, who successfully defended his freestyle heavyweight title in Los Angeles, was a character who attracted a lot of attention. He began as a cooper in a brewery and then became a church minister and a preacher against alcohol. For a year after the Games and his second gold medal triumph, he toured the States as a professional wrestler.

Rivalling even the great Ivar Johansson as the most famous of the pre-war Swedish wrestling masters was Carl Westergren, who invented the "Westergren roll" and specialized in the backhammer. He was an Olympic veteran, winning Greco-Roman gold medals at middleweight in 1920, at light-heavyweight in 1924 and then at heavyweight in 1932.

The heavyweight boxing champion in Los Angeles was Alberto Lovell, who outpointed Italian Luigi Rovati in the final. But the Games ended on a sad note for Argentinian Alberto. There were continual rows and arguments in the Argentine camp and the team manager was sacked for being too much of a disciplinarian. There was a total breakdown of discipline during the voyage home to Argentina and heavyweight hero Lovell was one of several Olympic competitors arrested for causing a disturbance on board ship.

One of the greatest oarsmen of all time, Henry Robert Pearce of Australia, won a second gold medal in Los Angeles, successfully defending the single sculls championship he had won in such impressive style in Amsterdam. The son of a London waterman, Pearce had emigrated to Australia and later became a Canadian citizen. He turned professional a year after his second Olympic victory and became the world professional sculling champion. Pearce was such a dominant force in the water that he used to be able to find the time and the breath to tell rivals how they could improve their performances!

It had been feared that because of the Depression, the Olympics would have to be cancelled in 1932, but thanks to the energy, industry and initiative of the Organizing Committee they became one of the most successful Games in the history of the Olympic movement.

OLYMPIC FUN AND GAMES

According to the records, French discus thrower Jules Noel finished fourth in his event in Los Angeles although neutral observers were convinced that he had produced a winning throw. Sadly for Jules, the attention of all the field judges had been distracted by an exciting moment in the pole vault and nobody in authority had seen exactly where the discus landed. Jules was allowed another throw but was unable to challenge the leaders. American John Anderson won with an Olympic record throw of 162ft 4½in (49.49m).

German Fuehrer Adolf Hitler seized the opportunity of the Berlin Olympics to show off the might of the Nazi organizational machinery to the world, and unlimited State money was poured into the Games to make them the best ever. Sadly, his motives were not for the glory of Olympic sport but for the projection of the ideology of the Third Reich.

The Nazi racial discrimination against non-Aryans, particularly anti-Semitism and the belief in the necessity of a color bar, had been well publicized before the Games and there was vociferous agitation for a boycott of the Berlin Olympics in both America and Britain. But the International Olympic Committee sought and received assurances from Hitler and his henchmen that there would be no racial discrimination against any competitors and that the Games would be promoted in a true Olympian spirit and without any political bias.

For the first time, the Games were preceded by the now traditional torch relay. The Olympic torch was lit by the rays of the sun at Olympia in Greece and was then carried in relays by nearly 3000 athletes, who each ran one kilometer on a route that took the torch from Greece through Bulgaria, Yugoslavia, Hungary, Austria, Czechoslovakia and finally to Germany, where it was brought to the capacity-crowded 100,000-seater stadium specially erected for the Games. Thousands of the Hitler Youth Movement lined up in a military-style parade in the field in the center of the stadium, which was festooned with swastika flags, completely swamping the Olympic flag. As the torch was brought on the final lap for the Olympic flame to be lit, Hitler led his followers in giving the Nazi salute and the stadium echoed to chants of "Sieg Heil!" As the 52-nation march-past began to the accompaniment of a massive military band, Hitler imperiously took the salute. The 500 German competitors and team officials brought up the rear, marching with well-rehearsed military precision.

These were the first Games shown on television, with an audience of nearly 200,000 watching on closed-circuit screens at 25 venues in and around Berlin. They saw a carefully-staged presentation to Hitler by Spyridon Louis, the first marathon winner in Athens in 1896, who was dressed in traditional Greek uniform. He presented the German Chancellor with the ancient symbol of peace, an olive branch.

The thorough preparations also embraced the German competitors and they collected 87 Olympic medals – 35 gold, 23 silver and 29 bronze. For the first time the United States was toppled as the leading nation in the Olym-

pics but to the annoyance of the Fuehrer the most impressive performances on the track and field came from a squad of black American athletes led by possibly the greatest Olympic champion of all time.

Adolf Hitler, surrounded by a forest of swastikas and without an Olympic flag in sight, opens the 1936 Games in Berlin.

JESSE OWENS
"THE BLACK ANTELOPE" POWERS TO FOUR GOLD MEDALS

James Cleveland Owens was one of eight children of an Alabama cotton-picker. He became known as "Jesse" because he used to introduce himself to organizers of athletics meetings as J. C. Owens. Born in Danville, Alabama, on 12 September 1913, he won an athletics scholarship to Ohio State University, where he came under the influence of expert coach Larry Snyder. He developed technique to go with his natural speed and while still only 18 ran a wind-assisted 10.3 sec, for the 100 meters and long jumped to within an inch of 25ft. Owens won the American long jump championship in 1933 and 1934, and on a sunny Saturday afternoon on 25 May 1935,

Jesse Owens leaping into Olympic history with a record in the long jump that lasted until the 1960 Games in Rome.

gave notice to the world that he was truly a supreme athlete.

A crowd of 10,000 gathered at the University of Michigan's Ferry Field sports stadium to watch the annual "Top Ten" track and field match between American university teams. Many of the spectators had been drawn by the presence of Jesse Owens, who, it was rumored, had been regularly beating the 26ft barrier in the long jump while training for this meet. Conditions were ideal for a world record attempt but the usually cheerful and chatty Owens was in a morose mood when he arrived at the stadium for what was to become the greatest afternoon of his life. He had strained his back in a fall down a flight of stairs and it was so stiff that he was unable to join his Ohio State University team-mates in warm-up calisthenics. Owens had been entered in four events and decided to try to run the stiffness out of his back in the 100 yards.

He was so stiff that he had to be helped off with his tracksuit before the start of the race. But the moment he came hurtling out of his blocks the pain disappeared and he was off on a sequence of astonishing record-breaking action that has never been equalled for consistency. At 3:15 P.M. he streaked to victory in the 100 yards, equalling Frank Wykoff's world record of 9.4 sec. At 3:25 P.M. Owens took his one and only long jump and smashed the world record by six inches with a leap of 26ft 8¼in (8.13m), a distance that was unsurpassed

for a quarter of a century. At 3:34 P.M. he was an impressive winner of the 220 yards in a world record 20.3 sec. At 4:00 P.M. Owens scissored over the 220 yards low hurdles in 22.6 sec to shatter the 11-year-old world record. His stunning streak of four world records had taken him a total of less than 46 minutes.

In Berlin Owens produced even greater feats, though his Olympic exploits were spread over days rather than minutes. He equalled or broke 12 Olympic records on his way to gold medals in the 100 meters, 200 meters, long jump and sprint relay. Jesse won everything but a hand-shake from Hitler, who left the Olympic stadium in disgust after seeing America's "Black Ante-lope" completely monopolize the explosive events.

In both the 100 and 200 meters Owens powered through all his four races in each event without ever being headed. His times for 100 meters on his way to the gold medal were 10.3 sec, 10.2 sec, 10.4 sec and 10.3 sec. The 10.2 sec run would have been a world record but for a following wind just a fraction over the permitted (for record purposes) two meters a second. In the 200 meters he clocked 21.1 sec, 21.1 sec, 21.3 sec and, in the final, 20.7 sec. By the close of the Games he had equalled the 100 meters Olympic record and had broken the 200 meters by half a second.

His superiority was such that he generated awe rather than excitement on the track but in the long jump he was locked in one of the most compelling contests in Olympic history. In the first of three qualifying jumps, Owens put a foot over the board and no jump was recorded. Tension mounted as he repeated the foul jump on his second attempt. He now faced the possi-bility of elimination, and it was then, according to Owens, that his German rival Luz Long sportingly advised him to mark his take-off point from behind the board so that he would at least record a distance and so qualify for the final. Owens was suffering from nervous tension at this point because he had not realized that his first jump was part of the competition and had treated it as a warm-up effort. But he took the advice of Long and qualified with a third jump of just over 23ft 5in, a mere sixteenth of an inch inside the qualifying distance.

After four of their six jumps in the final, Owens was in first place just an inch ahead of Long. With his fifth leap, the blond, muscular German equalled Jesse's best effort of 25ft 9¾in (7.86m). Suddenly the pressure had switched back onto the black American, who glided down the runway for his fifth jump and an Olympic best of 26ft 0½in (7.93m). Long poured all his effort into a final jump but tried too hard and fouled. Knowing that victory was his, Owens was completely relaxed for his sixth jump and leapt gracefully to a new Olympic record distance of 26ft 5¼in (8.06m), which went unbeaten until the 1960 Games. The sporting Long, killed on the Eastern Front just a few years later, warmly congratulated Owens to cut through the chauvinism that had brought an unpalatable edge to the Games.

Owens had not yet finished his record streak. In the heat of the 4 × 100 meters relay he ran the first leg to set the United States quartet on the way to a world record equalling time of 40.0 sec. The next day he gave the sprint squad an even faster send-off in the final and they spurted to victory in a world record shattering 39.8 sec. Frank Wykoff completed a unique hat-trick as a member of the relay team. It was his third gold medal in three successive Olympics and all of them came in the sprint relay.

It was humiliating for Hitler to sit and watch Owens and his black team-mates monopolizing events on the track, where Germany was restricted to just one silver medal. The Nazi propaganda machine had been spitting out spiteful stories about Aryan superiority and dismissed Owens and his black colleagues as nothing more than "black auxiliaries." All Hitler saw was a stunning show of black athletic power. Ralph Metcalfe collected his second successive silver medal in the 100 meters and joined Owens in the relay triumph. Mack Robinson, whose brother Jackie was to make his own sporting history as baseball's first black professional some years later, was runner-up to Owens in the 200 meters final. Archie Williams won the 400 meters with another black team-mate Jim LuValle in third place.

John Woodruff, a University of Pittsburgh freshman and youngest of the black Americans, unleashed a storming finishing burst to take the gold medal in the 800 meters.

Woodruff's victory meant that black Americans had won every track event from 100 to 800 meters. Fred Pollard looked likely to join his black team-mates as a gold medallist in the 110 meters hurdles but faltered over the final hurdle. He had to be content with third place behind white American Forrest Towns and Britain's Don Finlay, who had won a bronze medal in Los Angeles and was still winning British championships in 1949 at the age of 40.

There was also a sign of black supremacy in the high jump. Cornelius Johnson and Dave Albritton, black team-mates with spring in their heels, finished first and second. Johnson had arrived late at the stadium because of a traffic jam and did not enter the competition until the bar was already at an Olympic record 6ft 6in. He finally took the gold with a jump of 6ft 7⅞in (2.03m). Delos Thurber finished third to make it a 1–2–3 clean sweep for the United States.

The nine black Americans in the United States track and field team collected eight golds, three silvers and two bronze medals between them – not bad for mere "auxiliaries."

The most memorable race of the Berlin Games came in the 1500 meters, which featured the five runners who had filled the first five places in the 1932 Games in Los Angeles: Italian Luigi Beccali, Britain's Jerry Cornes, black Canadian Phil Edwards, America's popular Glenn Cunningham and Swede Eric Ny. Yet they were all overshadowed in the final by a remarkable runner from New Zealand.

Jesse Owens wins a heat of the 200 meters in an Olympic record 21.1 sec. He equalled or broke 12 Olympic records on his way to his four gold medals.

Jack Lovelock improved from seventh place in the Los Angeles 1500 meters final to first in Berlin.

JACK LOVELOCK
A TACTICAL TRIUMPH FOR "THE MAN IN BLACK"

Few people realized the potential of John (Jack) Lovelock when he finished seventh in the 1500 meters final in the 1932 Los Angeles Olympics. A student at Otago University, he did not really come to world prominence until switching to Oxford University for his pre-medical degree. It was while representing a combined Oxford and Cambridge team at Princeton in July 1933 that he suddenly emerged as a runner of great talent. He beat highly-rated United States star Bill Bonthron by six yards for a new mile world record of 4 min 7.6 sec. Lovelock then quietly went back to concentrating on his studies, moving to London Hospital and keeping a low athletics profile as he prepared without fuss for the 1936 Olympics.

British hopes rested on the slim shoulders of Sydney Wooderson (later to become world mile record holder) who had beaten Lovelock in the pre-Olympics AAA championships in 1936. But Wooderson was troubled by a foot injury and went out in the heats in Berlin. Lovelock believed in qualifying for finals with as little effort as possible and trotted into the final with a preliminary time of 4 min 0.6 sec, while the big race favorites were all through in times faster than 3 min 55 sec.

Lovelock, in the distinctive all-black strip of New Zealand, was content to take a backmarker place as the high-quality field sped through the first lap on a world record schedule pace. A master of tactics, he had quietly prepared in London to ensure that he would be at the peak of his power for this final.

Glenn Cunningham, "The Iron Horse of Kansas," took up the running on the second lap and Lovelock moved effortlessly through the field to take up third place behind Sweden's Ny with Beccali, Cornes and the German champion Fritz Schaumburg all tightly bunched on his heels. At 1000 meters the powerfully built Cunningham was still holding the lead but with Ny at his shoulder and forcing a faster pace that was really testing the men behind. Ny led the field through the bell but Cunningham, Lovelock and the defending champion Beccali were in close attendance and looking stronger than the Swede, who, tired by his own furious pace-making, dropped back as the leaders swept into the back stretch for the last time.

Cunningham was leading with Lovelock on his outside and Beccali menacing in third place but as they got to within 300 meters of the tape the blond New Zealander suddenly changed gear and accelerated away on a thrilling surge for the finish line. Cunningham gave chase but "The Man in Black" had timed his decisive move to perfection and there was no catching him. He powered through the tape in a world record 3 min 47.8 sec, four yards ahead of Cunningham, who was also inside Bill Bonthron's old world record. The first five finishers were all inside the Olympic record and Jerry Cornes in sixth place ran 1.2 sec faster than when taking the silver medal in Los Angeles.

It was the final big race for Lovelock, who retired from major athletics to concentrate on his medical work. He qualified as a doctor at St Mary's Hospital, London, which was where some 20 years later Sir Roger Bannister – the world's first four-minute miler – also studied medicine. In 1940 Lovelock fell off a horse while out riding and sustained serious head injuries that affected his eyesight. He died tragically in New York on 29 December 1949, when he fell under a subway car at Church Avenue Station.

Finland won the 5000 meters (Gunnar Hoeckert), the 10,000 meters (Ilmari Salminen) and the 3000 meters steeplechase (Volmari Iso-Hollo) but surprisingly failed to take the javelin gold medal. This went to German Gerhard Stoeck, who also collected a bronze medal in the shot put, which was won by his compatriot Hans Woellke. A third German men's victory came in the hammer when Karl Hein beat the 24-year-old Olympic record by nearly six feet with a throw of 185ft 4in (56.49m).

However, the field event that captured public imagination was the pole vault, which became as much a test of stamina as strength and skill.

Opposite: Earle Meadows was on top of the world when he won the longest pole-vault duel in the history of the Olympics.

EARLE MEADOWS

THE CHAMPION WHO PASSED AN
ENDURANCE TEST

The United States won 12 of the 23 men's track
and field events. None of their champions had
to work such long hours for success as pole
vaulter Earle Meadows. Twenty-five qualifiers
for the final of the pole vault started the competition at midday. It was more than 10 hours
later, with floodlight replacing daylight, that
Meadows finally proved his supremacy with a
winning height of 14ft 3¼in (4.35m), which was
a new Olympic record.

Meadows won the longest pole vaulting duel
in the history of the Games against a strong
challenge for air supremacy from Japanese
Shuhei Nishida and Suoe Oe. They tied for
second place at 13ft 11¼in (4.25m). Nishida took
the silver medal (as he had in Los Angeles) and
Oe received the bronze, but they agreed, on
returning to Japan, to have a private duel to
decide who should have the silver. Again they
finished on a tie and so they had their medals
split by a silversmith, who then re-made them
with one half silver and the other half bronze.

In another marvellous aerial battle on 29
May 1937, Meadows and fellow-American Bill
Sefton pushed the world record up to 14ft 11in
(4.54m). This survived for three years until the
great Cornelius "Dutch" Warmerdam broke
the 15ft barrier for the first time. By the time
Warmerdam had finished his distinguished
career, he had lifted the record to 15ft 7¾in
(4.76m). He was USA champion from 1937
until 1944 but sadly missed Olympic competition because of World War II.

The Americans made a 1–2–3 sweep of the
medals in the decathlon, with Glenn Morris
shattering the world and Olympic records to
beat his team-mates Bob Clark and Jack
Parker to the gold. German world record
holder Willie Schroeder was the favorite to win
the discus but was outpowered by Americans
Ken Carpenter and Gordon Dunn, with Italian
Giorgio Oberweger producing peak form to
take third place.

As in Los Angeles and Amsterdam, the hop,
step and jump was won by a Japanese with
Naoto Tajima setting a new Olympic record of
52ft 6in (16m) to beat countryman Masao
Harada by 14½ inches. The gold medal also went
to Japan in the marathon, Korean-born Kitei
Son moving away from Britain's Ernie Harper
in the closing stages to win by a margin of more
than 2 minutes in 2 hr 29 min 19.2 sec. Harper
was more experienced at running marathons
than Son and sportingly signalled to him to

slow the pace or risk exhausting himself in the early stages of the race. Son slowed down but the defending champion Juan Carlos Zabala of Argentina shrugged off Harper's warning and continued at a suicidal pace that eventually forced him to collapse. Son had the energy and stamina left to speed away from true-sportsman Harper over the last mile of the punishing race.

Marathon walker Harold Whitlock stylishly won the gold medal for Britain in the 50 kilometers walk and there was an unexpected gold for Britain in the 4 × 400 meters relay when the quartet of Freddy Wolffe, Godfrey Rampling, Bill Roberts and individual silver medallist Godfrey Brown beat a powerful United States squad that had to be content with second place. Godfrey Brown's sister, Audrey, won a silver medal in the women's 4 × 100 meters relay.

An American student was the golden girl of the track.

HELEN STEPHENS
SHE BECOMES THE FASTEST WOMAN IN THE WORLD

Germany was confident that it had the fastest women sprinters in the world but it was forced to make a reassessment when Helen Stephens, an 18-year-old from Fulton, Missouri, stepped onto the track for her Olympic debut. She won her heat of the 100 meters in a new world and Olympic record of 11.4 sec. This was later disallowed because of a following wind but she proved it was no fluke when winning the semi-final in 11.5 sec, a time she equalled in the final when beating defending champion Stella Walasiewicz of Poland (but based in the States) by two meters. The German favorite Kathe Krauss finished third.

The Germans were determined to prove their sprinting superiority in the 4 × 100 meters relay and seemed set to make their point when they smashed the world record in the heats with a time of 46.4 sec. They were well in the lead in the final when they dropped the baton, and the United States, with Helen Stephens running an impressive anchor leg, came through to take the gold medal in 46.9 sec.

Tribisonda Valla of Italy equalled the world record of 11.6 sec in the 80 meters hurdles and Hungarian Ibolya Csak won the high jump after a jump off against 16-year-old British schoolgirl Dorothy Odam. As Mrs Dorothy Tyler, she came second again in the London Olympics of 1948 and continued a memorable Olympic career by being placed seventh in 1952 and twelfth in 1956.

German women won the discus (Gisela Mauermayer) and javelin (Tilly Fleischer) and they also had an uncrowned champion off the track. The world hailed as a masterpiece the film Leni Riefenstahl made of the 1936 Olympics. It was not only an outstanding sporting film but remains a marvellous contribution to the art of cinema. A film maker of repute before the Games, Miss Riefenstahl used 30 cameramen, shot over one million feet of film and skillfully edited it all to make a motion picture that captured completely the art and glory of Olympic sport.

In the swimming pool, the Japanese were in a monopolizing mood and took 10 out of a possible 17 medals in the men's events and another two in the women's program, in which a 17-year-old Dutch girl was supreme.

HENDRIKA MASTENBROEK
FOUR MEDALS FOR THE DUTCH WINDMILL GIRL

Born in Rotterdam on 26 February 1919, Hendrika "Rie" Mastenbroek made her first big splash on the international scene when winning two European titles in 1934. In the same year she set the first of her seven world records in individual events, speeding through the 100 meters backstroke in 1 min 16.8 sec. She was at her peak in Berlin, taking gold medals in the 100 meters freestyle, 400 meters freestyle and as a member of the Dutch 4 × 100 meters freestyle relay. There was a minor set-back for her in the 100 meters backstroke when she was beaten into second place by her team-mate Dina Senff, who missed her touch at the turn yet still had time to return to the wall and then kick off for a winning burst.

Americans so dominated the diving that they took all six medals in the men's and women's springboard events and were first and second in both highboard competitions. The most popular of all the champions was Californian schoolgirl Marjorie Gestring, who at 13 years and nine months was the youngest ever female gold medal winner. With a superbly executed $1\frac{1}{2}$ backward somersault as a high-tariff close to her program, she came from behind to beat team-mates Kathy Rawls and Dorothy Poynton-Hill in the springboard event. Mrs Poynton-Hill closed her eventful Olympic career by taking the highboard championship.

For the first time in Olympic competition, the over-water arm recovery stroke was used by some of the competitors in the men's 200 meters breaststroke. This later became known as the butterfly stroke and was introduced as a specialty event in the 1956 Olympics. Japanese Tetsuo Hamuro stuck with his orthodox underwater recovery stroke and was an impressive

The dramatic moment when the German women's relay team dropped the baton on the final change-over. They had set a world record in the heats.

winner of the 200 meters breaststroke final in Berlin in an Olympic record 2 min 41.5 sec.

The biggest surprise in the swimming pool came in the men's 100 meters freestyle final. The powerful Americans and Japanese were so busy watching each other that they failed to see Hungarian Ferenc Csik come through on the outside lane to snatch the gold medal. But it was another Hungarian who was considered the greatest hero in the water sports.

OLIVER HALASSY
THE ONE-LEGGED WATER POLO HERO

When he was 11 years old Oliver Halassy was knocked down by a tram in his native Budapest and had to have his right leg amputated from below the knee. Despite his handicap, he became one of Hungary's greatest swimmers and was a European 1500 meters freestyle champion. But it was in water polo that he made his biggest impact at international level, playing in nearly 100 matches for Hungary. Oliver won a silver medal in Amsterdam in 1928 and gold medals at Los Angeles in 1932 and in Berlin in 1936. He was a tremendous inspiration to the Hungarian water polo team in Berlin's 18,000-seat swimming venue, where a capacity crowd was yelling for a German victory. Hungary and Germany were bitter water polo rivals with the Germans winning the gold in 1928 and finishing as runners-up to Hungary in 1932 and 1936.

There was more rewarding water sport for the Germans in the rowing. They won five of the seven events and a silver and a bronze medal in the other two. Jack Beresford, competing for Britain in his fifth successive Games, partnered Leslie Southwood to a stunning victory in the

Cornelius Van Oyen, dead-eye shot in the rapid-fire pistol event in Berlin. He won the gold medal for Germany, with team-mate Heinrich Hax just a point away in second place.

double sculls, where the Germans considered themselves invincible. In the eights, the United States crew crossed the line first in a thrilling finish to the final with only one second covering the three medal-winning boats. French school boy Noel Vandernotte, just 12 years old, won two bronze medals as a cox in the pairs and fours. His father, Fernand, and uncle, Marcel Vandernotte, were also bronze medal winners. Noel may have been the youngest of all Olympic medallists, although there were unofficial reports that a boy of about eight coxed a winning Dutch pair during the loosely organized Paris Games of 1900.

The equestrian three-day event triggered arguments and controversy that raged long after the Berlin Games had finished. Many of the riders considered the course too tough. Three horses had to be destroyed, putting the United States, Denmark and Hungary out of contention in the team event. It was considered that the German riders had been given every opportunity to get accustomed to the course and not surprisingly they won, with Ludwig Stubbendorf taking the individual gold medal on a horse named after a great Olympic hero Nurmi.

There were also complaints of bias toward the Germans on the cycling track. Arie van Vliet seemed certain to win the 1000 meters sprint for the Netherlands when he was the victim of an appalling obstruction by Germany's Toni Merkens. Dutch officials protested and it was upheld. This would usually have meant a disqualification but instead Merkens was awarded the gold medal and the German Cycling Federation had to pay a fine of 100 marks. Van Vliet got his consolation by winning the 1000 meters time trial in an Olympic record 1 min 12.0 sec and later became world champion.

Norwegian Willy Rögeberg was in dead-eye form with his small-bore rifle on the shooting range. He had 30 shots at a 50-meter target with his .22 caliber rifle and hit the bull with every shot to score a rare and remarkable perfect 300. It was a record for his event. Twelve years later in the London Games he collected a bronze medal in the free rifle event.

Germany's Alfred Schwarzmann was the most successful gymnast in Berlin, winning three gold and two silver medals. Sixteen years later, at the age of 40, he won a silver medal on the horizontal bars in the 1952 Olympics.

Top wrestling honors went to Kristjan Palusalu of Estonia, who won the gold medal in the heavyweight freestyle category and also in the heavyweight Greco-Roman division.

There were two Olympic champions in the

lightweight division in the weightlifting. Mohammed Mesbah of Egypt and Austrian Robert Fein lifted identical weights for a new Olympic and world record of 755lb. When they were weighed, their body weights were also equal and so both were awarded gold medals. The outstanding lifter in Berlin was Egyptian middleweight Khadr Touni, who had an extraordinary winning margin over defending champion Rudolf Ismayr (Germany) of $77\frac{1}{4}$lb.

When the Olympic flame was extinguished at the end of the Berlin Games it was considered that sport had just about triumphed over political propaganda. But the shadow of the swastika was greater than that of the Olympic flag at the closing ceremony. It was 12 years and a world war before the Olympic flame burned again.

OLYMPIC FUN AND GAMES

Peru defeated Austria 4–2 after extra time in the football (soccer) quarter-finals. It was later discovered that Peru had substituted a player, which was then against the rules, and it was ordered to play Austria again behind closed doors. Peru refused and was disqualified. Austria went on to reach the final, where it was beaten by Italy.

Fanny Blankers-Koen (nearest camera) rises at the first hurdle on her way to victory in the 80 meters hurdles. It was her hardest race of the London Games, a desperate finishing spurt taking her past Britain's Maureen Gardner a meter from the tape (opposite top). Maureen later married top British coach Geoff Dyson.

Bomb-scarred London volunteered to stage the 1948 Games and did an excellent job considering it was within three years of the end of World War II. It was the age of austerity in the United Kingdom but the Games helped lift the gloom for Londoners who were looking for a release valve after surviving the Blitz. There was neither the time nor the money to furnish the sort of facilities that had helped make the 1932 and 1936 Olympics so successful but by improvisation and makeshift methods the London Olympic Committee provided perfectly adequate venues for all the major sports.

The main track and field events were staged at Wembley Stadium, better known as the national soccer ground, which had been built to house the 1924 British Empire exhibition. A temporary cinder running track was laid and more than 4000 competitors from 59 nations took part in a moving opening ceremony that helped heal the deep wounds of war. It was estimated that more than half a million people watched the Games on the 80,000 television sets then in use in Britain.

The defeated Japanese and Germans did not send teams and the USSR was not affiliated with the International Olympic Committee. The United States was far and away the most successful nation with 35 gold medals. Sweden was second with 13 but it was the four gold medals collected by a Dutch housewife that captured public imagination.

FANNY BLANKERS-KOEN
THE GOLD RUSH OF THE HOMESICK MOTHER

Women's athletics had been something of a side-show until Fanny Blankers-Koen exploded onto the scene. She, more than anybody, made women athletes worthy of respect and attention, with a series of stunning performances at the London Olympics. Inevitably labelled "The Flying Dutchwoman," Fanny had set world records in the 80 meters hurdles, long jump and high jump during meets in occupied Holland in the war years. But by the time the 1948 Games came around she was a 30-year-old housewife and mother of two children. She was coached by her husband, Jan Blankers, who as a psychological build-up to the Olympics taunted her: "You are too old, Fanny."

Born in the Netherlands in 1918, Francina Koen was outstanding at all sports at school but, with the encouragement of her father to motivate her, started to concentrate on athletics from the age of 14. She used to cycle 18 miles to and from the training track where she was coached by Jan Blankers, a triple jump specialist who won an AAA championship in Britain and who married Fanny in 1940. At the age of 18, she competed in the Berlin Olympics, where she finished sixth in the high jump. Over the next 10 years she set or equalled world records in

the 100 yards, 100 meters, long jump, high jump and 80 meters hurdles. Fanny was determined to prove in 1948 that she was not too old to still dominate women's athletics.

She was entered in the Olympic 100 meters, 200 meters, 80 meters hurdles and 4×100 meters sprint relay, all the events to be decided over a period of nine days. She had to run 12 times in heats and finals – and broke the tape in every race. In the 100 meters final, she finished a clear winner by three meters over Britain's Dorothy Manley. She had to come from behind after a poor start in the 80 meters hurdles final, edging out Britain's Maureen Gardner in a photo-finish. Fanny was close to quitting the 200 meters because she felt homesick and missed her two children. But after sobbing in her husband's arms and releasing the nervous strain and pent-up emotion, she went out onto the Wembley track and won the 200 meters semifinal and final in devastating style. Audrey Williamson finished seven meters in her wake in the final, the third British girl to win a silver medal behind Flying Fanny. To complete her "full house" of gold medals, Fanny anchored the Dutch sprint relay team to victory after taking over the baton in third place and catching Australian leader Joyce King in the last two strides.

Fanny continued competing at top level for four more years. In 1950 she was running faster than ever, as she proved when breaking the

world record for 220 yards and winning three titles in the European championships in Brussels. The following year she switched to the pentathlon and set a world record 4692 points. She competed in the 1952 Olympics but a blood infection hampered her preparation and she failed to win any medals. After her retirement, the golden lady of athletics took an active part in the administration of Dutch sport.

Another lady who took the eye at Wembley was French all-rounder Micheline Ostermeyer. Her specialty event was the shot, which she duly won with a put of 45ft $1\frac{1}{2}$in (13.75m). She entered the discus just for the fun of it, having managed no better than third in the French championships. Micheline was as astonished as everybody else when she won with a throw of 137ft $6\frac{1}{8}$in (41.92m). After winning a third medal – a bronze in the high jump – she celebrated by giving a Beethoven piano recital at the French team's headquarters.

The high jump gold medal went to American Alice Coachman, with Britain's Dorothy Tyler beaten into second place in a jump off after they had tied at 5ft $6\frac{1}{4}$in (1.68m). As Miss Dorothy Odam, the British jumper had suffered exactly the same fate in the 1936 Games when she was just 16 years old. Under present-day rules, Mrs Tyler would have had a gold medal to show for her efforts.

One of the highlights of the men's track and field was the Olympic debut of Emil Zatopek (see 1952 Helsinki Games for his biography). The galloping Czech electrified the first-day crowd at Wembley by running away with the 10,000 meters title, beating silver medallist Alain Mimoun of France by more than three-quarters of a minute in an Olympic record 29 min 59.6 sec. Viljo Heino, the world record holder from Finland, had led for the first eight laps but then Zatopek took over and set such a killing pace that the Finn was forced to drop out of the race.

Zatopek might also have won the 5000 meters had he been more experienced. He needlessly used up a lot of energy in his heat when getting involved in an unnecessary duel with Sweden's Erik Ahlden, racing neck and neck for the tape when it was obvious that both would qualify for the final. Seventy yards behind race leader Gaston Reiff at the bell in the final, Zatopek unleashed one of his wild bursts of speed that were to become such a feature of his running. A fast-tiring Reiff was relieved to break the tape with Zatopek just 0.2 sec behind him in second place.

America retained the 100 meters title through an athlete who made the US team in freakish circumstances.

Emil Zatopek, a worried-looking man with plenty to smile about when he won the 10,000 meters to start a memorable Olympic career.

HARRISON DILLARD
THE FALL AND RISE OF A HURDLING HERO

There was no question that Harrison "Bones" Dillard was the best high hurdler in the world in the immediate post-war years. He was a stylish performer, famed for his technique and his speed between the hurdles. Competing for Ohio's Baldwin-Wallace College, Dillard was unbeaten in 82 consecutive races in the year leading up to the US Olympic trials in June 1948.

Born in Cleveland, Ohio, on 8 July 1923, Dillard was inspired to take up athletics by the exploits of his idol Jesse Owens, who encouraged him by presenting him with the running spikes in which he won his four Olympic gold medals in 1936. In June 1947, Dillard lowered the world record for 220 yards hurdles (once held by Owens) to 22.3 sec and 10 months later

Harrison ("Bones") Dillard (No 69) qualifies for the 100 meters final, in which he was a stunning winner in an Olympic record-equalling 10.3 sec.

brought the world record for 110 meters hurdles down to 13.6 sec.

He was the hottest of all favorites in the US Olympic trials but lost his famous rhythm in the final of the 110 meters hurdles, hit a barrier and crashed out of the race. The trials are the sole basis of selection for the US Olympic team and so Dillard was out of the event for which he had seemed destined for a gold medal. Dillard picked himself up, dusted himself off and started all over again – this time in the 100 meters. He scraped into the team for London by qualifying in third place behind 100 yards world record holder Mel Patton and 100 meters world record holder Barney Ewell.

Dillard qualified for the final in London by winning his semi-final in impressive style but it was thought unlikely that he could get the better of his power-paced team-mates Patton and Ewell. After one false start it was Dillard who was quickest into top gear in lane six, nearest the stands. Ewell was in the center lane alongside Panama's Lloyd La Beach and he set off on a dance of delight in premature celebration of victory after crossing the finish line ahead – so he thought – of all his rivals. He had not seen Dillard slicing through the tape to his right but a photograph showed the Cleveland Flash a clear winner in 10.3 sec, equalling the Olympic record held by his hero Jesse Owens.

There was a second gold medal for Dillard when he teamed up with Barney Ewell, Lorenzo Wright and Mel Patton to win the 4 × 100 meters relay by a comfortable margin from the British squad. At first it was announced that the Americans had been disqualified because of a baton change outside the first takeover zone but the judges reversed their decision after studying

The first barrier in the men's 110 meters hurdles final and there is little to choose between Americans Craig Dixon (nearest camera), William Porter (second lane) and Clyde Scott (farthest lane). It was even closer at the tape with Porter (above center) beating Scott by a stride, with Dixon inches away in third place,

film of the race and it was with some relief that the British runners handed their golds to the rightful winners.

Mel Patton gained consolation for finishing "only" fifth in the 100 meters final by spurting to victory in the 200 meters final. He beat the unlucky Barney Ewell by a stride in 21.1 sec, with Lloyd La Beach again in third place.

Harrison Dillard continued his remarkable Olympic career in 1952, this time winning his favorite 110 meters hurdles event by just inches from team-mate Jack Davis. Both were clocked at an Olympic record 13.7 sec. Dillard added a fourth gold medal to his collection when he helped the American sprint relay squad retain their title.

Even without the redoubtable Dillard in the 1948 110 meters hurdles, America still made a 1–2–3 clean sweep with William Porter winning in 13.9 sec from compatriots Clyde Scott and Craig Dixon. In the 400 meters hurdles, Roy Cochran – American champion from as far back as 1939 – won the final in an Olympic record 51.1 sec.

The most exciting and spectacular track final came in the 400 meters flat race. Herb McKenley, world record holder and favorite, led for 300 meters at what he later admitted had been a recklessly fast pace. He started to tire and tie up coming into the final stretch and his giant fellow-Jamaican Arthur Wint began to overhaul him. With one of the longest strides ever seen on an athletics track, the 6ft 4in Wint

came through dramatically to edge ahead of McKenley in the last desperate stages to win in 46.2 sec.

It was an eventful Olympics for Wint, who won a silver medal in the 800 meters and collapsed with a cramp in the 4 × 400 meters relay final, leaving the United States quartet with a comfortable run for victory. Wint was twice an Olympic runner-up to one of the greatest of all 800 meter champions.

MAL WHITFIELD
THE CARBON-COPY TWO LAP MASTER

Born in Bay City, Texas, on 11 October 1924, Mal Whitfield was a Bay City stroller who dominated 800 meter and 880 yard races in the immediate post-war years. He lost only three of 69 races over two laps between June 1948 and September 1954. A superb stylist with an economical stride, Whitfield became known as the carbon-copy champion. He won the 800 meters title in London in 1948 in a time of 1min 49.2 sec, with the long-striding Arthur Wint in second place. Four years later in the Helsinki Games, Whitfield retained his Olympic title. His time was again 1 min 49.2 sec and Wint was again in second place.

Though preferring the 800 meters, Whitfield was also a fine 400 meters runner and took the bronze medal behind Wint and Herb McKenley in the London final. He was anchor man for the

American 4 × 400 meters relay squad and broke the tape 25 meters ahead of his nearest rival after Wint had dropped out in mid-race because of a cramp.

In Helsinki, Whitfield finished sixth in the 400 meters final and was a silver medallist with the American 4 × 400 meters relay team (see Helsinki Games chapter). He continued competing after the 1952 Games and set a world record for the 880 yards on 17 July 1953 of 1 min 48.6 sec. A month later he created a new world best time of 2 min 20.8 sec for 1000 meters. He was American 800 meters champion again in 1953 and 1954 but just failed in his bid to win a place in the team for the 1956 Melbourne Olympics.

There were three gold medals for the United States in the field events – Guinn Smith (pole vault), Willie Steele (long jump) and Wilbur Thompson (shot) – but North American domination of the high jump was surprisingly ended by Australian John Winter with a leap of 6ft 6in (1.98m). Hungary gained their first victory in men's track and field since the 1900 Games when Imre Nemeth won the hammer with a throw of 183ft 11½in (56.07m). Twenty-eight years later, Imre's son – Miklos Nemeth – won the javelin gold medal in the 1976 Montreal Games.

Sweden kept the Scandinavians to the fore with victories in the 1500 meters (Henry Eriks-

Mal Whitfield, the carbon-copy champion, anchoring the United States to victory in the 4 × 400 meters relay. Right: Australian John Winter ends American domination of the high jump.

son), 3000 meters steeplechase (Tore Sjostrand), triple jump (Arne Ahman), 10 kilometers walk (John Mikaelsson) and 50 kilometers walk (John Ljunggren).

It was a bare Olympics for Finland's athletes. They gathered just one gold medal among them, Tapio Rautavaara winning their specialty event, the javelin, with a throw of 228ft 11in (69.77m). American Steve Seymour was second with a best effort of 221ft 8in (67.56m). His team-mate Martin Biles managed a throw

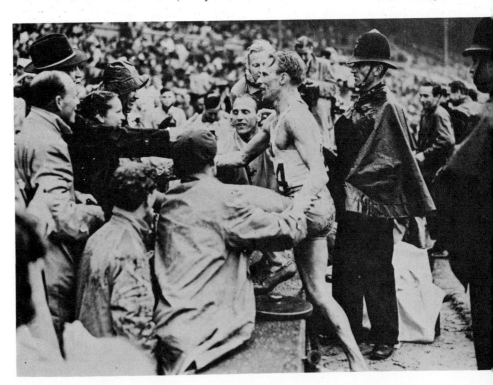

Henry Eriksson goes into the crowd to celebrate his 1500 meters victory with a group of Swedish spectators.

of 222ft 0½in (67.67m) in the qualifying round but could not reproduce this form in the final session and so finished out of the medal hunt.

Fortune Gordien, a prominent American discus thrower for more than 12 years, was just short of his peak power in the 1948 Games and had to be content with a bronze medal behind powerful Italian team-mates Aldolfo Consolini and Giuseppe Tosi. Gordien set new world record distances over the next three years but had to wait until 1956 to get another Olympic medal when he took the silver in Melbourne.

The most popular of all the men's champions was a 17-year-old Californian all-rounder.

BOB MATHIAS
THE BOY WHO PROVED HIMSELF A SUPERMAN

Bob Mathias in action in the discus event on his way to victory in the decathlon. He was a boy among men but emerged as the "Superman" of the London Olympics.

It was close to midnight on Friday, 6 August 1948, when Bob Mathias – three months short of his eighteenth birthday – proved himself a sporting superman at the London Games by winning the Olympic decathlon title. Mathias was competing in only his third decathlon competition. He had just graduated from high school and many people thought he would be out of his depth in a field that included the top 35 decathletes in the world. He had caused a stunning upset in June by winning the American championship but it was felt the pressure of Olympic competition would take its toll on a body that had not yet fully developed into its 6ft 3in, 217lb frame.

But Mathias thrived on the Olympic challenge and finished the first day in third position after five of the 10 exhausting events. The weather was appalling, with frequent rainstorms making Mathias feel a million miles away from his sunny California home. He gritted his teeth and forgot about the miserable conditions as he poured himself into the second day's events. After an impressive run in the 110 meters hurdles, he hurled the discus 144ft 4in (43.9m) to take the lead for the first time.

He had such a commanding lead by the time of the final event, the 1500 meters, that he virtually had only to complete the course to clinch victory. The race started just before midnight, with the track poorly floodlit by the lights usually reserved for greyhound racing. Among the crowd of around 250 spectators who had been in the stadium for 12 hours watching the struggle for supremacy were Bob's parents and two brothers, who had come from California to cheer him on. He lumbered heavily around the track in his least favorite event to clock a time of 5 min 11 sec, the third slowest

recorded among all the competitors, but he was still the winner of the gold medal by 165 points from his nearest rival, Frenchman Ignace Heinrich.

Mathias had forced himself to the edge of exhaustion in his quest for gold and when interviewed immediately after his triumph said: "This will be my last decathlon. I would not wish to go through that again." But once refreshed and over the torture of his two-day ordeal, he changed his mind and set his sights on the 1952 Olympic title.

In 1950, in the California town of Tulare where he was born, Mathias set a world record decathlon points total of 7453. It was a record that remained intact until the 1952 Games in Helsinki when he became the only athlete to retain the decathlon championship with a new record points haul of 7887, an astonishing 912 points ahead of silver medallist Milton Campbell, who retained the title for the United States in the 1956 Olympics.

Mathias was deprived of his amateur status in 1953 after appearing in a film based on his career. He became a politician and was elected to the House of Representatives as a Republican congressman for California.

The marathon was once again the most dramatic event of the London Games. Etienne Gailly, a 21-year-old Belgian paratrooper, led the way into the stadium but was so weakened by the pace he had set that he was struggling to stand, let alone run. In the last 385 yards, he was overtaken first by Argentinian Delfo Cabrera and then by Britain's Tom Richards. Gailly staggered across the finish line in third place to win a bronze medal and the sympathy of the spectators.

Above: William Smith has time to look round at the end of the 400 meters freestyle final to see his US team-mate Jimmy McClane finishing second.
Below: Karoly Takacs, Hungary's remarkable one-armed marksman.

America's swimmers gave an extraordinary show of power in the swimming pool. They made a clean sweep in the six men's events, 15 of their 18 representatives reaching the finals. New Olympic records were set in eight events and equalled in another and the US 4 × 200 meters relay team set a new world best. Their formidable relay team included 100 meters freestyle champion Walter Ris and the first two home in the 400 meters, William Smith and Jimmy McLane, who was also the winner of the 1500 meters. But the American victories were made a little hollow by the absence of Japanese swimmers. The Japanese staged their domestic championships in Tokyo to coincide with the Olympics and the winning times in their events were nearly all faster than those

set in the Olympic pool.

The American women met stronger opposition in the pool. Denmark took two gold medals through Greta Andersen (100 meters freestyle) and Karen Harup (100 meters backstroke) and the Netherlands won the 200 meters breaststroke through Petronella van Vliet. Ann Curtis was America's only individual swimming champion in the women's events. She won the 400 meters freestyle and anchored the 4 × 100 meters relay team to victory in a tight finish with the Danish girls.

American divers took 10 out of the 12 medals in the four diving events, including all the golds. Victoria Draves became the first woman to win both the highboard and springboard titles and Sammy Lee and Bruce Harlan won the men's events. Lee, born in Fresno, California, of Korean parents, became the first man to retain a highboard title in Helsinki four years later. He also won a bronze in the springboard in London and coached Bob Lee, who repeated the highboard double in the 1960 and 1964 Olympics. Lee was voted America's outstanding athlete in 1953 and continued taking a close interest in international diving after qualifying as a doctor of medicine.

In the boxing championships, one of the legendary figures of the gloved sport made his Olympic debut.

LASZLO PAPP
THE HUNGARIAN RING MASTER WINS THREE GOLDS

Born in Budapest on 25 March 1926, Laszlo Papp was one of the most skillful ring technicians in the history of Olympic boxing. He won a gold medal at middleweight in London in 1948 and was light-middleweight champion in Helsinki in 1952 and in Melbourne in 1956. A southpaw with a solid right jab and jolting left hook, Papp had to pull out everything he knew to outpoint British seaman Johnny Wright in the final in London and later in his career described it as the hardest contest he ever had as an amateur. His peak performance came in the 1956 final when he outpointed Jose Torres, who later became world professional light-heavyweight champion.

Papp became the first Iron Curtain boxer to be allowed to campaign as a professional. He won 27 and drew two of 29 professional fights and retired in 1965 as undefeated European champion. The Hungarian authorities refused to let him challenge for the world professional crown even though he successfully defended his European middleweight title six times. Papp became a successful coach to the Hungarian Olympic boxers after his retirement from the ring.

Another champion who went on to greater things after winning an Olympic title in London was flyweight Pascual Perez of Argentina, who became one of the greatest of professional world flyweight title holders. Vic Toweel, a South African beaten in the first series of the Olympic bantamweight division in London, won the world professional title in 1950.

Hungarian marksman Karoly Takacs was one of the most remarkable champions in London. He had been one of Hungary's top right-hand shots for more than 10 years when he lost his hand in a grenade explosion that nearly cost him his life in 1938. Takacs then perfected shooting with his left hand and was a member of the Hungarian national team that won the world title in Lucerne in 1939. He won the gold medal for rapid fire pistol shooting in the London Olympics and retained his title in Helsinki four years later.

There were three extraordinary fencing masters competing in the London Games. Christian d'Oriola, a 19-year-old Frenchman, won a gold medal with the French team in the foils event and also took the individual silver. It was reported that he sportingly allowed his 35-year-old countryman Jehan Buhan to beat him in the individual section. He won the individual and team gold medals in 1952, the individual gold again in 1956 and shared the team silver.

Danish doctor Ivan Osieer closed his Olympic fencing career in London, where it had started 40 years earlier. He had a silver medal (won in the épée event in 1912) to show for his efforts in seven Olympiads. His wife, Ellen Osieer, won a gold medal in the first women's individual championship in foils in Paris in 1924.

Hungarian Ilona Elek was as dominating in women's fencing as her countryman Laszlo Papp was in the boxing ring. She won the individual foil in 1936 and again in 1948 and was a silver medallist in 1952. She also won 11 gold medals in world championships, plus five silver and one bronze.

Ilona Elek (left), one of the greatest women fencers of all time, on her way to victory in the foil against Denmark's Karen Lachman.

Sweden continued to completely monopolize the modern pentathlon, their captain William Grut winning three of the five events and taking the individual gold medal. The Swedes were also announced as the winners of the team dressage in the equestrian events with nearly 100 points more than France. But it was later discovered that one of their team – Gehnall Persson – was not an officer (as was then required in the rules) and the Swedes were disqualified and their medals handed to the French team.

There was quite a family celebration after Sweden had won the soccer championship. The three Nordahl brothers – center-half Bertil, right-back Knut and famous center-forward Gunnar – became the only three brothers to win gold medals in the same competition in the same year.

The London Games were staged in true Olympic spirit with no sign of the chauvinism that had scarred and soured the 1936 Olympics. They played a valuable part in helping to restore some sense, sanity and stability to a war-weary world.

OLYMPIC FUN AND GAMES

The long and short of it: America had two contrasting champions in their team, bantamweight weightlifting gold medallist Joe di Pietro, who stood 4ft 6in, and basketball gold medallist Bob Kurland, who looked down from a height of just over 7ft.

*Emil Zatopek pounds towards
the tape and victory in the
5000 meters final in Helsinki.
He is chased by Frenchman
Alain Mimoun and German
Herbert Schade. They have
just swept past Britain's Chris
Chataway, who stumbled
against the curb coming into
the final straight.*

The Olympics came to the land of the midnight sun 12 years later than originally planned. Tokyo and Helsinki had been the two applicants for the 1940 Games. They were awarded to Tokyo but were then switched to Helsinki because of Japan's military movements in Asia. Finland was overtaken by the events of World War II but in 1952 the Finns made the long wait well worthwhile by staging an Olympiad that was superbly organized. They were literally inch perfect with their planning, even building the tower that rose above the main stadium 238ft 6⅜in high, which was the distance their great javelin-throwing hero Matti Jaervinen reached with his gold medal winning throw in Los Angeles in 1932.

The opening ceremony was charged with emotion when Finnish idol Paavo Nurmi brought the Olympic torch into the stadium and was then joined by the "father of middle distance running" Hannes Kolehmainen for the traditional ritual of lighting the Olympic flame.

For the first time since the Stockholm Games in 1912, the Russians returned to the Olympic fold to boost the entries to a record of nearly 6000 competitors representing 69 nations. The only slight anchor on the otherwise happy Games was that the Russians insisted on having an Olympic village separate from the Western competitors but this coldness rarely spilled over into the competition.

New Olympic records were set in 19 of the 24 men's events in the track and field championships with another two equalled, and there were three world records. Only two of the previous nine women's Olympic records survived and they also created three new world records. The star of the entire Games was the Czech middle and long distance runner who had made such a startling debut in the 1948 Olympics.

EMIL ZATOPEK
THE BOUNCING CZECH PULLS OFF THE "IMPOSSIBLE" TRIPLE

There has never been any other athlete quite like Emil Zatopek. He ran more miles than possibly any other person in history and looked as if he hated every second of it. When he ran, his head lolled from side to side and his face was contorted in agony with his tongue hanging out like somebody being strangled. He bounced around the track at uneven pace, sometimes slowing to converse with other runners and then tearing off on lung-bursting spurts that sapped the strength and stamina of his rivals. The fact that his strange tactics were successful is proved by his long-running record of victories. During a long and glorious career he set 18 world records from distances of 5000 meters to 30,000 meters.

Zatopek had revealed his potential to the world in the 1948 Games but nobody could have expected his extraordinary explosion of running power four years later when he completed what was considered the "impossible" triple of victory in the 5000 meters, 10,000 meters and the marathon, which he was attempting for the first time.

Born in Koprivnice, Moravia, on 19 September 1922, Zatopek did not become interested in running until the age of 18 when working in a shoe factory. He was persuaded to run at a local meeting and surprised himself by finishing second. By the time he was 22 he had broken the Czech records for 2000, 3000 and 5000 meters and after joining the army in 1945 he stepped up his punishing training schedule until he was running an average of 15 miles a day, often while wearing his heavy army boots.

His first major test came in the 1946 European championships in Oslo, when he finished fifth in the 5000 meters, won by Britain's Sydney Wooderson. This experience of top international athletics encouraged him to train even harder and by the time of the London Olympics in 1948 he had developed into one of the world's outstanding middle distance runners. He won a gold medal in the 10,000 meters and a silver in the 5000 meters, yet had still not reached his peak. That came in Helsinki in 1952.

Zatopek's 1952 gold rush started on Sunday, 20 July, when he lined up with 30 other runners for the 10,000 meters. He dominated the race after five laps, during which he seemed almost bored by the procession. Suddenly he unleashed a long sprint that wrote off most of his competitors. Only Britain's Gordon Pirie and French Algerian Alain Mimoun could present

any sort of a challenge but they too were dropped when he put in a devastating last lap of 64.00 sec to clinch a convincing victory in 29 min 17.0 sec, which slashed 42.6 sec off the Olympic record he had set in London.

He was back on the track two days later for his heat of the 5000 meters when he was content to stroll across the finish line in third place after spending much of the race chatting to his rivals. The final was far from casual, with Zatopek having to work furiously hard for his victory. With 300 meters to go, Britain's Chris Chataway was in the lead with German champion Herbert Schade, Mimoun and Zatopek chasing at his heels. Chataway, close to exhaustion, stumbled against the curb and sprawled on the track as Zatopek made his dash for victory. Mimoun and Schade tried to respond but could not match the Czech's finishing speed as he broke the tape in a new Olympic record of 14 min 06.6 sec.

That same afternoon Zatopek's wife, Dana, who was born on exactly the same day as he was, won the gold medal in the javelin with an Olympic record throw of 165ft 7in (50.47m).

The fourth family gold medal came on Sunday, 27 July, in the toughest race of them all, the marathon. Zatopek had never run the 26 mile 385 yard course before and was so unsure of what sort of pace to set that he decided to follow the British favorite Jim Peters. But soon after the halfway distance Zatopek, unimpressed by the slowness of the race, went out on his own and reached the stadium more than two minutes ahead of his nearest rival. The agonized look on his face was replaced by a broad grin as he crossed the finishing line in an Olympic record 2 hr 23 min 3.2 sec.

Zatopek, who had run a total of more than 38 miles in eight days, wound down his memorable Olympic career in Melbourne in 1956 when he finished sixth in the marathon, which was won by the persistent Alain Mimoun, who had won three silver medals behind the great Czech.

Dana Zatopek continued to compete after her husband's retirement and followed her fourth place in the javelin in Melbourne with a silver medal in her fourth Olympics in Rome in 1960.

Emil was severely censured for publicly supporting the Dubcek government in their stand against Russian domination in 1968. He lost his Communist Party membership, his rank of colonel in the Czech army and his position of coach to the Dukla athletic team. But he never lost the esteem and admiration of the followers of world sport who considered him one of the greatest athletes of all time whose integrity, sportsmanship and sheer talent were legendary.

Zatopek had been expected to make an impact on the Helsinki Games but few people had ever heard of the winner of the blue ribbon event of the Olympics, the men's 1500 meters.

JOSEF BARTHEL
TEARS FROM THE "UNKNOWN" OLYMPIC CHAMPION

Nobody was all that impressed by the victory of Luxembourg's Josef Barthel in heat one of the 1500 meters in 3 min 51.6 sec. There were some favorable comments about him when he then won his semi-final in 3 min 50.4 sec but as this was the fastest time of his career all the experts were convinced he would be out of his depth in the final, where he would be confronted by world-class runners like British champion miler Roger Bannister, crack German Werner Lueg, classy American Bob McMillen and powerful Frenchman Patrick El Mabrouk.

The modest Barthel, with a smile that showed off gold teeth, shrugged when asked what he considered his chances of getting Luxembourg's first track gold medal. Even he did not really consider himself in the class of his famous rivals but he had been well prepared for the Games and was determined to give the final all he had. German coach Woldemar Gerschler, the man behind the success of pre-war German ace Rudolph Harbig, had trained Barthel and was one of the few people in the

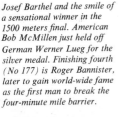

Josef Barthel and the smile of a sensational winner in the 1500 meters final. American Bob McMillen just held off German Werner Lueg for the silver medal. Finishing fourth (No 177) is Roger Bannister, later to gain world-wide fame as the first man to break the four-minute mile barrier.

world who knew he was capable of great things.

There was a lot of pre-race tension among the favorites but the unfavored Barthel was untroubled by nerves. He knew he had nothing to lose because nobody seriously expected him to challenge for the gold medal. Even a false start could not unnerve him and when the field finally got away at the second time of asking he moved along effortlessly and economically with the main bunch while German Rolf Lamers set off at a cracking pace. The first lap was covered in 57.8 sec and Lamers was still leading at 800 meters, reached in 2 min 01.4 sec. It was a much faster pace than Barthel had ever experienced but he was still in contact with the leading bunch.

Werner Lueg led by two meters at the bell with Barthel, Lamers, Bannister, El Mabrouk and the tall McMillen in pursuit. Lueg started to falter as he came off the final bend. Barthel was at his shoulder, sensed that he was losing his drive and sprinted past him before anybody else could respond. Bannister, later to become famous for being the first man to break four minutes for the mile, had burned himself out and only McMillen could challenge the speeding Barthel, who raised both hands and showed a flash of gold teeth as he hit the tape half a meter ahead of the fast-finishing American.

The enormity of what Barthel had achieved finally hit him when the time was announced as a new Olympic record of 3 min 45.1 sec, more than five seconds faster than he had ever run

before. As he stood on the victory rostrum while the appreciative Finnish crowd listened to the first Olympic rendering of the Luxembourg national anthem, Barthel sobbed as the emotion of the moment swept over him.

There were only wide, beaming grins when the relay runners of Jamaica finally got on the victory rostrum.

HERB McKENLEY
A GOLD AT LAST FOR THE OLYMPIC SILVER MAN

The 4 × 400 meters relay was one of the final events of the 1952 Games and presented great Jamaican sprinter Herb McKenley with a last chance to win a longed-for gold medal. McKenley had seemed destined to be labelled with a "second best" tag. At London in 1948 he had been beaten in the last strides of the 400 meters final by his team-mate Arthur Wint. Jamaica had been favored to win the 4 × 400 meters relay but that hope evaporated when Wint collapsed with a cramp during his leg of the race.

In the final of the 100 meters in Helsinki McKenley appeared to many people to have broken the tape just ahead of America's Lindy Remigino. But the official race photograph showed Remigino inches ahead of the Jamaican. The first four across the finishing line were all credited with a time of 10.4 sec. Remigino, who won a second gold in the sprint relay, had only just squeezed into the US team. He was third in a photo-finish in the Olympic trials. McKenley collected yet another silver medal in the 400 meters final, this time finishing just inches behind his countryman George Rhoden. Both were clocked at an Olympic record 45.9 sec.

Running the third leg of the relay for Jamaica, McKenley was determined to make no mistake. He took over the baton in second place, four yards behind American Charlie Moore, who had won the 400 meters hurdles in an Olympic record 50.8 sec. McKenley ran the race of his life, overhauling Moore and handing anchorman George Rhoden a two yard lead. Nobody in the world could give the individual gold medallist any sort of an advantage and he held his lead right through the tape. Jamaica was the winner in a world record 3 min 3.9 sec. The American quartet was also inside the old world record. McKenley's individual leg was timed at 45.1 sec, then the fastest recorded over 400 meters.

America had three remarkable champions among their six gold medallists in the field events. High jump winner Walter Davies had been a polio victim as a boy and had taken up

athletics to help him recover strength in his limbs. Pole vault champion Bob Richards was a preacher known as "The Vaulting Vicar." He won nine US titles and was three times American decathlon champion. In the 1956 Melbourne Games, he retained his pole vault title but was unplaced in the decathlon. Shot put champion Parry O'Brien was one of the greatest specialists at his event of all time. He was just 20 when he won the gold medal in Helsinki. After retaining the title in 1956, he won the silver medal in 1960 and was placed fourth in 1964. The man who pioneered the step-back style of shot putting, O'Brien beat the world record 14 times and was the first man to break the 60ft barrier. He had 116 consecutive victories between 1952 and 1956 and won 18 US titles. O'Brien was 34 when he produced the greatest put of his career with a mighty effort of 64ft 7½in (19.7m) in 1966.

Brazil's first ever Olympic track and field gold medallist was triple jumper Adhemar Ferreira da Silva, who dominated his event for seven years. He broke his own world record four times in the Helsinki final and retained his championship in Melbourne. Da Silva also won three Pan American titles.

In the women's events, Marjorie Jackson took both sprint gold medals for Australia and her team-mate Shirley Strickland won the 80 meters hurdles in a world record 10.9 sec. Miss Strickland – later Mrs De La Hunty – won more medals than any other woman athlete in history during a marvellous Olympic career which started in London in 1948 when she collected bronze medals in the 100 meters and 80 meters hurdles and a silver in the sprint relay. She got another bronze in the Helsinki 100 meters final and in her homeland of Australia in 1956 retained the 80 meters hurdles title and

Herb McKenley became accustomed to this kind of photo-finish. Farthest from the camera, the Jamaican was just beaten at the tape in this 100 meters semi-final by American Lindy Remigino (No 981). There was a repeat finish in the final, with Remigino beating McKenley to the gold medal by half a stride.

105

when she got a bronze. Her team-mate Nina Romashkova won the Helsinki discus championship with a throw of 168ft 8½in (51.42m). As Mrs Ponomareva, she took the bronze medal in 1956 and re-established herself as Olympic champion in 1960. She made headlines of the wrong kind when she was arrested for alleged shoplifting in London and was featured in front-page scandal stories.

In the Olympic pool it was an American diver who made the biggest splash.

PAT McCORMICK
FOUR GOLD MEDALS FOR THE DIVING MUM

Born in Seal Beach, California, on 12 May 1930, Pat Keller was champion of her state while a teenager but missed selection for the 1948 Olympic team. She was 22 and married to airline pilot Glenn McCormick by the time the 1952 Games came around. She travelled to Helsinki and took the gold medals in both the platform and springboard events.

Many people thought her diving career was over when she gave birth to a son in the summer of 1956 but five months later she went to Melbourne and successfully defended both her

Shirley Strickland (No 31) is congratulated by her competitors in true Olympic spirit after winning the 80 meters hurdles.

Britain's high jumper, Dorothy Tyler, competing in her fourth Olympics.

won another gold – her seventh medal – in the 4 × 100 meters relay.

Russia failed to record a single victory in the men's athletics but collected two gold medals in the women's events. Galina Zybina took the shot put title with an Olympic record of 50ft 1½in (15.28m). She was the silver medallist at Melbourne four years later and completed a full range of Olympic medals in Tokyo in 1964

titles. Her winning margin in the springboard event of 16.47 points is the greatest ever recorded in Olympic competition. She was voted American Woman Athlete of the Year for 1956 and in 1965 became the first woman elected to the US Swimming Hall of Fame.

Hungarian women swimmers won four of the five events in the pool. Their 4×100 meters relay team smashed the world record with a time of 4 min 24.4 sec. Three members of the squad also won individual medals: Katalin Szoke (winner, 100 meters freestyle), Judit Temes (third, 100 meters freestyle) and Eva Novak (silver in the 400 meters freestyle and 200 meters breaststroke). The Hungarian husband and wife team of Dezso Gyarmati and Eve Szekely also won gold medals in Helsinki, Eve in the 200 meters breaststroke and Dezso in the water polo final. Both had won silver medals in the London Olympics before getting married. Dezso went on to win a second gold medal with the Hungarian water polo team in Melbourne and a bronze in Rome in 1960.

The United States had five out of the 10 gold medallists in the boxing ring, including Norvel Lee, who had gone to Helsinki as a reserve in the heavyweight division and finished up winning the light-heavyweight title. He was summoned into action after first-choice Chuck Spieser had been taken ill. Two Helsinki finalists later made a fortune fighting each other for the world professional heavyweight championship.

FLOYD PATTERSON
THE OLYMPIC CHAMPION WHO WALKED INTO "INGO'S BINGO"

Aged just 17, Floyd Patterson was the baby of the United States boxing squad but he looked like a man among boys when he started his campaign to win the middleweight gold medal. Taught to box in a reform school, the fast-punching stylist from Brooklyn overwhelmed all his opponents with the speed and power of his combination attacks. Ringside experts thought he might have problems in the final when he faced Romanian champion Vasila Tita but he eliminated all doubts by storming to a first round knockout victory.

His team-mate Ed Sanders won the gold medal in the heavyweight class when his opponent in the final, a Swede called Ingemar Johansson, was disqualified for "not giving of his best." The Olympic officials even withheld the silver medal from the humiliated Swede, who vowed to show them they had made a grave error in their judgment. He earned their respect

and apologies nearly seven years later when sensationally stopping Floyd Patterson in three rounds in a world heavyweight championship contest. Patterson walked into the Swedish boxer's fearsome right-hand punch, which was nicknamed "Ingo's Bingo." Patterson became the first man to regain the world heavyweight championship when he knocked out Johansson in five rounds a year later, and they met for a third time in 1961, with Patterson winning by a knockout in the sixth round.

The Helsinki Games featured two outstanding champions in the water sports. Dane Paul Elvstrom won the second of four yachting gold medals in 1952. He was also a champion in 1948 in the Firefly and a Finn gold medallist in 1952, 1956 and 1960. A fitness fanatic, he prepared in such a way for his competitive races that he was able to hang over the side of his boats for longer periods than his rivals and so get an important advantage. He won 11 world championships in seven different classes between 1957 and 1974. His amateur status was brought into question after he had started a company selling his own specially designed sails and pleasure boats.

Sweden's Gert Fredriksson was another water master in action in Helsinki. One of the greatest canoeists of all time, he won the kayak singles in 1952, which was a title he also captured in 1948 and 1956. He was also the 10,000 meters champion in 1948 and 1956 and shared in a kayak pairs win over 1000 meters in 1960 when he was 40. His medals collection was boosted to eight by a silver in the 10,000 meters in 1952 and a bronze in the 1000 meter kayak singles in 1960. He also won seven world canoeing championships. All these triumphs came after what were considered his peak power years during World War II.

Bernard Malivoire, a 12-year-old French schoolboy, coxed Raymond Salles and Gaston Mercier to victory in the coxed pairs final, to become the youngest recorded gold medallist.

Great Britain had to wait until the final event of the Games to win their only gold medal. Colonel Harry Llewellyn coaxed his famous mount Fox Hunter to a clear round in the Prix de Nations equestrian team championship to clinch the gold medal for Britain. Relaxing before the start of this vital final round, Colonel Llewellyn had gone to the stable and slept side by side with Fox Hunter.

Another colonel – Frenchman André Jousseaume from the famous Cadre Noir at Saumur – wound down a memorable Olympic career with a bronze medal in the individual dressage event. It was his fifth medal in four Olympics. He won dressage team golds in 1932 and 1948,

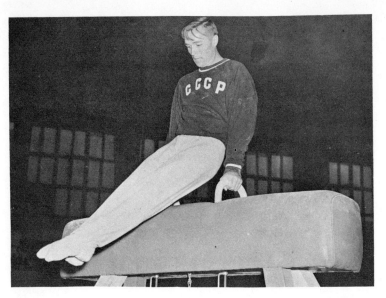

Viktor Chukarin, winner of seven gold medals in the Olympic gymnastic competitions of 1952 and 1956.

a silver in team dressage in 1936 and another silver in the individual event in 1948. Another military man with a fine Olympic record in dressage events was Swedish Major Henri St Cyr. He won four gold medals in the individual and team classes in 1952 and 1956 and also competed with distinction in the Olympics of 1936, 1948 and 1960.

Russia made its greatest impact in gymnastics, winning 22 medals in all, including eight golds. Its outstanding champions included the gifted Viktor Chukarin, who collected a total of seven gold medals in the Games of 1952 and 1956. He was a fine all-round performer and inspired a whole generation of gymnasts who were to continue to keep Russia in the forefront in a sport fast growing in popularity.

On the cycling track, Australian theologian Russell Mockridge won the 1000 meters time trial and the 2000 meters tandem in his first competition with partner Lionel Cox. An out-standing all-rounder with a quiet, pleasant personality, Mockridge later turned professional and showed his versatility by competing in the marathon Tour de France in 1955. He was tragically killed in a car accident in 1958.

The 1952 soccer final featured a Hungarian team that developed into one of the greatest sides in the history of the game. Included in the squad that won the gold medal were world stars Gyula Grosics, Mihaly Lantos, Jozsef Bozsik, Zoltan Csibor, Peter Palotas, Gyula Lorant, Nandor Hidegkuti and the legendary Ferenc Puskas.

Sweden was surprisingly forced to take second place in the modern pentathlon by Hungary but Lars Hall emerged as the individual winner for the Swedes, a title he retained in 1956. World champion in 1950 and 1951, Hall is the only person to win successive individual gold medals in the testing modern pentathlon, which is a trial of strength and stamina as well as all-round skill. It is the supreme examination of the all-round sportsman and was suggested for the Olympic program by Baron de Coubertin. There are five events: shooting, swimming, fencing, horse riding and cross-country running. Lars Hall was expert at all of them and is recognized as one of the great giants of the sport. He was the first non-military winner of the title.

There were new peaks of strength and power reached in the weightlifting. The United States won four golds, Russia three and there were seven world records, five more equalled and 18 new Olympic best performances. John Davis, the 1948 heavyweight champion from America, was the only man to retain his title.

When the Olympic flame was finally extinguished at the end of these Games in Helsinki, it was generally agreed that in terms of both personalities and performances they had been the most successful yet staged and were made particularly memorable by the enthusiasm and friendship of the Finnish spectators.

OLYMPIC FUN AND GAMES

Jean Boiteaux had just won the Olympic 400 meters swimming gold medal for France when startled officials were disturbed to see a spectator dive fully clothed into the pool. He swam to where the new champion was recovering his breath and kissed him on both cheeks. No disciplinary action was taken when it was discovered that the invader was Jean's father celebrating his son's victory.

For the first time the Olympic Games were celebrated in the Southern Hemisphere and out of season for many competitors, who had to make special preparations to hit their peak form in November and December of 1956.

The Olympics had gone ahead despite political and military turmoil in the world, with the Russians suppressing an attempted uprising in Hungary and British and French troops invading Suez. Egypt, Iraq, Lebanon, the Netherlands and Spain withdrew on political and moral grounds but the tough and decisive Avery Brundage, Detroit-born President of the International Olympic Committee from 1952 to 1972, insisted: "The Games will *not* be cancelled. We will not let any country use the Olympics for political purposes. The Games provide competition between individuals not nations."

Nearly 90,000 spectators crammed the Melbourne Cricket Ground to see the opening ceremony performed by Prince Philip, the Duke of Edinburgh. The warmest applause from the sun-drenched crowd was reserved for the contingent of Hungarian competitors who had made it to Melbourne despite the upheaval in their homeland. Missing from the parade of more than 3000 competitors representing 67 nations were the show jumpers of the world. Because of Australia's strict quarantine regulations, the equestrian events were staged in Stockholm in the summer, with Germany's Hans Winkler winning the first two of his record five gold medals. The Olympic torch was brought from Stockholm to Melbourne and was carried on the final lap by Australia's world junior mile record holder Ron Clarke who was to be such a formidable middle-distance runner over the following decade.

American competitors picked up 32 gold medals but Russia emerged as the top nation with a haul of 98 medals, 37 of them gold. Two of their gold medals were won on the track by one of the greatest middle-distance runners of all time.

VLADIMIR KUTS
"THE IRON MAN" OF THE TRACK

In a relatively short career in international athletics, Vladimir Kuts rewrote the Olympic and world record books for middle distance events. Born in the Ukraine on 7 February 1927, he did not start taking an interest in running until 1950 at the age of 23. He had concentrated on rowing, skiing and boxing while serving as a marine in the Russian navy and it was almost by accident that he discovered his talent for running faster and farther than any of his navy colleagues.

Within a year of giving all his attention to the track he was rated sixth in Russia at both 5000 and 10,000 meters. The world sat up and took notice of him when he ran away with the 1954 European 5000 meters championship with favorites Emil Zatopek and Britain's Chris Chataway unable to get anywhere near him. He shattered the world record by more than 12 seconds and lowered the record three more times during the following three years.

Kuts was known as "The Iron Man" of the track. He ran the Zatopek way, killing off his opponents with murderous changes of pace. Chataway, who later became an influential

Vladimir Kuts, the Russian "Iron Man," wins the 5000 meters in Melbourne to complete a golden double.

Bobby Joe Morrow, smooth winner of the 100 meters final in 10.5 sec. The flags in the background indicate the strength of the wind into which the sprinters were running.

voice in British politics, handed him a rare defeat in a world record run over 5000 meters in London in October 1954. This inspired Kuts to increase his training runs and he was at the peak of his form for the Olympics in Melbourne.

On the first day of the Games he had a titantic battle with Britain's Gordon Pirie in the 10,000 meters. Pirie had beaten Kuts and his 5000 meters world record earlier in the year but the Russian was determined not to concede second-best again. He set a torturous pace, destroying the field with sudden lung-bursting sprints. Only Pirie managed to stay with him but he too was broken after 20 of the 25 laps and was so exhausted that he dropped back to eighth place. Kuts went on to win by 50 meters, beating Zatopek's Olympic record by more than 30 seconds.

Five days later he employed the same ruthless front-running tactics in the 5000 meters, this time while under attack from the British trio of fine middle-distance aces Pirie, Chataway and Derek Ibbotson. They tried everything they could to break the Russian Iron Man but he was too strong on stamina for all of them.

Chataway, troubled by stomach cramps, was the first to crack and then Pirie and Ibbotson were slowly dropped by the red-vested Kuts, who ran with robot-like precision without

expression or any signs of discomfort. He smashed Zatopek's Olympic record by more than 27 seconds, winning in 13 min 39.6 sec, with Pirie 11 seconds away in the silver medal position and Ibbotson third.

In October 1957 Kuts ran his final major race in Rome, bringing the world 5000 meters record down to 13 min 35.0 sec, which went unbeaten for seven years. He became plagued by ill health and died of a heart attack at the age of 48.

An American sprinter from Texas rivalled Kuts as the star of the track in Melbourne.

BOBBY JOE MORROW
THE GREATEST OF ALL THE WHITE SPRINTERS

It is generally agreed that Bobby Joe Morrow was the greatest white sprinter in Olympic history until the emergence of Valeri Borzov in 1972. Between 1955 and 1958 he was beaten only once in a championship race and was equally capable over 100 and 200 meters. Standing 6ft $1\frac{1}{2}$in and powerfully built, Morrow was a supreme stylist who looked elegant and composed even when going flat out at world record speed. Born in Harlingen, Texas, on 15 October 1935, he was an outstanding footballer at school but was convinced that he should concentrate n athletics while studying at the Abilene Christian College.

He was never beaten to the tape on his way to three gold medals in Melbourne. In four rounds of the 100 meters he twice equalled the 10.3 sec Olympic record set by his idol Jesse Owens and clocked 10.5 sec when running into a stiff wind in the final. Australian Hec Hogan was slightly ahead of him at the halfway point but Morrow smoothly accelerated to win by a full meter from team-mate Thane Baker, with Hogan in third place.

Morrow was even more impressive in the 200 meters, hitting top gear coming off the bend to streak away to victory in an Olympic record 20.6 sec. He had been nursing a slight thigh muscle injury but heat treatment and a tight bandage prevented him breaking down in the final. Morrow led a clean 1–2–3 sweep for America, with 1952 champion Andy Stanfield and Thane Baker following him home.

He then combined with Ira Murchison, Leamon King and Thane Baker to retain the 4 × 100 meters relay title for the United States. Morrow ran a storming anchor leg to break the tape in a world and Olympic record 39.5 sec.

The following year Morrow equalled the world record 9.3 sec for 100 yards three times and in 1958 helped his Abilene Christian College sprint relay team beat the world record for the 4 × 220 yards relay. He was handicapped by injury in 1959 but made a recovery in time to challenge for a place in the 1960 US Olympic team, only narrowly missing out in the trials after clocking 20.8 sec for 200 meters.

Morrow led an American gold rush in the track and field events. The men picked up 15 golds in 24 events, one more than at Helsinki in 1924. One of the most surprised and surprising of all the winners was Charlie Jenkins in the 400 meters. His team-mate Lou Jones, the world record holder, was a clear favorite but ran out of finishing pace after taking a commanding lead in the outside lane. As Jones started to fade coming into a strong head wind in the final stretch, four runners swept past him in one of the closest blanket finishes ever seen outside the 100 meters. Just three tenths of a second separated them at the tape with Jenkins winning by a stride from Germany's Karl-Friedrich Haas. The judges were unable to pick between Russian Ardalion Ignatyev and Finn Voitto Hellsten for third place and so both were awarded bronze medals, the first instance of a tie on the track in Olympic competition.

For the fourth successive Olympics America provided the winner of the 800 meters. Britain's stylish Derek Johnson was leading with 30 meters to go but with a superhuman effort race favorite Tom Courtney drove himself into first place to win in an Olympic record 1 min 47.7 sec. Courtney was so exhausted by his last-gasp victory that he had to receive medical treatment.

The United States had two outstanding Olympic champion hurdlers on its team. Lee Calhoun won the 110 meters hurdles in 13.5 sec in a desperately close finish with countryman Jack Davis. They had dead-heated in the US Olympic trials. It was the second time Davis had been beaten to a gold medal in a photo-finish, Harrison Dillard edging him into silver medal place in the Helsinki Games. His namesake Glenn Davis won the 400 meters hurdles title in Melbourne in an Olympic record 50.1 sec.

Both Calhoun and Glenn Davis retained their hurdling titles in Rome in 1960, the only men to win two Olympic gold medals in their respective events. Calhoun had been suspended by the Amateur Athletic Union in 1958 for appearing with his bride on an American television "give away" show and accepting gifts valued at around $2000. He set a world record of 13.2 sec for the 110 meters hurdles soon after his reinstatement and in the 1960 Rome final again won in a photo-finish, this time from countryman Willie May.

Glenn Davis, an exceptionally fast sprinter as well as hurdler, retained his 400 meters Olympic championship in Rome in 49.3 sec, just 0.1 sec outside the world record he had set in 1958. He briefly held the world 440 yards flat world record and collected a third gold medal in America's triumphant 4 × 400 meters relay team in Rome. It was his last major race before switching to American football as a professional.

The 1500 meters saw an end to the American domination on the track with victory going to Irish outsider Ronnie Delany. Ireland's selectors had wondered whether it was worth the expense of sending Delany to Australia after a poor run of results in Dublin, where he had twice been beaten by Britain's Brian Hewson. But Delaney produced winning form where and when it mattered.

Hewson was first to make a break approaching the final bend but as a rush of runners passed him in the final frantic 150 meters it was the green vest of Delany that was seen to flash past on the outside. The Irishman went through the tape with his arms opened wide in a gesture of triumph. German champion Klaus Richtzenhain was second and Australian hero John Landy, the second man to break four minutes for the mile, spurted through to take the bronze medal. The first nine finishers broke the Olympic record.

111

Alain Mimoun – at last an Olympic winner ahead of Emil Zatopek. Below: Little sign of the drama to come in the 3000 meters steeplechase as eventual winner Chris Brasher coasts along in fifth place.

Delany, who had prepared for the Olympics at America's Villanova University, dropped to his knees after crossing the finishing line. The sporting Landy, who had read the Olympic oath at the opening ceremony, went across to help the champion up and then apologized for intruding. Delany was on his knees to pray.

Britain's Chris Brasher was a candidate along with Charlie Jenkins and Delany for being the most unexpected champion on the track. He had finished 11 out of 12 in the 1952 3000 meters steeplechase final and was best known for having helped pace Roger Bannister to the first four-minute mile. A bespectacled Cambridge University cross-country and track blue, he had gone to Melbourne as third string for the steeplechase, behind John Disley and Eric Shirley. Brasher produced a race of a lifetime to win by 15 meters in an Olympic record 8 min 41.2 sec. But Britain looked likely to be robbed of their only athletics gold medal of the Games when it was announced that Brasher had been disqualified for obstructing Norway's Ernst Larsen on the last lap. It was not until three hours after the race that the jury of appeal decided that the result should stand after Larsen had sportingly spoken up in Brasher's defense. Brasher is now a distinguished journalist in Britain, a lecturer on mountaineering and a leading light in the mushrooming sport of orienteering.

One of the most heart-warming sights of the Games came at the end of the marathon (which had incidentally got off to an hilarious false start!). French Algerian Alain Mimoun, three times a silver medallist behind Emil Zatopek, shrugged aside photographers and officials after his victory to stand anxiously at the trackside waiting for the sixth man home to finish. It was the great Czech Emil Zatopek and as he crossed the finishing line Mimoun gave his old rival and friend a welcoming hug.

The United States won seven of the nine field events, including the decathlon, in which Milton Campbell beat fellow American Rafer Johnson into second place. Johnson had his great Olympic moment to come four years later.

Charlie Dumas, the first man to beat the 7ft barrier in the high jump, set an Olympic record of 6ft 11½in (2.12m) after a long duel with Australian Charles Porter, who took the silver medal. The Reverend Bob Richards, "The Vaulting Vicar," retained his pole vault title, but not without drama in the qualifying competition, when he only managed to clear 13ft 1½in (4m) at his third attempt. He finally beat countryman Bob Gutowski into second place with an Olympic record height of 14ft 11½in (4.56m).

Gregory Bell overcame the handicap of a

gusting wind to take the long jump title with a leap of 25ft 8¼in (7.83m), just six inches ahead of his team-mate John Bennett.

There was only one record in the men's track and field events in Melbourne. Norwegian Egil Danielsen made a spectacular winning javelin throw of 281ft 2½in (85.71m), more than 40ft further than his own next best throw. Americans dominated the other throwing events, with Parry O'Brien retaining his shot put title with an Olympic record 60ft 11¼in (18.75m) and 20-year-old Al Oerter capturing the first of his all-time record four successive Olympic discus championships (see the Mexico 1968 chapter for Oerter's biography). The most successful of the throwing experts in Melbourne was the man who won not only a gold medal but also a wife.

HAL CONNOLLY
LOVE BREAKS THROUGH THE IRON CURTAIN

Three weeks before the Olympics, hammer thrower Hal Connolly broke the world record with a mighty hurl of 224ft 10in (68.52m). While training in Melbourne's Olympic village for the Games, Hal watched Czechoslovakia's Olga Fikotova taking practice throws with the discus. It was love at first flight. Hal was so smitten by Miss Fikotova that he failed to produce his best form in the hammer-throwing circle but still managed to win the gold medal with a throw of 207ft 3½in (63.19m). Olga won the women's discus. She had also won Hal's heart.

Czech officials put diplomatic and political red tape in their way to try to take the heat out of the romance but Connolly, of Irish stock and reviving the Irish-American dominance in the hammer, was used to beating the odds. He had been born with a withered left arm three inches shorter than his right, which did not stop him from developing into one of the world's greatest ever hammer-throwing exponents. And now Czech politicians were not going to stop him marrying Olga Fikotova.

He and Olga made a personal plea to the President of Czechoslovakia for permission to marry and after weeks of stony silence they were at last given the go ahead to become husband and wife. On 27 March 1957, they were married in Prague, where they went through two ceremonies, one in a Roman Catholic church and the other in a civil court-room. Emil Zatopek was the best man and his wife, Dana, the matron of honor. Hal took his bride home to California and celebrated by breaking the world hammer-throw record another five times. They competed together at

three more Olympics without managing to repeat their Melbourne triumphs.

Twelve years after winning the gold medal in Melbourne, Olga produced a lifetime's best discus throw of 175ft 5in (53.46m). In the 12-year interval she had become the mother of four children, including twins. She has since made a career as a writer and both she and Hal have been involved in the civil rights movement in sport.

Olga and Hal captured the hearts of the Australian public with their romance. But the Aussie spectators at the main stadium saved their loudest cheers for their own darling of the track.

BETTY CUTHBERT
THE BLUE-EYED BLONDE WITH THE GOLDEN TOUCH

Born at Merrylands, near Sydney, on 20 April 1938, Betty Cuthbert was so keen to see the Olympics in her homeland that she bought tickets for all the track and field programs the moment they went on sale. But Betty, an 18-year-old blue-eyed blonde with a trim figure and a sparkling personality, was able to pass the tickets on to her brother after she had gained a place in the Australian team as a sprinter. Her brother had the pleasure of seeing

Betty Cuthbert clinches her third gold medal as she beats Britain's anchor-runner, Heather Armitage, to the tape in the 4 × 100 meters relay final.

Dawn Fraser, winner of three successive gold medals in the 100 meters freestyle, has to settle for a silver in the 400 meters in Melbourne. Dawn (left) congratulates winner Lorraine Crapp, with bronze medallist Sylvia Ruuska looking delighted with herself in the center of the picture.

four years later in Rome.

In the women's long jump, Elzbieta Krzesinka of Poland equalled her own world record of 20ft 10in (6.35m) to take the gold medal. Russia collected two gold medals through the massive, 240lb Tamara Tyshkyevich in the shot and Inese Jaunzeme in the javelin.

The Australians made a winning splash in the swimming pool, with a now legendary swimmer making her Olympic debut.

DAWN FRASER
AUSTRALIAN MERMAID WINS THE FIRST OF HER RECORD GOLDS

Despite suffering from bronchial asthma throughout her career, Dawn Fraser became one of the immortal heroines of the swimming pool. She started her unique Olympic medals collection in Melbourne by winning the 100 meters freestyle and sharing in the 4 × 100 meters freestyle relay victory. "Dawnie" – as she was known to all her friends – also took a silver in the 400 meters freestyle.

She became the only swimmer to have won an Olympic title in the same event at three successive Games when completing her hattrick of victories in the 100 meters freestyle in Tokyo in 1964. During her remarkable career, she won 23 national championships, 39 world record plaques, six Commonwealth Games gold medals, four Olympic golds and four silvers. Noted for her boisterous personality, she went too far in celebration of her historic third successive gold medal in the Tokyo Olympics. She was involved in taking the Japanese flag from the Emperor's palace, a prank for which she was suspended from international swimming by the Australian governing body. The ban was later lifted and Dawnie – born in New South Wales on 4 September 1937 – was honored by Queen Elizabeth, head of the Commonwealth, by being made a Member of the British Empire.

The Australians were in almost complete control in the Olympic pool in Melbourne. Jon Henricks, John Devitt and Gary Chapman made it a 1–2–3 for the Aussies in the 100 meters freestyle and Scots-born Murray Rose won both the 400 and 1500 meters freestyle events. American George Breen had set a new world record in a heat of the 1500 meters but had to settle for a bronze medal in the final.

Rose, who emigrated to Australia while a child, was also a member of the winning 4 × 100 meters freestyle relay team and took his gold medal haul to four in 1960 when he retained his 400 meters title. In each of his 400 meter

Betty win three gold medals and become the heroine of the Games. She trimmed the Olympic record for the 100 meters to 11.4 sec in a heat and won the final in 11.5 sec from Germany's Christa Stubnick and from another fleet and lovely Aussie, Marlene Matthews.

The same trio shared the medals in the 200 meters, finishing in the same order but this time with Betty an even more emphatic winner in an Olympic record 23.4 sec that triggered a frontpage splash headline in one Australian newspaper: "BETTY YOU BEAUT!"

Her third gold medal came in the 4 × 100 meters relay when she anchored the Australian quartet to a new world and Olympic record of 44.5 sec. Sharing in her triumph was Mrs Shirley De La Hunty, who had already retained the 80 meters hurdles title that she had won as Miss Shirley Strickland in 1952.

Betty Cuthbert, who had a twin sister, Midge, was unable to retain either of her titles in the 1960 Rome Olympics because of a hamstring injury. But she had recovered her old zip and zest by the time of the 1964 Tokyo Olympics and won the 400 meters in 52.00 sec. She equalled or broke a dozen world records during her career and shares with the great Fanny Blankers-Koen the record of winning four Olympic gold medals on the track.

Mildred McDaniel achieved a world record high jump in Melbourne of 5ft 9¼in (1.76m) and her 17-year-old American team-mate Willye White won a silver medal in the long jump, an event in which she was to finish eleventh in the 1972 Games in Munich. There was a glimpse of America's bright future in the sprint relay team. They finished third in the final with a squad that included a 16-year-old schoolgirl called Wilma Rudolph, who was to win three gold medals

riumphs, Japan's Tsuyoshi Yamanaka was second exactly 3.1 sec behind. Rose, who also won a silver and a bronze medal in Rome, set 5 world records between January 1956 and July 1964. Born in Nairn, Scotland, on 6 January 1939, he was at the time of the 1956 Games the youngest ever triple gold medal winner. His first world record was 9 min 34.3 sec for the 880 yards freestyle. Eight and a half years later he set his last world record in the same event, this time clocking 8 min 55.5 sec.

David Theile was another outstanding Australian Olympic swimming champion. He won the first of his two gold medals in the 100 meters backstroke in a world record 1 min 02.2 sec, with his team-mate John Monckton 1.0 sec away in second place – the biggest winning margin ever recorded in this Olympic event. Theile retained his title in Rome in 1960 and added a third gold medal as a member of Australia's 4 × 100 meters relay team.

By its usual standards, the United States had a disastrous time in the water. Only Bill Yorzyk (200 meters butterfly) and Robert Clotworthy (springboard diving) won golds in the men's events. Pat McCormick retained both her springboard and high-diving titles and Shelley Mann won the women's 100 meters butterfly.

The remarkable Joaquin Capilla won Mexico's first diving title eight years after his first Olympic medal. He won the bronze medal in this event in the London Games in 1948 and was the silver medallist in 1952. A bronze medallist in the springboard diving in Melbourne, Joaquin came from a family of skilled divers. His brother, Alberto, was also in the Mexican diving team in Helsinki and Melbourne.

There was uproar in the pool when Hungary met Russia in a water polo match that became a war. The game was almost literally a blood bath. Police were called to calm players and spectators alike after a Hungarian player's eyebrow had been gashed during a clash with a Russian opponent. The Hungarians eventually won 4–0 and went on to take the gold medal.

Highlight of the boxing was another triumph for Hungary when Laszlo Papp became the first boxer to complete a hat-trick of gold medals by outpointing future professional world light-heavyweight champion Jose Torres in the light-middleweight final. Peter Rademacher won the heavyweight gold medal for the United States and in his very next contest fought Floyd Patterson for the world professional heavyweight championship, losing in six rounds.

Britain won two boxing gold medals with 18-year-old Londoner Terry Spinks taking the flyweight title and Scottish airman Dick McTaggart winning the lightweight championship and the award for best stylist. It was in shooting, wrestling, gymnastics and rowing that the Russians overhauled the United States in the medals table. Viktor Chukarin won three more gold medals in the gymnastics to add to the four he collected in 1952. The Melbourne Games marked the start of the wonderful Olympic career of Larisa Latynina, who in three Olympiads won nine titles. She won four golds, a silver and a bronze in Melbourne with a stunning display of technical proficiency in a complete range of gymnastic events. Only her brilliance prevented Hungary's graceful Agnes Keleti from dominating the women's gymnastics. She won four golds to add to the one she collected in the floor exercises in 1952. Miss Keleti was one of several Hungarian competitors who elected not to return to Hungary after the 1956 Games. She later became gymnastics coach to the Israeli national team.

Russian oarsman Vyacheslav Ivanov, the world's leading sculler in the 1950s and 1960s, made his Olympic debut and impressively won the single sculls. It was a title he retained in 1960 and again in 1964. Ivanov possessed enormous strength that enabled him to produce finishing sprints just as opponents thought they had him beaten. The silver medallist in Melbourne was Australian Stuart McKenzie, his rival in many major events over the next decade.

Two American sons of famous Olympic champions, John B. Kelly, Jr, and Bernard Costello, Jr, were not quite able to match the performances of their fathers. (John Kelly and Paul Costello had won the double sculls together in 1920 and 1924.) Kelly, Jr, had to be

Golden partners – Sweden's Petrus Kastenman kisses his mount Illuster after they had won the individual event in the 1956 equestrian Olympics, which were staged in Stockholm.

content with a bronze medal behind Ivanov and McKenzie in the single sculls, and Costello, Jr, took a silver in the double sculls.

Yale University pulled off America's eighth successive victory in the eights but not without a scare. They had to haul their way through the *repêchage* after being beaten into third place in their heat. In the final, they just beat a powerful crew from Canada.

Gillian Sheen was a surprise winner of the foil event for Britain in the fencing. But there was no surprise when Italy's Edoardo Mangiarotti dominated the men's fencing in the épée and foil. A natural right-hander, he had been coached by his father to fence left-handed, which he felt would give him an advantage over opponents. Mangiarotti learned his lessons so well that he won two golds and a bronze medal in Melbourne. He was continuing an Olympic career that had started in 1936 and that continued until the 1960 Games in Rome, where in front of his own supporters he won a gold and a silver to take his medals haul from five Olympics to 13 (four individual and nine team).

Hungarian Rudolf Karpati was another fencing master in action in Melbourne. A team winner in the saber in 1948 and 1952, he took the individual gold medal in 1956 and 1960 and was again in the winning Hungarian team in both events to take his personal gold collection to six medals.

Leandro Faggin of Italy was the outstanding star on the cycling track. A powerful and versatile rider, he showed the full range of his talent in the Melbourne Games by setting an Olympic record for the 1000 meters and then leading his colleagues to the 4000 meters team pursuit championship. He later turned professional and dominated world pursuit cycling, winning three world professional titles.

Britain's road race team was in contention for the gold medal until their leading rider Bill Holmes was sent crashing when a spectator stepped out to take a photograph of him. Holmes lost two valuable minutes and the British team were narrowly beaten into second place by France in the gruelling 116-mile race.

Finland's Rauno Makinen had been taught to wrestle as a youngster by his father, Kalle, who won a freestyle bantamweight gold medal in the 1928 Amsterdam Olympics. Rauno proved to have been a fine pupil when in 1956 he won the Greco-Roman featherweight wrestling gold medal. Shot putter Jiri Skobla of Czechoslovakia also tried to emulate his father, who had been Olympic heavyweight weightlifting champion in Los Angeles in 1932. Jiri had to be content with a bronze medal behind American giants Parry O'Brien and Bill Nieder.

In a tense weightlifting duel, America's Paul Anderson and Argentinian Humberto Selvetti lifted exactly the same poundage in the heavyweight division. Anderson, who had gone on a crash diet to get himself at what he considered his best weight for the contest, won by virtue of his lighter body weight. In 1957 he set a world record when he raised 6270lb (2844kg) off trestles by using his back. It was more than any human had ever lifted before.

Once again the Olympics had proved that sport was a cementer of nations and in a lighthearted and happy closing ceremony all the competitors paraded as a single body rather than in team formation. It epitomized the spirit of a Games that had been enjoyable because of its close, almost family-like atmosphere.

OLYMPIC FUN AND GAMES

Russian Vyacheslav Ivanov was so excited about his victory in the single sculls that he tossed his gold medal up in a gesture of sheer delight. As he reached out to catch his prized possession he succeeded only in knocking it into the waters of Lake Wendouree, where the rowing events were staged. The 18-year-old Muscovite dived into the water but was unable to retrieve his medal. He was later presented with a replacement medal by the International Olympic Committee. Ivanov received gold medals again in 1960 and 1964 and each time clung on tightly to the greatest rewards in the world of sport.

There was a flavor of ancient and modern Olympics in the 1960 Games in Rome. The wrestling, for instance, was staged in the Basilica of Maxentius, where 2000 years before the Romans had held similar sporting contests. The marathon started by the Capitol and finished at the Arch of Constantine. Cash from football pool profits boosted the finances of the Italian organizing committee and it was able to build a magnificent Sports Palace and a cycling Velodrome which revealed modern Italian architecture at its imaginative best. The Italians joyously celebrated the greatest occasion in their history since the fall of the Roman Empire and gave a warm and friendly welcome to the record total of more than 5000 competitors from 84 nations.

For the first time in half a century, the United States failed to dominate the track and field events. The gold medals were shared out between nine nations in the men's events, with New Zealand experiencing its finest hour with two magnificent championship-winning performances on the track on the afternoon of 2 September.

PETER SNELL
TRIPLE GOLD FOR THE QUIET MAN FROM OPUNAKE

Peter Snell was virtually an unknown force when he arrived in Rome to compete in the 800 meters. He had a personal best time of 1 min 49.2 sec, which meant he was not rated in the top dozen entries, but only Snell and his wise coach Arthur Lydiard knew the hard groundwork he had put in as preparation for his Olympic challenge. With Lydiard driving him on, he had been running a regular 100 miles in training every week to build up his stamina to go with his natural speed. Every weekend Snell would leave the track and go on punishing 20-mile runs in the Waitakere Ranges outside Auckland. It was exhausting work which was to prove invaluable in Rome during a testing schedule that involved running four rounds of the 800 meters in three days.

Born in Opunake on 17 December 1938, Snell had concentrated his main sporting energies on lawn tennis as a youngster and did not switch seriously to athletics until he was 18. He overcame a stress fracture of a bone in his foot during his build up to the Rome Games and was approaching peak form when summoned for the first round. He cruised to an impressive victory in a personal best of 1 min 48.1 sec. The same day he qualified comfortably for the semi-finals with a controlled run in 1 min 48.6 sec.

Snell looked full of running when he won his semi-final in 1 min 47.2 sec with world record holder Roger Moens in second place. In the final, Moens appeared to have the race won as he kicked off the final bend but the powerfully built New Zealander proved the stronger and overhauled the Belgian in the last five meters to win in an Olympic record 1 min 46.3 sec. The

The 80,000-seat Olympic Stadium in Rome, scene of the track and field events in the 1960 Games. The stadium was the focal point of the Foro Italico, which was originally planned by Mussolini and was finally built in 1953.

117

quiet, unassuming man from Opunake had emerged from obscurity to become a world star and added to his reputation in 1964 by winning the 800 and 1500 meters (see the chapter on the Tokyo Games).

Within an hour of Snell's stunning victory in Rome, the finishing tape was again broken by an athlete wearing the black vest and shorts of New Zealand.

MURRAY HALBERG
THE CHAMPION WHO WAS DRIVEN ON BY COURAGE

During a schoolboy rugby match, Murray Halberg suffered the sort of terrifying injury that would have put most people off sports for life. He was taken to a hospital with damage to his side that left him with a withered left arm and a paralyzed shoulder. Halberg, however, adjusted to his handicap and turned to athletics for his sporting outlet. Coached, like Peter Snell, by Arthur Lydiard, he developed into a master middle-distance runner and reached the pinnacle of his career in Rome when, at the age of 27, he ran away with the 5000 meters title.

He was a cunning tactical runner and realized that there were faster finishers in the field of 12 finalists. After sitting casually in last place for the first 1000 meters, Halberg gradually worked his way towards the front. Australia's Dave Power led with three laps to go when Halberg suddenly sprinted to the front and unleashed an astonishing lap of 61.8 sec. None of his rivals tried to go with him because they considered it a suicidal pace bound to destroy Halberg. He had run himself to the edge of exhaustion by the start of the last lap but with sheer will-power and courage he kept going to break the tape in 13 min 43.4 sec, slow by world standards but fast considering the baking-hot conditions.

Halberg's last lap time was 73 sec, his slowest of the race, and Germany's fast-finishing Hans Grodotzki was cutting back his lead all the time although he was still eight meters adrift at the tape. Grodotzki also collected the silver medal in the 10,000 meters, in which Halberg finished fifth. The following year the brave New Zealander broke the world two and three mile records and bowed out of major athletics after retaining his British Empire and Commonwealth three miles title in Perth in 1962.

The 10,000 meters gold medal in Rome went to Russian Pyotr Bolotnikov, who shattered his countryman Vladimir Kuts' Olympic record by 13 sec with a time of 28 min 32.2 sec. However, another athlete from "Down Under" provided the most majestic performance on the track.

HERB ELLIOTT
A WORLD RECORD FOR "THE HUMAN DEER"

Most people expected Herb Elliott to win the gold medal in the 1500 meters final in Rome but few expected him to do it in quite such devastating fashion.

Born in Perth on 25 February 1938, Elliott first had dreams of Olympic glory while watching the Melbourne games in his homeland in 1956. Within two years he had developed from a promising schoolboy miler to the fastest man in the world over both 1500 meters and the mile. In 1958 he set world records over both distances and also won the 880 yards and mile titles in the Commonwealth Games in Cardiff. Some experts wondered whether he had reached his peak too early to be a real threat in the Rome Olympics but his demanding coach Percy Cerutty prepared him to a perfect pitch for the Games. His tough training schedule included torturous runs up and down the sand dunes at Portsea, after which track running was almost a relief.

Elliott was content to run with the pack for the first 800 meters in the final but then, with a flapping towel signal from coach Cerutty, he started a finishing sprint 600 meters from the tape. He surged smoothly and powerfully away from his rivals to win in a world record 3 min 35.6 sec. Frenchman Michel Jazy was 20 meters away in second place and the first six to finish were all inside the Olympic record of

3 min 41.2 sec.

The man they called "The Human Deer" ran four more under-four minute miles after his Rome triumph and then retired at the age of 22, before what is reckoned to be a miler's prime. Throughout his career he broke the four-minute mile barrier on 17 occasions and was never beaten in a 1500 meter or mile race. He was once offered $160,000 to turn professional but he preferred to run for fun.

For the first time since the 1928 Games, both sprint titles eluded the United States. The 100 meters gold medal went to West Germany's Armin Hary, a cool, confident character who specialized in blitz starts in which he anticipated the gun. He proved that his 10.0 sec world record run in Zurich three weeks before the Games was a true form pointer when he beat American Dave Sime by a stride in 10.2 sec with Britain's Peter Radford a meter away in third place.

Hary collected a second gold medal in the 4 × 100 meters sprint relay after the winning United States squad had been disqualified for a faulty change-over. Roman idol Livio Berruti streaked to a popular victory in the 200 meters in 20.5 sec, with American Lester Carney second. The Roman crowd celebrated by light-

Armin Hary (farthest from camera) takes the 100 meters gold medal, beating American Dave Sime (nearest) by a stride. Britain's Peter Radford finishes third.

ing hundreds of newspapers as torches and Berruti, who always ran in dark glasses, removed them and waved them above his head as he ran a lap of honor to thunderous cheers.

The United States at last got a track gold medal from the unlikely source of Otis Davis, who sneaked to Rome as third-string 400 meter runner two years after taking up athletics at the age of 26. Davis beat New York-born

Peter Snell (opposite, above) gives an indication of his potential as he coasts to victory in the 800 meters semi-final; and Herb Elliott, a world record breaker when winning the 1500 meters (opposite, below). Italian idol Livio Berruti wins the 200 meters (left) with American Lester Carney in second place.

119

German Carl Kaufmann in a photo-finish, both timed at a world record 44.9 sec. Davis, who had gone to Oregon University on a basketball scholarship, shared in another world record when he anchored the United States 4 × 400 meters relay team to victory in 3 min 2.2 sec, and again it was Kaufmann whom he pushed back into a silver medal place on the last leg.

Glenn Davis was also a member of the relay squad after he had retained his 400 meters

hurdles championship. Lee Calhoun won the 110 meters hurdles for the second successive Olympics as America took all six medals in the two hurdles events. It was something of an anti-climax for Glenn Davis, who had been looking forward to a duel with South African Gert Potgieter, who had emerged as a world class 400 meter hurdler. But Potgieter was seriously injured in a car crash two weeks before the Games, the last Olympics in which South Africa participated before they were banned because of their apartheid policies of government.

Poland made an impressive impact in the athletics, the versatile Zdzislaw Krzyszkowiak winning the 3000 meters steeplechase and the great Jozef Szmidt capturing the first of his two gold medals in the triple jump. Both these talented Poles, accomplished in a wide range of events, set new Olympic records when winning their titles.

Don Thompson, a bespectacled bank clerk from London who was nicknamed "Little Mouse," won the exhausting 50 kilometers walk after getting accustomed to Rome-type conditions by training in the steaming bathroom of his home in England. But the long-distance champion who made the greatest impression on the Romans was a marathon man from Ethiopia.

ABEBE BIKILA
THE BARE-FOOT CHAMPION FROM BLACK AFRICA

A member of the Emperor's Household Guard in Ethiopia, Abebe Bikila brought black Africa its first gold medal in athletics when he padded bare-footed through the streets of Rome to win the marathon in a world best time of 2 hr 15 min 16.2 sec. It heralded the start of the emerging power of Africans in the world of athletics and there was further proof of the talent waiting to be tapped when Moroccan Rhadi Ben Abdesselem finished second just 200 yards behind Bikila. The 28-year-old Ethiopian was given rousing support by the Roman crowd as he hurried through streets that had become moonlit in the closing stages of a race that started after the afternoon heat had given way to the cool of the evening.

Bikila became the first runner ever to retain an Olympic marathon title when he won again in Tokyo in 1964. He overcame all odds because just five weeks before the Games in Japan he underwent an appendix operation. An estimated crowd of more than 500,000 lined the marathon route in Tokyo to see Bikila – this time wearing running shoes – lope easily and economically to his second gold medal in the record time of 2 hr 12 min 11.2 sec. While waiting for the second man to enter the stadium, the astonishing Bikila entertained the crowd with a series of energetic physical exercises. Silver medallist Basil Heatley of Britain crossed the finish line four minutes later. Bikila attempted to pull off a hat-trick of marathon victories but a leg injury forced him to retire at 17 kilometers in the 1968 race in Mexico, which was won by his compatriot Mamo Wolde.

There was a tragic sequel to the Bikila story. He was severely injured in a car accident and was confined to a wheelchair following treatment at the Stoke Mandeville paraplegic hospital in England. A brave and cheerful character, he took up competitive paraplegic sports, including archery, but he was never able to shake off the after-effects of his injuries and he died, aged 41, on 25 October 1973.

America's athletes fared much better in the field events in the Rome Games with Don "Tarzan" Bragg (pole vault), Ralph Boston (long jump), Al Oerter (discus), Bill Nieder (shot) and Rafer Johnson (decathlon) all collecting gold medals. Nieder only got into the US team as a replacement for injured Dave Davis and he beat defending champion Parry O'Brien into second place with an Olympic record put of 64ft 6¾in (19.68m), with their team-mate Dallas Long in third place.

Ralph Boston removed Jesse Owens' 1936 long jump record from the books with a leap of 26ft 7¾in (8.12m), just a centimeter ahead of his countryman Irving Robertson. Don Bragg became the first man to clear 15ft in the Olympic pole vault, winning with a final effort of ¯15ft 5in (4.70m). The silver medal went to American Ron Morris, who also cleared 15ft after squeezing into the 12-man qualifying pool in last place.

The lead in the decathlon continually changed hands as Rafer Johnson and American-trained Chuan-Kwang Yang of Formosa duelled for supremacy. Johnson, later a Presidential bodyguard, finally won by 58 points as they both shattered the previous Olympic record. Yang's silver medal was the first to be won by a Chinese in any Olympic sport.

Poland's Janusz Sidlo, silver medallist in the javelin in Melbourne, had the longest throw in Rome (279ft 4in; 85.14m) yet failed to win the title. His best throw came in the qualifying rounds, marks that are not counted in the final stages. Sidlo finally finished eighth, with the gold medal going to Russian Viktor Tsibulenko with a throw of 277ft 8¼in (84.64m). It was a case of third time luck for Tsibulenko, who

Irena Press (nearest camera), one of the famous Russian sisters, on her way to victory in the 80 meters hurdles final.

had finished fourth in 1952 and third in 1956.

Defending champion Hal Connolly was favored to retain his hammer title after setting a new world record of 230ft 9in (70.33m) three weeks before the Games. But he was more than 20ft below his best in Rome and the gold medal went to Russian Vasili Rudenkov.

There was a shock defeat in the high jump for world record holder John Thomas of the United States. He was pushed back into third place by Russian seven-foot specialists Robert Shavlakadze and Valeri Brumel. The women's high jump, however, went to form, with remarkable Romanian Iolanda Balas clearing 6ft 0⅞in (1.85m) for a decisive victory. She dominated her event from 1958 until 1966 and won again in the 1964 Tokyo Games with an Olympic record of 6ft 2¾in (1.90m). A tall, leggy blonde of 6ft 0¾in, she raised the world record no fewer than 14 times with what was an old-fashioned but effective scissors style of jumping.

Russia won six of the 10 women's track and field events, with the Press sisters making it a family double. Irina won the 80 meters hurdles and Tamara the shot. Nina Ponomareva regained the discus title she had won in 1952, with Tamara Press in second place. But the outstanding woman athlete of the Games was a 20-year-old tearaway from Tennessee.

WILMA RUDOLPH
"THE TENNESSEE TIGRESS" WITH THE DAZZLING SMILE

Wilma Rudolph won lots of friends in Rome with her dazzling smile and pleasant personality. She also won three gold medals. A bronze medallist in the sprint relay at the age of 16 in Melbourne, she became the third woman since World War II to win the 100 and 200 meters and share in a 4 × 100 meters relay triumph.

Wilma Rudolph, "The Tennessee Tigress," speeds to a gold medal in the 100 meters, with Britain's Dorothy Hyman in second place.

The seventeenth of 19 children, Wilma was paralyzed in the left leg by an illness at the age of four and was not able to walk normally until she was seven. She said that she had to learn to run fast to be sure of getting to the dinner table before her brothers and sisters had eaten all the food. Born at Clarksville, Tennessee, on 23 June 1940, her potential was spotted by famous Tennessee Tigerbelles coach Ed Temple when he watched her moving at speed around a basketball court. A matter of weeks later she clinched a place in the relay squad for the Melbourne Olympics.

The experience in Australia proved invaluable and Wilma was equipped in both talent and temperament to produce her full power in Rome. In a heat of the 100 meters she equalled the world record of 11.3 sec and in the final recorded an extraordinary 11.0 sec dead, but a following wind robbed her of a world record. She had to battle against a strong head wind as she came off the bend in the final of the 200 meters but still powered smoothly to victory by three meters in a time of 24.0 sec. Her third

gold medal came as anchor runner for the sprint relay team that set a world record of 44.4 sec in the qualifying round.

America's swimmers made up for their disappointing performances in the Melbourne Games by winning 11 gold medals and breaking five world records. Many people thought it should have been 12 golds but the judges placed Lance Larson of the United States second to Australian John Devitt in the 100 meters freestyle final. Slow-motion television replays showed that Larson had touched first, and to avoid the possibility of any future human errors of judgment, electronic timing was introduced for subsequent Olympics.

Many of the Australian team went down with stomach upsets ("the Roman tummy") before the swimming finals and it was left to Olympic veterans Dawn Fraser, Murray Rose, Jon Konrads and David Theile to produce winning form and make the Aussies second to the United States in the medals table. Britain was the only other country to win a gold medal in the pool with Anita Lonsbrough, a 19-year-old from Yorkshire, breaking the world record to touch first in the 200 meters breaststroke.

Jon and Ilsa Konrads, born in Latvia but raised in Australia, pulled off a family double. Ilsa followed Jon's success in the 1500 meters freestyle by taking a silver medal with the 4 × 100 meters relay team.

Jeff Farrell, a 23-year-old navy officer from Kansas, had been the pre-Games favorite for the 100 meters freestyle but an appendix operation just six days before the Olympic trials cost him his place in the team. He managed to qualify for two relay squads – still bandaged after his operation – and was rewarded for his courage and determination with two gold medals in Rome in the 4 × 200 meters freestyle relay and the 4 × 100 meters medley relay.

In the women's events, the incredible squad of American teenagers were in smashing splashing mood. Chris Von Saltza, 16, won the 400 meters freestyle; Carolyn Schuler, 17, took the 100 meters butterfly; Lynn Burke, 17, was first in the 100 meters backstroke; and they all collected two more gold medals each in the relays.

Ingrid Krämer, a 17-year-old diver from Dresden, became the first non-American winner of the springboard diving title and completed the double on the highboard. As Mrs Engel, she retained the springboard championship in 1964 and was runner-up on the highboard. Four years later in Mexico – then Mrs Gubin, having divorced and re-married – she finished fifth in the springboard event. While on her way to victory in Tokyo she complained that the water was too cold and took hot showers between each dive.

The boxing events brought to the fore a face and fists that were to become familiar to millions. Cassius Marcellus Clay won the light-heavyweight title by outpointing European champion Zbigniew Pietrzykowski of Poland in the final. Clay was just 18 but already had the sort of showmanship and arrogant but likeable manner that was to make him the best known of all twentieth-century sportsmen after changing his name to Muhammad Ali.

Years later, Ali revealed that he had thrown his gold medal in the Ohio River in a gesture of disgust and despair over racial inequality in the United States. But he had been so proud of his prize in Rome that on the night of his victory he slept with the medal around his neck.

The most popular winners were local heroes Francesco Musso (featherweight), Giovanni Benvenuti (welterweight) and Franco de Piccoli, a southpaw heavyweight who brought the excited crowd in the Palazzo dello Sport to their feet when he knocked out giant Russian Andrei Abramov – the European champion – in the first round. Benvenuti later became world professional champion at light-middle and middleweight.

The gymnastics featured several all-time great Olympic performers. Russian Boris Shakhlin continued where he had left off in Melbourne, winning four gold medals to go with the two he had won in 1956. By the time he closed his great Olympic career in Tokyo in

1964, he had won a total of 13 medals – seven gold, four silver and two bronze. Japan's Takashi Ono had to live in the shadow of Shakhlin but still managed a considerable collection of medals. He won three golds in Rome and after four Olympiads (1952–64) had 13 medals – five gold, four silver and four bronze.

In the women's gymnastics, Russian ballerina of the bars Larisa Latynina was again the dominant force but her team-mate Polina Astakhova gave her some stiff opposition and won two

Cassius Clay, later world famous as Muhammad Ali, punches his way to golden glory in the light-heavyweight division of the Olympic boxing competition.

Italy won the first Olympic gold medal in the Rome Games when its team finished first in the 100 kilometers team road trial cycling event.

golds, a silver and a bronze in Rome. Polina, although frail to look at, had great strength and determination to go with her natural grace, and after a career spanning three Olympiads (1956–64) had nine medals to show for her efforts, five of them gold.

The tragic death of Danish rider Knud Jensen during the road race threw a shadow over the cycling. It was later revealed that the use of drugs – a rising menace in Olympic sport – had been a contributory factor. The Russians won the road race to stop an Italian clean sweep of all the cycling gold medals. Sante Gaiardoni

led the Italian five-title victory dash by achieving the unique double of the 1000 meters sprint and the 1000 meters time trial. He became a professional world champion and retired after marrying an opera singer in 1971.

In basketball, the United States gained its fifth successive title and Russia was runner-up for a third time. A feature of the American play was the deadly shooting of Jerry Lucas, a 6ft $7\frac{1}{4}$in Ohio State University undergraduate. Against Japan, Lucas shot 14 times from the floor and made all 14. He made over 70 per cent of his field goal attempts during the Games, in which the superbly drilled US squad averaged a record 102 points a game.

India had been matching the American basketball domination in hockey but was finally dethroned by Pakistan after 32 years as champion.

The soccer final was scarred when Yugoslavian captain Milan Galic was sent off for disputing a disallowed goal with the referee. His team-mates kept their heads and beat Denmark 3–1.

In the show jumping, Italy's Raimonde d'Inzeo beat his brother Piero for the gold

Above: Pakistan defeats India in the hockey final to end 32 years of Indian domination of this event.

Raimonde d'Inzeo, riding Posillipo, jumps to gold in the grand prix show jumping event. His brother, Piero, took the silver medal.

medal. They completed a full set of medals for the family when they collected a bronze in the team event, which was won in grand style by Germany, with Hans Winkler taking the third of his five gold medals from five Olympics (1956–72). Australia was the surprise winner of the three-day event, its first success in Olympic equestrian competition.

The Bay of Naples provided a picturesque setting for the yachting in which Crown Prince Constantine of Greece won a gold medal in the Dragon class. Norwegian Peter Lunde completed a remarkable family hat-trick when he won a gold medal in the Flying Dutchman event. His father had won a silver medal in the 5.5 meters class at the 1952 Games and his grandfather was an Olympic sailing gold

medallist in 1928. They are the only father, son and grandson to have won Olympic medals.

Hungary's Aladar Gerevich won his sixth successive gold medal in the team saber event. It was a medal collection that started in Los Angeles in 1932. In all he won 10 Olympic medals.

Turkey dominated the wrestling with seven gold medallists and Russia was the most successful nation in the weightlifting with five champions. There were so many competitors in the weightlifting that competitions sometimes went on until after three in the morning.

The friendly Games of Rome ended in a blaze of glory. After the Olympic flame had been extinguished, the stadium was illuminated by spectators burning newspapers and using them as torches. They clearly did not want the Olympic light to go out after it had brought so much pleasure into their lives.

The Olympic yachting was held in the picturesque Bay of Naples, with Crown Prince Constantine of Greece winning a gold medal in the Dragon class.
Left: In the light-heavyweight freestyle wrestling division, Ismet Atli (on left) was one of Turkey's gold medallists.

OLYMPIC FUN AND GAMES

Wim Esajas is one person who would not describe his 1960 Olympic experience as fun. He travelled all the way to Rome from Surinam, Dutch Guiana, as the sole representative of his country. His event was the 800 meters. On the day of his heats, Wim rested at the Olympic village in preparation for his afternoon activity on the Olympic track. Unfortunately for Wim, the heats were run in the morning. He was eliminated without setting foot on the track.

Japanese student Yoshinori Sakai mounts the steep steps at the Olympic stadium in Tokyo for the traditional opening ceremony of lighting the Olympic flame.

close of the Games their showpiece had won the respect and admiration of the watching world. Even a political row that led to the barring of Indonesia and North Korea could not dent the Olympic spirit generated by the enthusiastic Japanese hosts, and despite wet and miserable weather the Games were regarded as a triumph for Tokyo in particular and for the Olympic movement in general.

A record number of 94 nations sent more than 5500 competitors and Olympic records tumbled in all sports. After 163 events, the final medals table showed Russia in the lead with 96 (30 golds, 31 silver and 35 bronze). The United States finished second with 90 medals, 37 of which were won in the swimming pool.

These were the Games in which Olympic immortals Dawn Fraser (swimming), Hans Winkler (show jumping) and Vyacheslav Ivanov (sculling) each won his or her third successive gold medal but it was an American hat-trick hero who claimed the world's attention and admiration in the track and field arena.

AL OERTER
THE DISCUS THROWER WITH THE MIDAS TOUCH

It was against doctor's orders that Al Oerter went to the discus-throwing circle in Tokyo to defend the title he had won in Melbourne in 1956 and again in Rome in 1960. He looked more like a case for a hospital than a gold medal. There was a brace around his neck to ease the nagging pain of a slipped disc and his ribs were bound with surgical tape and packed with ice to guard against further damage to cartilages torn in a pre-Games training session.

He was understandably well below his world record best of 206ft 6in (62.94m) with his first four throws and looked doomed to lose his Olympic title to his great Czech rival Ludvik Danek. The Czech was leading with a throw of 198ft 6½in (60.51m) when Oerter prepared for his last-but-one throw. Gritting his teeth against the pain in his side, Oerter made up his mind to gamble on one massive fling regardless of the fact that he had been advised to take it easy. By now he had removed the restricting brace from around his neck. Oerter spun his powerful 6ft 4in, 260lb-frame around in the circle and then fired the discus a stunning distance of 200ft 1½in (61m). It won him his third successive gold medal and for the third time he had triumphed with a new Olympic record throw.

Only standing jumper Ray Ewry (1900–1908 and hammer thrower John Flanagan (1900–

The Japanese unashamedly used the 1964 Olympics as a giant public relations operation to finally wipe away the scars of World War II. They went out of their way to show that they were not only masters of organization but also warm and friendly people, and everybody visiting Tokyo for the Games was given a wonderful welcome and made to feel at home.

It was the first time the Games had been held in Asia and the Japanese spared no expense or energy to make them memorable and a testimony to their organizational ability and thoroughness. Their final bill exceeded $2 billion but the Tokyo Olympic Committee considered every yen well spent, because by the

1908) had ever scored a hat-trick of title wins in track and field events. But Oerter, born at Astoria, New York, on 19 September 1936, was not finished yet. At the Mexico Games four years later, this dedicated competitor was back in action and adjusted his style to a waterlogged throwing circle to produce a lifetime's best throw of 212ft 6½in (64.78m) for a unique fourth successive Olympic title. He had won a gold medal for each of his four children and seemed satisfied but in 1979 he got the flavor of the Olympics again and started a comeback at the age of 42 with the Moscow Games in mind.

Oerter's third title win came on the second day of the Tokyo Games, in which the United States captured 12 of the men's track and field championships. They got an unexpected triumph on the first day in the 10,000 meters.

BILLY MILLS
HE LEADS AN AMERICAN LONG-RUNNING BREAKTHROUGH

In the history of the Olympics, the United States had never won either the 5000 or 10,000 meters on the track. There seemed little likelihood of them breaking the sad sequence of failure in Tokyo, where Australia's outstanding middle and long distance runner Ron Clarke was favored for both events.

The 10,000 meters was run on the first day and American hopes rested on the shoulders of Billy Mills, a 26-year-old US Marine lieutenant who was a descendant of American Indians. Mills stuck bravely to the heels of world record holder Clarke as the tall, stately Aussie set the sort of blistering pace that brought him a cluster of 17 world records during a distinguished career in which he was always able to beat the clock but – when it really mattered – not his competitors.

At the bell, Clarke was leading with only the crop-haired Mills and Tunisian Mohamed Gammoudi in contention. They had to take a zig-zag course around the back stretch as they lapped a procession of runners exhausted by Clarke's early pace-making. Mills moved up onto the Australian's shoulder ready for a challenge, but then suddenly with 250 meters to go Gammoudi surged through the gap between them and made a break for the tape. He opened up a lead of 10 meters and seemed to have the race won, but then Clarke, followed by Mills, attacked coming off the bend. It was Mills who proved the stronger and the swifter and he overhauled Gammoudi 40 meters from the finishing line on his way to a stunning

Two stunning middle-distance track victories for the United States. Billy Mills (above) overtakes Ron Clarke as he presses for home in the 10,000 meters. Bob Schul (left) hits the tape in the 5000 meters final.

victory in an Olympic record 28 min 24.4 sec. It beat his previous best for the distance by some 45 seconds. The only other time that the United States had won a medal in the event was back in Stockholm in 1912 when Louis Tewanima had taken the silver behind the great Finn Hannes Kolehmainen. Tewanima, like Mills, was of American Indian descent.

Bob Schul, a cocky and confident character from Ohio, was convinced he could make it a

double for the United States by winning the 5000 meters. He played a shrewd waiting game and outmaneuvered his European rivals after Ron Clarke had again been found short of finishing speed. Clarke did much of the pace making but dropped away to ninth as the sprint for home started on the final lap.

Michel Jazy, the French flier noted for his exploits over 1500 meters, seemed the probable winner but he did not have the strength to maintain his long run for the tape. He was overtaken first by crack German Harald Norpoth and then by Schul, who unleashed his challenge as he entered the final stretch. Schul went away from Norpoth to win by three meters, with his 30-year-old American team-mate Bill Dellinger driving past the shattered Jazy to snatch third place. The last 400 meters was covered in an exceptionally fast 54.8 sec.

The most successful track athlete in Tokyo was New Zealander Peter Snell, who followed up his gold medal win in the 1960 800 meters by winning both the 800 and 1500 meters. Since the Rome Games, Snell had blossomed into a magnificent athlete with world records at 800 meters, 880 yards and one mile. He retained his 800 meters title with ease, taking the lead in the final with 200 meters to go and winning comfortably in 1 min 45.1 sec, which was just outside his world record.

Snell was content to let his countryman John Davies set the pace in the 1500 meters final. Many people thought Davies was Snell's superior over the longer distance but Peter the Great proved them wrong with a superbly timed finish that took him to victory in 3 min 38.1 sec. Snell was timed at 25.4 sec for the last 200 meters as he swept to victory by 1½ sec over Czech Josef Odlozil, with his compatriot Davies in third place. It was the first 800/1500 meters Olympic double since Albert Hill of Britain had pulled it off in 1920.

However, the fastest man of all on the track in Tokyo was a black tornado of a sprinter from Florida.

BOB HAYES
"THE FASTEST HUMAN IN THE WORLD"

Several sprinters have been given the title of "The Fastest Human in the World." Nobody could argue that the description was an exaggeration when referring to Bob Hayes. He had given notice of his blitzing speed in 1963 when he became the first man to run 100 yards in 9.1 sec and the first to break six seconds for the indoor 60 yards dash. Hayes specialized in anchor leg relay runs and on one occasion in 1962 had been timed at an astonishing 7.8 sec from a flying start for a 100 yards relay leg. That would mean his average speed was 26.22 mph.

There was nothing stylish or smooth about Hayes. He relied on strength, driving his heavy frame along the track with a rolling, pigeon-toed action that left coaches shaking their heads in disbelief that he could travel so quickly with such an unorthodox method. After scorching to victory in his Olympic semi-final 100 meters in a wind-aided 9.9 sec, Hayes recorded a legal world record-equalling 10.00 sec in the final with Cuban Enrique Figuerola second and Canadian Harry Jerome third.

Hayes, born in Jacksonville, Florida, on 20 December 1942, produced the most incredible run of his career in the final of the men's sprint relay. Slack baton changing meant he was lying in fifth place when he started the final leg. By the time he sliced through the tape he was in first place, bringing the United States team home in a world record 39.0 sec. He was timed over the last 100 meters at a mind-boggling 8.9 sec. This was Hayes' final race as an amateur. When he returned home to the United States he signed as a professional footballer with Dallas Cowboys and became one of the game's great players.

In contrast to the sheer power of Hayes, 200 meters champion Henry Carr was a technically correct and majestic mover. He purred to victory in the final in an Olympic record 20.3 sec, with his American team-mate Paul Drayton just 0.2 sec away in second place. Carr collected a second gold medal when he anchored the United States team to victory in the 4 × 400 meters relay. British team captain Robbie Brightwell made up for a disappointing run in the individual 400 meters final by running a storming last leg to bring his squad home in second place just ahead of Wendell Mottley of Trinidad and Tobago. The first three teams were inside the old world record, with the United States winning in 3 min 0.7 sec. Mike Larrabee, a 30-year-old veteran of the US track team, won the individual 400 meters title in 45.1 sec and shared in the relay triumph.

Randy Matson, giant United States shot putter, naturally thought he had won the title with a mighty heave of 66ft 3¼in (20.20m) in the fourth round of the final. It was the first time the 65ft and 66ft barriers had been broken in the Olympics. But within two minutes Matson was back in second place. His country-man Dallas Long, the bronze medallist in Rome, was next to put and went into a winning lead with an effort of 66ft 8½in (20.33m). Parry O'Brien, champion in 1952 and 1956 and silver medallist in 1960, finished in fourth place. There was consolation for Matson in Mexico when he won with a put of 67ft 4¾in (20.54m).

Fred Hansen maintained the American stranglehold on the pole vault title with an Olympic record victory at 16ft 8¾in (5.10m). He cleared this at his third and final attempt after passing up his chance of attempting 16ft 6¾in (5.05m), a height that brought Germany's Wolfgang Reinhardt the silver medal. Hansen, a Texas dental student, had to show stamina as well as strength and skill. The competition lasted 13 hours and finished under floodlights.

John Thomas cleared an Olympic record 7ft 1¾in (2.18m) in the high jump but had to be satisfied with a silver medal behind his great Russian rival Valeri Brumel who took the gold at the same height but with fewer failures.

There was another gold medal for Russia in the hammer, with 31-year-old Romuald Klim beating his old Hungarian throwing foe Gyula Zsivotsky with an Olympic best 228ft 10in (69.74m). Zsivotsky got his revenge in Mexico

Valeri Brumel clears the 7ft barrier in the high jump. He finally takes the gold with a leap of 7ft 1¾in.

Abebe Bikila (left) does some calisthenics after retaining his marathon title. Britain's Ken Matthews (below) joyously breaks the tape at the end of the 20 kilometers walk that started in style (bottom).

Olympic record effort of 55ft 3½in (16.85m). Just two months earlier he had been hospitalized for a knee operation that seemed certain to keep him out of the Games.

There was the anticipated double for the United States in the two men's hurdles finals with Hayes Jones adding a gold to the bronze medal he had won in the 1960 110 meters hurdles and Rex Cawley winning the 400 meters hurdles in 49.6 sec. But the usual supremacy of the American decathletes was broken when Germany's Willi Holdorf took the gold medal. For the first time since the 1912 decathlon, America did not have a man in the first three.

Britain's track and field team had one of their most successful Olympiads. Basil Heatley chased the marathon master Abebe Bikila home in the marathon, Ken Matthews won the 20 kilometers walk, John Cooper was second to Rex Cawley in the 400 meters hurdles, Paul Nihill was the silver medallist behind Italian ace Abdon Pamich in the 50 kilometers walk and Maurice Herriott was second to versatile Belgian Gaston Roelants in the 3000 meters steeplechase.

But the most impressive performance by a British athlete came from long jumper Lynn

four years later, beating Klim to the title by just three inches with a record throw of 240ft 8in (73.36m).

Competing in appalling conditions, Finland's Pauli Nevala overcame the handicap of pouring rain to win the javelin with a throw of 271ft 2in (82.66m). Poland's Jozef Szmidt retained the triple jump title he had won in 1960 with an

Davies, the first Welshman to win an Olympic title and the first Briton since 1908 to win a Games gold medal in the field events. A water-logged runway, adverse wind and bitter cold put many of the more fancied jumpers out of their stride, but Davies thrived on the conditions and in the fifth round produced a lifetime's best leap of 26ft 5¾in (8.07m) to take the title with just 1½in to spare over defending champion Ralph Boston. Coached by well-known British television commentator Ron Pickering, "Lynn the Leap" became the only athlete to complete a "grand slam" of Olympic, European and British Commonwealth long jump championships. He will be in Moscow for the 1980 Games as British team manager.

There was a rare double for Britain in the long jump events.

MARY RAND
A FULL SET OF MEDALS FOR BRITAIN'S GOLDEN GIRL

Britain had longed for a golden girl of athletics ever since women had been entered in track and field events for the first time in 1928. They had provided many "silver ladies" but had never managed to produce a gold medal winner. That was all changed in Tokyo when an attractive blonde housewife, Mary Rand, became the first woman to break the 22ft barrier in the long jump to take the gold medal with a leap of 22ft 2¼in (6.76m). Mary, married to Olympic oarsman Sydney Rand, completed a full set of medals in Tokyo. She took a silver in the pentathlon behind Russian Irina Press and was a bronze medallist with the British sprint relay squad.

It was as Mary Bignal, a schoolgirl at the famous Millfield School in her native English county of Somerset, that she first showed her potential as an outstanding athlete. An exceptional all-rounder, she competed for Britain in 63 international events during her career. A recurring leg muscle injury prevented her defending her long jump title in Mexico but she went to the Games as a television commentator. While in Mexico she met her present husband Bill Toomey, the 1968 US Olympic decathlon champion, with whom she now lives in California.

Six days after Mary's gold medal win in Tokyo, her room-mate Ann Packer won a surprise second gold medal for Britain. Ann's specialty event was the 400 meters, in which she won a silver medal behind Australia's amazing Betty Cuthbert, a winner of three gold medals in the 1956 Melbourne Olympics. Ann

entered the 800 meters almost as an after-thought. She had little experience in two-lap running but her natural speed gave her a vital edge over her rivals and she came gliding on the wide outside off the final bend to win in a world record 2 min 1.1 sec. As she sprinted gracefully through the tape she ran into the arms of British team captain Robbie Brightwell, whom she married a few months later.

American women won just two gold medals in track and field. Wyomia Tyus held off her team-mate Edith McGuire to take the 100 meters title in 11.4 sec (see Mexico Games for her biography) with Poland's Ewa Klobu-

Mary Rand becomes the first woman to break the 22ft barrier as she wins the long jump gold medal for Britain.

Tamara Press (left) retains the Olympic shot put title for Russia, and Romanian Iolanda Balas (right) retains the high jump championship she won in Rome.

Miss Klobukowska anchors Poland to the Olympic gold medal in the sprint relay. She later failed a "sex test" but was allowed to keep her medal.

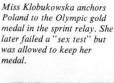

kowska in third place. Miss Klobukowska later failed a "sex test" and had her world records taken away from her but not her Olympic medals. She was in the Polish sprint relay team that surprisingly beat the United States into second place in a world record 43.6 sec.

Edith McGuire was an impressive winner of the 200 meters in an Olympic record 23.0 sec. just 0.1 sec outside her own world record. Poland's talented Irena Kirszenstein was second, to add another silver medal to the one she had won in the long jump. She was also a member of the Polish sprint relay team and was to make a great impact on athletics over the next 12 years under her married name of Irena Szewinska (see Montreal Games for her biography).

Tamara Press – Irina's elder sister – won two more gold medals, retaining the shot title she had won in Rome and capturing the discus championship, in which she had finished second in 1960.

Iolanda Balas retained her high jump title as expected but the victory in the javelin of her Romanian team-mate Mihaela Penes was a total surprise. At 17 years and 2 months, Mihaela was the youngest ever track and field Olympic champion.

Improving world standards in international sport were never made more obvious than in the Tokyo Olympic swimming pool, where during eight days of competition 52 Olympic records were broken. There were world records in eight of the 10 men's races and four more in the women's events. It was a bonanza for the United States swimmers, who captured 13 of the 18 titles. Four gold medals went to one swimmer.

DON SCHOLLANDER
THE FREESTYLER WINS THE FREEDOM OF THE WATER

Until the emergence of Mark Spitz, Don Schollander's feat in winning four gold medals in the Tokyo pool was an Olympic swimming record. An outstanding freestyle swimmer, he won the 100 and 400 titles and twice anchored the United States to relay victories in world record times. During his competitive career, he set 13 individual world records between 1963 and 1968. The 200 meters freestyle was unquestionably his strongest event. He was the first man to break the two-minute barrier and set nine world records over the distance. His front crawl technique was considered close to perfection.

Born in Charlotte, North Carolina, on 30 April 1946, Schollander was brought up in Oregon but developed his swimming in California with the Santa Clara club. In Tokyo, he beat Britain's Bobby McGregor by a touch to win the 100 meters freestyle in 53.4 sec and was a more convincing winner of the 400 meters freestyle in a world record 4 min 12.2 sec. In the 4 × 200 meters relay, his "split" time for the last leg was 1 min 55.6 sec, two seconds faster than any of the other 31 swimmers in the final. The 18-year-old student might have won a fifth gold medal at Tokyo but for surprisingly being left out of the US medley relay team. Four years later in Mexico Schollander added a fifth gold to his collection as a member of the US 4 × 200 meters freestyle relay team. He was beaten into second place in the individual 200 by powerful Australian Mike Wenden.

Schollander, 5ft 11in tall and weighing a trim 174lb, won three gold medals in the 1967 Pan American Games and by the close of his career in 1968 had won 11 individual American titles and shared in 10 team event championships. He studied law at Yale University and then became a stockbroker before becoming an Olympic coach and a member of the select

United States Olympic Committee.

Dick Roth won the 400 meters individual medley race for the United States after postponing an appendix operation. Japanese doctors advised that he should have immediate surgery after he had complained of stomach pains but Roth refused to miss the Games. He left the hospital, won his final in an Olympic record 4 min 45.4 sec and then immediately after the medal presentation ceremony returned to the hospital for his operation.

There was consolation for Australia's near-swamping by the United States in that they won three individual titles and all of them in Olympic record times – Bob Windle (1500 meters freestyle), Ian O'Brien (200 meters breaststroke) and Kevin Berry (200 meters butterfly). O'Brien and Berry also broke world records on their way to gold. But it was Dawn Fraser who provided the greatest success story for Australia by becoming the first swimmer to win the same event in three successive Olympics. She won the

Don Schollander gives a victory wave after helping the United States team win the 4 × 100 meters freestyle relay for one of his four gold medals.

A flying start to the women's 100 meters freestyle, which was won in an Olympic record time by defending champion Dawn Fraser.

Ingrid Engel-Kramer was in spectacular form as she retained her springboard diving championship for East Germany.

Waldemar Baszanowski prepares to make a world and Olympic record lift to win the lightweight class in the Tokyo weightlifting competition.

100 meters freestyle in an Olympic best time of 59.5 sec, with American "whiz kid" Sharon Stouder in second place. Sharon won the 100 meters butterfly and shared in the two US relay gold medal successes.

The only European to win a gold medal was Galina Prosumenshchikova, first in the 200 meters breaststroke final in a new world record of 2 min 46.4 sec. A 15-year-old Moscow schoolgirl, she gained Russia's first ever swimming gold medal and gave television and radio commentators nightmares with her name – the longest of any Olympic champion.

East German diver Ingrid Engel-Kramer retained her springboard title but lost her highboard championship by just 1.35 points to American Lesley Bush. Ken Sitzberger and Bob Webster won the men's diving titles for the United States.

America had only one gold medallist in boxing – a Philadelphia slaughterhouse worker called Joe Frazier. He won the heavyweight title

and used his success as a launching pad into the professional ranks, where six years later he became world champion and had a series of memorable battles with Muhammad Ali. There was a lot of controversy and bad temper over some of the decisions in the boxing. Spanish featherweight Valentin Loren was suspended for life from amateur boxing when he punched the referee after being disqualified in the first minute of his contest against Cheng Hsu of Formosa.

Russian sculler Vyacheslav Ivanov got a shock on the way to his third successive gold medal. He was sensationally beaten in a heat of the single sculls by American Don Spero but got through to the final after easily winning his *repêchage*. His opponent in the final, as in 1960, was Germany's Achim Hill, who finished four seconds behind as Ivanov powered to his golden hat-trick. The eights title returned to the United States when the crew from the Vesper Boat Club beat a German eight in a storming finish.

Hans Winkler was another treble gold medallist in the grand prix show jumping event with Germany. He had won in 1956 (individual and team) and in 1960 (team) when riding Halla but this time he captured his gold medal on Fidelitas. French veteran Pierre d'Oriola, Olympic show jumping champion back in 1952, found his old flair to produce a crucial clear round to take a second gold medal after a 12-year gap. His ride brought France their only gold medal of the Tokyo Games in the very last event. The French team was runner-up to Germany in the grand prix event.

The only time the polite Japanese spectators almost forgot their sporting manners was in their specialty sport of judo when Dutch world champion Anton Geesink's victory in the open division was greeted with stunned silence. The capacity crowd found it difficult to applaud the sight of their idol Akio Kaminaga being pinned to the mat, a loser after 9 min 22 sec. They had the consolation of winning gold medals in the other three weight divisions.

There was also success for the host country in the gymnastics with Yukio Endo leading the Japanese to five victories in eight events. Two world-renowned Russian gymnasts, Boris Shakhlin and Larisa Latynina, closed their memorable Olympic careers with gold medal victories, and Czechoslovakia's Vera Caslavska started her gold medal collection that was to make her an Olympic immortal (see Mexico Games for her biography).

Japan emerged as the top nation in the wrestling, winning four gold medals. Their outstanding performer was Osamu Watanabe, whose victory in the final of the featherweight freestyle division was his 186th successive win.

At 6ft 3in and 350lb, Russian weightlifter Leonid Zhabotinsky was not only the biggest man at the Tokyo Games but also the strongest. He won the heavyweight gold medal with a world and Olympic record total lift of 1262lb. "The Great Zhabo," as he became known, reigned supreme as the strongest man in the world for the next five years, retaining his world championship in 1965 and 1966. He successfully defended his Olympic title in Mexico with a lift that was identical to his Tokyo record. In 1969, at the age of 31, Zhabo suddenly and inexplicably retired in mid-contest during a world championship duel with American Joe Dube. He quit competitive events but had literally left a great impression on the world of weightlifting.

Italian cyclist Sergio Bianchetto retained the 2000 meters tandem title he had won in Rome, this time partnered by Andrea Damiano. In 1960, his team-mate on the bicycle made for two was his former school pal Giuseppe Beghetto. In the individual 1000 meters sprint in Tokyo he was beaten into second place by his countryman Giovanni Pettenella, who also collected a silver medal in the 1000 meters time trial behind Belgian Patrick Sercu.

In the major team sports, the United States again won the basketball without losing a game and for the fourth successive time Russia was the runner-up; India was restored as hockey champion, beating Pakistan 1–0 in a tense final; Hungary regained the soccer title it won in 1952, with Ferenc Bene scoring 12 goals in the tournament and helping the Hungarians to a 2–1 victory over Czechoslovakia in the final; Russia won the men's title and the highly-trained Japanese the women's title in the new Olympic sport of volleyball; and Hungary won the water polo championship for the third time in four Olympics.

Avery Brundage, American President of the International Olympic Committee, said on his arrival home in the United States: "These Games were a triumph for Japan and a triumph for the Olympic movement. The entire Japanese nation from newsboy to industrial tycoon adopted the Games as his own project and went out of his way to please the visitors. Thanks to their efforts and to the Olympic spirit that prevailed throughout, the Games were a phenomenal success."

A new sport enters the Olympics: volleyball. Russia has the first men's champions, pictured here on the way to a 3–0 victory over the United States.

OLYMPIC FUN AND GAMES

South Korean flyweight Dong-Kih Choh was so disgusted at his disqualification for punching after being ordered to "stop boxing" that he staged a sit-down strike in the ring. He sat cross-legged in the middle of the ring and turned a deaf ear to all pleadings and demands that he should leave. His stubborn squat held the boxing program up for nearly an hour. He was finally persuaded to leave after a promise had been made to him that an inquiry would be held into his disqualification. Mr Choh took no further part in the tournament.

Olympic balloons are released into the thin air of Mexico City at the start of the 1968 Games.

Below: The high altitude suited African runners like Mamo Wolde (No 329) and Nafta Temu (No 575). Temu beat Wolde in this 10,000 meters race but the Ethiopian won the marathon.

The Olympic spirit just about managed to shine through the storm clouds of controversy that hung over the Mexico Games almost from the moment the IOC awarded the XIX Olympiad to a city 7347 feet above sea level. There was world-wide criticism of the decision and it was even suggested by some gloomy experts that athletes unaccustomed to competing at altitude would be risking death in Mexico's thin air. Because of the reduced atmospheric pressure and air density, it was obvious that Olympic and world records would tumble in the explosive events such as the sprints and rapid-power field events but the major concern was for the competitors in endurance events who could be in trouble because of a lack of oxygen.

Despite the uproar and heated debate, a record number of 112 nations entered nearly 8000 competitors and the Mexicans shrugged off a domestic crisis to give everybody a warm and friendly welcome. In a bloody battle just 10 days before the opening ceremony, government forces had shot and killed more than 250 students and wounded over 1000 others during a demonstration in Mexico City against the regime in power. But there was never a hint of the internal troubles at the Games and the Mexican people proved an enthusiastic and appreciative audience as they watched a series of phenomenal performances that, despite everything, made the 1968 Games among the most memorable there had ever been.

Happily, the forecasts of fatalities were proved unfounded but there were many disturbing moments when sea-level athletes collapsed in their events and had to be revived with oxygen from the team of medical experts who were constantly on hand. It was quickly clear that athletes living at high altitude all their lives were going to have a big advantage in the distance events.

On the opening day, Kenyan Naftali Temu won the 10,000 meters in 29 min 27.4 sec. He produced a sprint finish to overhaul Ethiopian Mamo Wolde, who collected the silver medal and later added a gold when he succeeded his countryman Abebe Bikila as marathon champion. Tunisian Mohamed Gammoudi came in third just in front of Mexican idol Juan Martinez. The time was the slowest since the 1948 Games in London and 1 min 48 sec outside the world record set by Australian Ron Clarke, who collapsed unconscious after finishing in sixth place.

It was the altitude athletes who also triumphed in the 5000 meters and 3000 meters steeplechase. Gammoudi and Kenyans Kip Keino and Temu finished in that order in the 5000, with Mexican Martinez again in fourth place. There was an extraordinary performance by Kenyan Amos Biwott in the steeplechase. A 19-year-old novice at the event, he had no idea about tactics and technique. When the bell rang to signal the start of the final lap he appeared to have no chance of winning, for he was 30 yards behind the leaders and in last place. But he suddenly unleashed a frantic burst of speed that took him from last to first inside 300 meters and he was five meters ahead of his countryman Ben Kogo at the tape.

The most talented of the Kenyan team was a police inspector from Nairobi.

KIPCHOGE KEINO
THE LEADER OF THE BLACK AFRICAN ATHLETIC EXPLOSION

A remarkably versatile runner, Kipchoge "Kip" Keino astonished track experts by entering the 1500, 5000 and 10,000 meters in Mexico, where two events would have been too demanding for most athletes. He had competed in the 1964 Tokyo Olympics just two years after taking up track running and finished fifth in the 5000 meters and unplaced in the 1500 meters. The following year he revealed his enormous potential when he broke the 3000 and 5000 meters world records and ran a 3 min 54.2 sec mile.

Many people thought he was taking on too much in Mexico and there seemed little hope for him winning any medals when he dropped out of the 10,000 meters with two laps to go because of violent pains in his stomach. But he recovered to qualify for the final of the 5000 meters, in which he was just beaten in a desperate sprint finish by the powerful Mohamed Gammoudi.

Keino then ran in two preliminary rounds of the 1500 meters and in the final faced great American miler Jim Ryun, the Kansas kicker who had been in devastating form the previous year when he lowered the world mile record to 3 min 51.1 sec and the 1500 meters record to 3 min 33.1 sec. An attack of glandular fever had knocked some of the power out of Ryun but he was still a hot favorite to win the gold medal. With his team-mate Ben Jipcho helping to take the strain, Keino set out with the express intention of running the feared finishing kick out of Ryun. Jipcho took the field through a fast

first lap in 56.0 sec and then with two laps to go Keino moved to the front and quickly opened a commanding lead. Ryun had been content to cruise along with the back markers and suddenly found himself 25 meters adrift of the Kenyan. It was not until after the bell that Ryun made his familiar finishing spurt, but Keino had already got the race wrapped up and went through the tape 20 meters clear in 3 min 34.9 sec, a personal and Olympic best performance. Ryun flashed through the last lap in 55.7 sec to take the silver medal in 3 min 37.8 sec, 4.7 sec slower than his world record but a creditable time considering the high altitude.

Keino, born on 17 January 1940, had lost some of his blistering speed by the time of the Munich Olympics in 1972 but still managed to take a silver medal in the 1500 meters behind Finn Pekka Vasala. He had never taken the steeplechase seriously but decided to "have a go" at the event in Munich. His hurdling was, to say the least, loose and unorthodox but he still managed to outmaneuver his experienced rivals to win in an Olympic record 8 min 23.6 sec, with

It's a one-two for Kenya in the steeplechase (left) as Amos Biwott takes the gold and Benjamin Kogo the silver.

"Kip" Keino, the king Kenyan and leader of the black African explosion in track athletics, wins the 1500 meters in a new Olympic record, with American Jim Ryun nearly 3 sec back in second place.

Ralph Doubell equals the world record as he inches ahead of Wilson Kiprugut in the 800 meters final.

his compatriot Ben Jipcho in second place.

Australian Ralph Doubell had to equal the world record for 800 meters of 1 min 44.3 sec to stop another Kenyan gold medal win in Mexico. He produced a powerful finish to beat Kenya's Wilson Kiprugut by 0.2 sec. American Tom Farrell made up a lot of ground off the final bend to take the bronze medal in 1 min 45.4 sec.

The American squad, which had prepared for the Games at a special high altitude camp in Lake Tahoe, Nevada, came into their own in the explosive events and captured nine medals in the men's 100, 200 and 400 meters and in the two relays.

Jim Hines, coached by 1956 triple gold medallist Bobby Morrow, stormed to victory in the 100 meters in a world record equalling 9.9 sec and ran a stunning anchor leg in the sprint relay final to take the United States to the gold medal and a world record of 38.2 sec. Born at Dumas, Arkansas, on 10 September 1946, Hines turned professional after the Games and was clocked at 20.2 sec over 220 yards in 1969 when running against a race-horse.

It was Tommie Smith, wearing dark glasses, who produced the outstanding sprinting feat of the Games when he raced gracefully to victory in the 200 meters in a sensational world record

Jim Hines proves himself the fastest man on two legs as he slices through the tape at the end of a world record run in the 100 meters.

138

Hines, Smith and Evans all produced magnificent performances but even they had to take a back seat to a remarkable world record set in the long jump.

Tommie Smith flings his arms wide (left) as he shatters the 200 meters world record.

BOB BEAMON
HE LEAPS INTO THE TWENTY-FIRST CENTURY

Could the 28ft barrier be broken for the first time? This was the main topic of conversation as the world's four greatest long jumpers prepared for battle in the Olympic final in Mexico on 18 October 1968. The four favorites were reigning Olympic champion Lynn "The Leap" Davies, joint world record holders Ralph Boston of the United States and his perennial rival Igor Ter-Ovanesyan, and the wildly unpredictable Bob Beamon, a black American who had jumped to within an inch of the world best of 27ft 4¾in (8.34m). In the thin, rarified air of high altitude Mexico it was considered that the fierce competition could motivate somebody into passing the magic 28ft mark. The erratic Beamon struggled to qualify for the final but his team-mate Ralph Boston, the 1960 Olympic champion, commented: "Don't get him mad or he's likely to jump clean out of the pit."

Lee Evans becomes the third black American to break a world record in the explosive track events as he ducks through the tape in the 400 meters.

time of 19.8 sec. But Smith will sadly be remembered for his actions *after* the race rather than his phenomenal speed during the run, in which he beat Australia's Peter Norman and his fellow black American John Carlos with ease. When they went to the rostrum for the medals presentation, Smith wore a black leather glove on his right hand, Carlos one on his left. As the United States national anthem was played, they both bowed their heads and raised their gloved hands in a "black power" salute. In the other hand, each waved a Puma running shoe aloft. They later explained that one hand represented idealism and the other commercialism. "If I do something good like win a race, then I am an American," said Smith. "But if I do something bad, then I am a Negro."

There was sympathy for their cause but savage criticism for using the Olympic platform to promote it. Both were suspended from the United States team by the US Olympic Committee and ordered home. Their demonstration against commercialism caused embarrassment among many competitors who it was known were taking money from shoe manufacturers for wearing a particular brand of spikes on the track. Members of the IOC knew that athletes were accepting under-the-counter payments but could do nothing either to prove it or to stop it. The amateur ideals of Baron de Coubertin were being savaged.

Lee Evans chopped 0.3 sec off the world record for the 400 meters when he broke through the 44.0 sec barrier to win the final in 43.8 sec. He later shared in another world record when helping the United States relay team take the 4 × 400 meters title in 2 min 56.1 sec. He and his three team-mates – Vince Matthews, Ron Freeman and Larry James – averaged just over 44.00 seconds apiece for their 400 meter legs.

Bob Beamon jumps into the twenty-first century as he shatters both the 28 and 29ft barriers in the men's long jump final. In this picture sequence he is up, down and away past the electronic measuring device. His incredible leap had to be measured with an old-fashioned steel tape.

On a gray, overcast afternoon three of the lesser-known competitors gave the final an undistinguished start by registering no jumps. Then Beamon, tall and gangling, came onto the runway. For 30 seconds he jogged and skipped at the end of the track and then suddenly started his run-up, revving up to full sprint speed as he neared the take-off board. He hit the board soundly with his right foot and launched himself into space for the greatest man-motivated leap on earth. The spectators and other competitors gasped with astonishment as he propelled himself through the thin air. He appeared to be walking in space and landed at the far end of the pit beyond the range of a sophisticated modern measuring device.

The judges had to call for an old-fashioned steel tape and after agonizing minutes the electric indicator board flashed the unbelievable figures: 8.90 meters – 29ft 2½in. It was the shortest field events *competition* in history. Beamon had jumped into the next century, establishing a record that experts forecast could survive for 50 years. Beamon, born in New York on 29 August 1946, said after his record-smashing leap: "My first reaction when I heard the distance was that maybe the high altitude had gone to my head and that I was dreaming. I thought maybe I could just beat 28 feet but to go over 29 feet was just mind blowing."

After one more jump in the competition of 26ft 4½in (8.03m), Beamon retired to the shelter of the grandstand to escape the rain that had come cascading down immediately after his winning leap. East German Klaus Beer pushed Boston and Ter-Ovanesyan back into third and fourth places with a jump of 26ft 10½in (8.19m) for the silver medal. Britain's Lynn Davies was psychologically shattered after setting his sights on a "gold or nothing" target and he finally finished a dispirited ninth.

All the jumping competitions produced the unusual and the unexpected. The first five in the triple jump all broke the old world record, with Russian Viktor Saneyev leading the way with a prodigious effort of 57ft 0¾in (17.39m). Four years later in Munich and without the benefits of thin air, Saneyev retained his title with a triple jump of 56ft 11¼in (17.35m).

Dick Fosbury gave a new style to the world on his way to victory in the high jump at an Olympic record 7ft 4¼in (2.24m). His unorthodox method of jumping backwards over the bar became universally known as "The Fosbury Flop" and has been copied by many of the leading high jumpers. A 6ft 4in, 184lb bouncing athlete from Portland, Oregon, Fosbury cleared his winning height at the third attempt to beat his team-mate Ed Caruthers, who took the silver with a straddle-style leap of 7ft 3½in (2.22m).

Eight pole vaulters beat the Olympic record in a tense seven-hour contest that finished with three men tied at the world record height of 17ft 8½ in (5.40m). Once again the gold medal went to the United States, with Bob Seagren beating West German Claus Schiprowski and East German Wolfgang Nordwig because he had fewer failures at lower heights.

Janis Lusis, Russia's world record holder in the javelin, added the Olympic title to his two European championships with a winning throw of 295ft 7in (90.10m). This marvellous competitor took the silver medal at Munich four years later and finished eighth in the 1976 Montreal Games.

After Randy Matson (shot) and four-timer Al Oerter (discus) had collected more gold medals for the United States, Bill Toomey proved himself the world's greatest all-rounder when he took the decathlon title with an Olympic record points haul of 8193.

Jose Padraza won a silver medal for Mexico in the 20 kilometers walk, overhauling Russian Nikolai Smaga in the last 400 meters with what observers considered a fair imitation of running. But he was unable to catch Russian walking master Vladimir Golubnichi, who regained the title he had won in 1960. He had taken third place in 1964 and completed his collection of medals by getting the silver in Munich in 1972. East German Christoph Hohne won the 50 kilometers walk with 10 minutes to spare over his nearest rival.

The United States retained the 110 meters hurdles title through Willie Davenport in an Olympic record equalling 13.3 sec and an American-trained runner won the 400 meters hurdles in superb style.

DAVID HEMERY
THE COOL ENGLISHMAN WITH THE SUPREME STYLE

For the first time in history, the 1968 400 meters hurdles final brought together eight runners who had all been inside 50 seconds for this "killer" event of the track. The line-up from the inside lane was Rainer Schubert (West Germany), co-holder of the European record at 49.1 sec; Gerhard Hennige (West Germany), who shared the European record; Geoff Vanderstock (US), who had set a world record 48.8 sec in the US Olympic trials; Roberto Frinolli (Italy), the European champion; Viacheslav Shomarokhov (Russia), a 28-year-old deaf mute noted for his strength and stamina; David Hemery (Great Britain), born in England and trained in Boston; Ron Whitney (USA), the Olympic record holder at 49.0 sec; and on the outside John Sherwood (Great Britain), who shared the Commonwealth and UK record of 49.3 sec with Hemery. It was expected to be the closest of all finals with Americans Vanderstock and Whitney slight favorites.

Hemery, a law and business studies student at Boston University, ran the race of his life to dominate the final from gun to tape. He had cut back the stagger on Whitney by the time he had glided over the second hurdle and at the halfway mark the 6ft 1½ in blond Briton was so far ahead of the rest of the field that everybody thought he had gone off too fast and would "blow up" in the finishing straight. But Hemery, upright and graceful, changed from a 13-stride

Randy Matson wins the shot put with a new Olympic record heave of 67ft 10¼ in (above left). Below: David Hemery (No 402) breaks the tape and the world record in the 400 meters hurdles.

141

pattern between hurdles to 15 strides and increased his speed and his lead. He approached the final tenth hurdle as if it was the first and dashed to the finish line an astonishing eight meters clear of runner-up Hennige, with Sherwood bravely hurling himself across the line to snatch the bronze medal to go with the silver his wife, Sheila, had won in the long jump. Hemery's winning time was a new world and Olympic record of 48.1 sec. It was such a fast race that only the last man, Frinolli (50.1 sec), failed to break the 50.0 sec barrier.

Born in Cirencester, Gloucester, on 18 July 1944, Hemery had been coached in his early days as a 110 meter hurdler by veteran English expert Fred Housden. In America he came under the intoxicating influence of Boston track and field coach Billy Smith, who convinced him he should switch to the 400 event. Hemery's world record lasted until the 1972 Olympics in Munich when John Akii-Bua, the English-coached Ugandan, won the gold medal in the incredible time of 47.82 sec. Hemery finished a gallant third behind his old rival Ralph Hann of the United States in 48.52 sec. He completed a full house of medals when helping Britain take the silver medal in the 4 × 400 meters relay.

The outstanding champion on the track in the women's events was a girl from Georgia who had done it all before.

WYOMIA TYUS
A UNIQUE DOUBLE FOR THE ROCKET-GIRL FROM GEORGIA

It was pouring with rain when Wyomia Tyus went down in her starting blocks for the 100 meters final in Mexico. Just 11.0 sec after the starter's gun had fired, Wyomia was slicing through the tape on the saturated track to break the world's record and become the first athlete, male or female, to win a sprint title in two successive Olympics.

Like her great predecessor Wilma Rudolph, Wyomia was a member of the famous Tigerbelles club. Born at Griffin, Georgia, on 29 August 1945, she had been a top-ten rated world sprinter since the age of 17. She improved her personal best time for the 100 meters by 0.3 sec on her way to the gold medal in Tokyo and took a silver medal in the sprint relay. Still only 23 by the time of the 1968 Games, she followed her success in the 100 meters by anchoring the US team to the gold medal and a world record of 42.8 sec.

Irena Szewinska of Poland took the bronze medal in the 100 meters and captured the 200 meters title with a world record run of 22.5 sec. There was a stunning upset in the 400 meters when Frenchwoman Colette Besson produced a flying finish to beat British favorite Lillian

Wyomia Tyus creates Olympic history as she becomes the first ever athlete to retain a sprint title, winning the 100 meters in a world record 11.00 sec.

Board by a stride in an Olympic record equalling 52.0 sec. Lillian, pin-up girl of British athletics, was just 20 and approaching her peak when she tragically died of cancer soon after proving herself the best 800 meters runner in Europe in 1969.

The pressures and strain of top-level competition were underlined when in the 800 meters semi-final, world record holder Vera Nikolic of Yugoslavia ran off the track 300 meters from the finish and, clearly distressed and overwrought, ran to a bridge just outside the stadium and had to be restrained by an official as she attempted to throw herself to the ground below. In the final of the race, America's Madeline Manning showed fine judgment coming into the home stretch and accelerated just at the right time to leave her rivals stranded. She hit the tape in an Olympic record 2 min 0.9 sec, the third fastest time ever recorded.

Maureen Caird, a 17-year-old from New South Wales, became the youngest ever track athletics champion in the Olympics when she won the 80 meters hurdles in a world record equalling 10.3 sec, with her team-mate Pam Kilborn a tenth of a second away in second place. There was another teenage triumph when 18-year-old Czech high jumper Milena Rezkova cleared 5ft 11¾ in (1.82m) to beat two Russians to the gold medal. It was one of the most popularly received victories because the crowd was well aware that Russian troops had invaded Czechoslovakia to put down a threatened rebellion just two months earlier.

Romanian Viorica Viscopoleanu did "a Beamon" in the long jump. She virtually won the competition with her very first jump in the final, a world record leap of 22ft 4½in (6.82m). Lia Manoliu, a 36-year-old engineer from Bucharest, won another gold medal for Romania in the discus. Her throw of 191ft 2½in (58.28m) was 10 feet below her world record but she was content just to have the gold medal in what was her fifth Olympics. She had won bronze medals in 1960 and 1964.

East German Margit Gummel set a world record of 64ft 4in (19.61m) in winning the shot and West German Ingrid Becker won the pentathlon with a points total of 5098, clinching the title with her last-event performance when she ran the 200 meters in 23.5 sec.

The United States was once again the monopolizer in the swimming pool. It captured 10 of the 15 men's titles and American women swimmers were first in 11 of their 14 events. Two American men won two individual titles: Mike Burton (400 and 1500 meters freestyle) and Charles Hickcox (200 and 400 meters medley). Burton retained his 1500 meters title

in Munich and later became a member of the US Olympic Committee. Hickcox, 6ft 3in tall and a student at Indiana University, showed remarkable stamina in testing conditions by winning a third gold medal as a member of the 4 × 100 meters medley relay team and took the silver medal in the 100 meters backstroke behind crack East German Roland Matthes.

A sign of the toll on swimmers at high altitude was that John Ferris, bronze medallist in the 200 meters individual medley won by Hickcox, collapsed at the medal ceremony and had to be given an emergency intake of oxygen.

The American domination was interrupted by Matthes and Australian Mike Wenden. A versatile swimmer but specializing in the backstroke, Matthes influenced a generation of swimmers with his style and technique. He won the 100 meters and 200 meters backstroke titles in Mexico and again in Munich and was a bronze medallist in the shorter event at Montreal in 1976. He added to his medals collection by taking a silver with the East German 4 × 100 meters medley relay team in 1968 and a bronze in 1972.

Australian Mike Wenden was among the world's best front-crawl sprinters for eight years from 1966. He set one of only three world records in the Mexico Olympic pool with a dashing 52.2 sec in the 100 meters freestyle final. In the 200 meters freestyle he beat the holder Don Schollander in 1 min 55.2 sec. Wenden also picked up a silver and a bronze

Milena Rezkova clears the high jump bar at a height of 5ft 11¾in to take the gold medal.

Debbie Meyer, a triple gold medallist in the swimming pool in Mexico.

Vera Caslavska, poetry in motion as she performs a vault of near perfection.

with the Australian freestyle relay teams. But it was a 16-year-old from Maryland who claimed most attention in the swimming pool.

DEBBIE MEYER
A TRIPLE HIT FOR THE MISS FROM MARYLAND

Born in Annapolis, Maryland, on 14 August 1952, Debbie Meyer had only three years in top-level competition before retiring in 1970 but in her short career she set 16 world freestyle records. Three of them came in the 1968 US Olympic trials and she maintained her form in Mexico when she became the first swimmer, male or female, to win three individual gold medals in one Olympic Games. She took $11\frac{1}{2}$ sec off the 1964 Olympic record in the 400 meters freestyle and also won the newly intro-

duced 200 and 800 freestyle titles. Coached by Sherman Chavoor at the Arden Hills Club, Debbie's favorite challenge was the 1500 meters freestyle and she broke the world record for this event on four occasions.

Her team-mate in Mexico, Claudia Kolb, won both the 400 and 200 meters individual medley to add two gold medals to the silver she collected in Tokyo in the 200 meters breast-stroke. Catie Ball, American holder of all the world breaststroke records, failed to make any impression in Mexico because of a stomach upset and the breaststroke titles went to Yugoslavian Djurdjica Bjedov (100 meters) and American Sharon Wichman (200 meters).

Both the springboard diving titles went to America (Bernie Wrightson and Sue Gossick) but the highboard gold medals went to countries gaining their first titles in the pool. Milena Duchkova won the women's highboard for Czechoslovakia and Italian Klaus Dibiasi was the men's champion for the first of his record three successive titles (see Montreal Games for his biography).

Gymnastics had by now caught the public imagination thanks to coverage by television, and it was a Czech woman who emerged as the queen of the Mexico Games.

VERA CASLAVSKA
MEDALS AND MARRIAGE FOR THE BALLERINA OF THE BARS

No woman in Olympic history could match the medals collection of Vera Caslavska at the close of the Mexico Games. Her tally was a record of seven golds, an individual silver and three team silvers. Vera started her gold rush at Rome in 1960, continued in Tokyo in 1964 and reached her golden peak in Mexico. There was an extra edge to her performance in 1968 because she was competing against the crack Russians, only two months after Soviet troops had entered her native Prague. Anger, sorrow and pride were mirrored in her beautiful face as she competed with the zest and enthusiasm of a woman possessed. Vera was competing for Czechoslovakia and was unbeatable.

She brought the Mexican spectators to their feet during her near-perfect floor exercise when she went gracefully and energetically through her program to the tune of the "Mexican Hat Dance." When the six presentation ceremonies were staged, Vera was in every one of them as, much to the delight of the crowd, she collected four gold medals and two silver.

Vera announced her retirement at the end of the championships and as a romantic finale got married in Mexico City to Czech 1500 meters runner Josef Odlozil, silver medallist in Tokyo in 1964.

In the men's gymnastics, the Japanese won 12 of a possible 22 medals and took five of the eight titles. Their individual stars were Akinori Nakayama (winner of three gold medals in Mexico and again in Munich) and Sawao Kato (who won two individual gold medals for combined exercises and four team golds in Mexico and Munich). Miroslav Cerar, unbeaten in the pommelled horse discipline from 1958 to 1970, retained the title in his speciality event that he had won in Tokyo in 1964. He also collected a bronze medal on the horizontal bar.

Bill Steinkraus won a first ever show jumping gold medal for the United States while riding Snowbound. It was the veteran rider's fourth Olympics. He won a bronze medal with the US team in 1952 in Helsinki and collected team silver medals in 1960 and again in 1972. Captain of the US equestrian team from 1955 until his retirement in 1972, he was one of the favorites for a gold medal in Tokyo in 1964 but his intended partner, Sinjon, had to be pulled out at the last minute because of lameness.

Great Britain won the three-day event. Their team was Derek Allhusen (individual silver medallist on Lochinvar), Richard Meade, Ben Jones and Jane Bullen who, at 20, became the first woman ever to win any sort of a medal in this gruelling event.

George Foreman was an impressive winner

of the boxing heavyweight title. He later made even more of an impact by taking the professional world championship from Joe Frazier, subsequently losing it to Muhammad Ali in Zaire. Two outstanding boxers retained titles that they had won in Tokyo – Russian light-middleweight Boris Lagutin and Polish light-welterweight Jerzy Kulej.

There were two formidable French riders in action on the cycling track. World champion Daniel Morelon won the 1000 meters sprint

Bill Steinkraus on Snowbound, a winning partnership for the United States in the Olympic grand prix show jumping competition.

Daniel Morelon and Pierre Trentin (right) power to victory on their way to a gold medal for France in the 200 meters tandem event.

145

title, in which he had taken the bronze in 1964. He won the title again in 1972 and was the 1976 silver medallist. One of the greatest amateur riders of all time, he also won a gold medal in the 2000 meters tandem event in Mexico. His partner on the tandem was Pierre Trentin, who also collected a gold in the 1000 meters time trial and a bronze in the 1000 meters sprint. While in Mexico Trentin set a world amateur record for the kilometer of 1 min 3.91 sec.

The four Petterson brothers of Sweden won silver medals in the Olympic road time-trial cycling race – the only time in the history of the Games that four brothers have collected medals in the same event. The previous family record was held by the three Nordahl brothers of Sweden, who played in the championship-winning soccer team in London in 1948. Another family win was made by Yoshinobu Miyake, who took the gold medal for Japan in the featherweight weightlifting division, while his brother Yoshiyuki won a bronze medal in the same division.

The most successful rowing crew since World War II made their Olympic debut when the Einheit Dresden coxless four (Dieter Grahn, Frank Forberger, Frank Ruhle and Dieter Schubert) won the gold medal in their event.

The East Germans, unbeaten in any major championship regatta, retained their title.

Aleksandr Timoshinin won the first of his two gold medals in the double sculls. In Mexico he was partnered by Russian team-mate Anatoli Sass. He teamed up with Gennadi Korshikov to win his second title at Munich.

Scotsman Rodney Pattisson won the first of two consecutive yachting gold medals for Britain. At Acapulco, with Iain Macdonald Smith as his crew, he helmed his Flying Dutchman *Superdocious* to victory despite a disqualification in their first race. At Kiel in 1972, Pattisson retained his title. This time his boat was *Superdoso* and Chris Davies was his crew.

In the team sports, the United States almost inevitably won the basketball; Russia won both the men's and women's volleyball; Pakistan beat Australia (shock victors over India) in the hockey final; Hungary beat Bulgaria 4–1 in a stormy soccer final in which four players were ordered off by the referee.

Gary Anderson, a self-taught left-handed marksman, retained his free rifle title for the United States at the shooting range, and Britain's Bob Braithwaite had 187 consecutive hits to take the gold medal in the clay pigeon shooting with 198 points.

OLYMPIC FUN AND GAMES

British boxer Chris Finnegan won the gold medal in the middleweight division but it was eight hours after the final before he was officially confirmed as champion. He was unable to supply a sample for the urine test and two Olympic officials had to accompany him until the early hours of the morning. It took eight pints of beer before Chris could oblige!

The Munich Games were bloodied by the most horrifying tragedy in the history of the Olympics. A tournament that had opened rich with promise of great sporting achievements and keen but friendly rivalry between nations was suddenly brought to a standstill by murder and terrorism in the Olympic village. Palestinian guerrillas invaded the village in the early hours of the morning on 5 September, shot and killed two members of the Israeli team and held nine others hostage. They demanded the release of 200 Palestinian political prisoners held in Israel and threatened to shoot each of the hostages if their demands were not met. The Games were suspended as millions of people watched the sickening drama on world-wide television. Finally, after 15 hours of negotiation and tense talks, the hostages and their captors were flown by helicopter to a nearby airbase for what should have been a flight to the Middle East. Shortly after the helicopter landed, West German police marksmen opened fire but before they could kill the five terrorists a hand grenade was detonated and all nine Israeli team members died in the explosion.

On the following day a service of mourning and memorial was held in the main Olympic stadium for the 11 Israelis killed. The Games then continued, heavy with the horror and despair wrought by the terrorists. Avery Brundage, coming to the end of his long and controversial reign as President of the International Olympic Committee, was determined that the appalling tragedy should not extinguish the Olympic flame. The Baron de Coubertin ideals of unity and fellowship through sport had to be seen to be preserved.

At a colossal cost of $600 million, the Munich Olympic Committee had provided facilities and stadia unequalled in the 76-year history of the Games. They built a sports complex that was on the scale of a small town rather than a village, with the competitors housed in blocks of luxury flats alongside the modern structure of the main stadium and Olympic pool. It all resembled something out of a science-fiction movie and was a thousand years removed from the first of the modern Games in Athens in 1896.

After some of the most stupendous sporting competition ever witnessed in the Olympic arena, the unofficial medals table showed Russia as the most successful nation, with 50 golds in a total of 99 medals, just five ahead of the United States. The most startling feature of the Games was the rapid improvement of East Germany right across the sports board. They were third in the medals table, winning 20 golds in their total of 66.

There was a reminder of past Olympics in the track and field with a stunning revival of Finnish supremacy in the middle-distance events.

LASSE VIREN
A POLICEMAN ON THE GOLD MEDAL BEAT

Lasse Viren, a slim, fair policeman from Finland with a wispy beard, was following in famous footsteps when he pulled off a shock double in the 5000 and 10,000 meters in Munich. Only his countryman Hannes Kolehmainen (1912), Emil Zatopek (1952) and Vladimir Kuts

(1956) had achieved this golden one-two before. The fact that Viren repeated the double dose in 1976 (see the Montreal Games) put him into the land of legend along with those immortal flying Finns Kolehmainen and Paavo Nurmi.

In the 10,000 meters, British world record holder David Bedford, tough Tunisian Mohamed Gammoudi and versatile Belgian

Valeri Borzov wins the 100 meters and (bottom) prepares to receive the baton on the last leg of the sprint relay.

Emiel Puttemans were the pre-race favorites, and Viren looked unlikely to be able to live with them after he had taken a tumble just before the halfway point. But Viren got up and quickly made up the lost ground and in the final 600 meters increased the pace until none of his rivals could stay with him. With a last lap spurt of 56.4 sec, Viren went through the tape in a world and Olympic record 27 min 38.4 sec. Puttemans took the silver medal and Miruts "The Shifter" Yifter of Ethiopia the bronze.

Viren, born in the Finnish village of Myrskyla on 22 July 1949, had defending champion Gammoudi, Britain's Ian Stewart, strong American Steve Prefontaine and the persistent Puttemans to contend with at the bell in the 5000 meters final. Gammoudi made a great effort to hold onto his title but Viren glided away to beat him by five yards with Scotsman Stewart third. With a time of 13 min 26.4 sec, Viren had created a new Olympic record and before the year was out he had lowered the world record to 13 min 16.4 sec.

Inspired by the performances of Viren, Pekka Vasala made it a track triple for Finland when he timed his home stretch challenge to perfection to beat reigning champion Kip Keino to the line in the 1500 meters final in 3 min 36.3 sec. Keino gained consolation by taking a gold medal during a rare excursion over the 3000 meters steeplechase course.

Jim "The Stork" Ryun had prepared hard for the Games in a bid to win the elusive 1500 meters title for America for the first time since Mel Sheppard's victory back in 1908. Ryun had the talent but not the luck. He fell following a collision in his heat and was unable to catch the leaders in what should have been a simple qualification race. American officials protested on Ryun's behalf but the Olympic judges refused to give Ryun a second chance. It was a Games of other disappointments for the US track and field team. Their supremacy in both the sprints and the pole vault was broken.

VALERI BORZOV
THE RED ROCKET MAN GETS A DOUBLE-GOLD LAUNCH

Running seemingly almost without effort, Valeri Borzov became the first non-American since Canadian Percy Williams in 1928 to win both the Olympic 100 and 200 meters titles. He shattered America's grip on the sprint championships in such a stylish manner that he was reckoned to rival even America's 1956 triple gold medallist Bobby Morrow as the greatest white sprinter of all time. There was, however, an emptiness about Borzov's win in the 100 meters. Eddie Hart and Rey Robinson, joint world record holders at 9.9 sec, were eliminated in the quarter-finals without stepping foot on the track. The two Americans had been given the wrong times at which to report to the stadium and turned up too late to take part in their heats. Borzov was able to casually look around him as he powered smoothly to victory in the final in 10.14 sec with American third string Bobby Taylor second in 10.24 sec. A sneer campaign started that Borzov would never have won had the two American favorites gone to the starting line but he silenced all the disbelievers when he scorched to victory in the 200 meters in a European record 20.0 sec.

Born near Lvov on 20 October 1949, Borzov was said to be a man-made sprinter rather than a "natural." A group of physiologists and coaches in Kiev fed facts and data on all previous great sprinters into a computer and then programmed Borzov to perfect the right style, body weight and technique. Whatever they did, the methods worked and Borzov became the finest non-American sprinter the world had ever seen. He collected a silver medal in the sprint relay in Munich and after recovering from a series of injuries took the bronze medal in the 100 meters in Montreal.

America's sprinters regained some pride in the 4 × 100 meters relay when they took the title with a world-record-equalling 38.19 sec. But for the first time they were unable to contest the 4 × 400 meters relay after the United States squad was withdrawn because of another black power demonstration following the 400 meters individual final. Vince Matthews and Wayne Collett, winner and second in the 400 meters, had turned their backs on the American flag as it was raised during the victory ceremony. They chatted and joked while the national anthem was being played and when they left the rostrum Matthews twirled his gold medal around by the chain as if it were worthless and Collett gave a "black power" salute. Both were suspended from the Games and ordered home and America decided against entering a scratch team in the relay that they had won nine times at past Olympics. In their absence, Kenya took the title with Great Britain in second place. David Hemery was a member of the British team, so collecting a full set of medals.

Hemery finished third in the 400 meters hurdles final when defending the title he won in such fine style in Mexico. John Akii-Bua, the popular winner from Uganda, beat American Ralph Mann into second place with a world record 47.82 sec. Akii-Bua revealed at the post-race press conference that he was one of 43

children of a father with eight wives. He prepared for his Olympic challenge by wearing a 25lb jacket while hurdling in training runs.

America had one of the great characters of the Games in Dave Wottle, who won the 800 meters by just three-hundredth of a second in a desperately close finish with Russian Yevgeni Arzhanov. Wottle, who always ran in a peaked golf cap, tantalized and teased his rivals and the crowd by continually racing at the back of the field and leaving his victory swoops until the last moments of the race. In the final, Wottle almost left his throttle run too late but his exhausted Russian rival stumbled two meters from the tape and the tall American forced his way across the line with literally inches separating them. Wottle amused and warmed everybody with his almost casual approach to the Games. He got married just prior to leaving the United States and brought his bride to Munich with him on their honeymoon.

Frank Shorter, Munich-born American citizen, brought the United States its first marathon victory since the eventful run of John Hayes in the famous "Dorando race" of 1908. A German student made a hoax run into the stadium and was mistakenly greeted as the winner, a stunt which took some of the gloss off Shorter's triumph. He performed wonders to beat the previously undefeated Belgian Karel Lismont by a margin of more than two minutes in 2 hr 12 min 19.8 sec. Title-holder Mamo Wolde came home in third place.

Frenchman Guy Drut gave notice of his potential over the 110 meters hurdles when he split the crack American trio. Rod Milburn hurdled beautifully to retain the title for the United States in 13.24 sec. Drut finished in second place in 13.34 sec, edging out Americans Tommy Hill and defending champion Willie Davenport, but Drut's day of glory was to come four years later in Montreal.

The biggest upset for the Americans was to not win their specialty event, the pole vault. East German Wolfgang Nordwig pushed 1968 champion Bob Seagren back into second place with an Olympic record effort of 18ft 0½in (5.50m). It was the first time an American had failed to win in the Olympic pole vault. Seagren was furious because at the last moment he was barred from using the "catapult" fiberglass pole with which he had previously set world records and won the Olympic gold in Mexico.

However, long jumper Randy Williams saved the United States from a complete washout in the field events. He damaged a leg muscle while warming up and gambled all on his first jump in the final. His boldness paid golden dividends with a title-winning leap of 27ft 0½in (8.24m).

Mary Peters, British heroine in the pentathlon, gives her all in the long jump section of her event. Mary trained for the Games in the divided city of Belfast and was one of the most popular of all winners for the cheerful way she represented the people of Ireland.

For the first time since 1956 there was a new champion in the discus. Form suggested it would be American Jay Silvester but once again he failed to produce his best form in an Olympics and had to be content with the silver medal when veteran Czech Ludvik Danek, who had spent so much of his career in the shadow of Oerter, produced a winning distance of 211ft 3in (64.40m) with his very last throw.

Shot putter George Woods collected his second successive silver medal, finishing just half an inch behind Poland's Wladyslaw Komar, who won with an Olympic record of 69ft 6in (21.18m).

Russia proved a force in the field events, with Yuri Tarmak (high jump), defending champion Viktor Saneyev (triple jump), Anatoli Bondarchuk (hammer) and Nikolai Avilov (decathlon) all winning gold medals. Saneyev was the only 1968 track and field champion to successfully defend his title. His countryman Janis Lusis made a mighty effort to hang onto the javelin championship he had won in Mexico but was beaten by just half an inch when East German Klaus Wolfermann set an Olympic record 296ft 10in (90.48m).

East German women captured six of the gold medals in the 14 women's events in the athletics stadium: Renate Stecher (100 and 200 meters), Monika Zehrt (400 meters), Annelie Ehrhardt (100 meters hurdles), Ruth Fuchs (javelin) and their 4 × 400 meters relay team. It was Renate Stecher who anchored the East German team to a silver medal in the sprint relay to close an impressive Games in which her power and speed on the track had been one of the big talking

points. In both the 100 and 200 meters she beat Australian Raelene Boyle into second place, setting a world record in the longer event of 22.4 sec. Silvia Chivas collected Cuba's first ever medal in women's track and field with a bronze in the 100 meters. The bronze medallist in the 200 meters was defending champion Irena Szewinska of Poland.

Two West German heroines brought the capacity crowd to their feet. Heide Rosendahl won the long jump with a leap of 22ft 3in (6.78m) and was just beaten to the gold medal in the pentathlon by Britain's popular Mary Peters. Heide got a second gold medal as a member of West Germany's world-record-equalling sprint relay squad (42.81 sec). Ulrike Meyfarth became the youngest ever Olympic track and field champion in the high jump. The 16-year-old West German schoolgirl – a gangling 6ft 4in tall – won with an Olympic record jump of 6ft 3¾in (1.92m).

The success of Mary Peters in the pentathlon was one of the happiest stories of the Games. She had prepared for her third and final Olympics in the divided city of Belfast and at 32 years of age and after 17 years of competition, a gold medal looked beyond her. But she responded to an electric atmosphere in the Olympic stadium by setting a world record points total of 4801, beating Heide Rosendahl by just 10 points.

For the first time since women's athletics was introduced into the Olympic program in 1928, the United States failed to win a single gold medal. All they had to show for their efforts were a bronze in the 400 meters (Kathy Hammond), a bronze in the javelin (Kathy Schmidt) and a silver medal in the 4 × 400 meters relay.

By their standards, Russia also had a quiet time in the women's track and field. Ludmila Bragina was their star performer, winning the newly introduced 1500 meters in 4 min 1.4 sec. This was an improvement on the world record she herself had set in the semi-finals and in her heat she had also beaten the previous world's best time.

Another world record fell to Russian shot putter Nadezha Chizhova, who won by a margin of more than $2\frac{1}{2}$ ft with a title-clinching effort of 69ft (21.03m). Her team-mate Faina Melnik won the discus with an Olympic record 218ft 7in (66.62m).

There was, however, nobody in the track and field who could match the medal-winning charge of a swimmer from California who became the most successful gold prospector in the history of the Olympics.

MARK SPITZ
A MAGNIFICENT SEVEN GOLDS FOR THE HUMAN TORPEDO

When he was just 17, Mark Spitz won five gold medals at the 1967 Pan American Games in Winnipeg, setting world records in the 100 and 200 meters butterfly. A year later at the Olympics in Mexico he was set to win six swimming golds and he talked cockily of how he was going to leave everybody for dead. But he finished with "only" two golds in the relays and his critics claimed he was a better talker than he was a swimmer. Spitz vowed that in future he would let his swimming do his talking for him and put his mind to preparing for the 1972 Olympics in Munich.

Born in Modesto, California, on 10 February 1950, Spitz could swim almost before he could walk and from the age of six was taking special coaching lessons, later joining the famous Santa Clara Swim Club of California. When his local rabbi complained that swimming was interfering with Mark's after-school Hebrew lessons, his father explained: "Even God likes a winner."

It was while studying dentistry at Indiana University that Spitz began to make the breakthrough as a world-class swimmer. During the build-up to the Munich Olympics he set world records for the 100 meters and 200 meters freestyle and the 100 meters butterfly. He had held the 200 meters butterfly record on six different occasions and two weeks before the Games opened he recaptured that one as well. Swimming coaches noted his performances and wondered if he had "peaked" too early.

Mark Spitz butterflies through the water on his way to one of his seven gold medals.

"Can he do it in the Olympics when and where it matters?" they asked, remembering his fade-out in Mexico.

The answer was an emphatic yes. The Spitz Blitz in Munich started on the first day of the swimming championships. He won the 200 meters butterfly in a new world record of 2 min 0.7 sec and then anchored the American squad to a world record and the gold medal in the 4 × 100 meters freestyle relay. Brash to the point of arrogant in Mexico, Spitz put up a much more reserved and modest front in Munich and would only say: "I'm making no predictions. I am still nervous about what happened four years ago."

On the second day of competition he added the 200 meters freestyle title to his collection, again in a new world record. When receiving his medal, Spitz waved his pool-side shoes at the photographers and was accused by the Russians of breaking his amateur status by advertising the manufacturers' trademark. He was cleared by the International Olympic Committee and showed that the incident had not affected his concentration by winning the 100 meters butterfly and the 100 meters free-style and by anchoring the US relay squads to victories in the 4 × 200 meters freestyle and the 4 × 100 meters medley finals. Spitz had spurted to seven golds and with every one of them had come a world record.

With nine Olympic gold medals – including the two from the Mexico Games – Spitz equalled the long-standing record haul by Finland's fabulous Paavo Nurmi. His overall medal haul is 11, nine gold and a silver and bronze won in 1968. He never swum competitively again after the Munich Games and made a great commercial success of his life by unashamedly cashing in on his golden glory in the swimming pool.

The Olympic pool in Munich was boiling with record activity. During the championships there were 30 world and 84 Olympic records broken or equalled. With Spitz leading the way, the United States was the most successful team, with 17 golds from a possible 29.

The Americans celebrated an eighteenth gold medal when Rick DeMont beat Brad Cooper of Australia by a touch in a thrilling 400 meters final. But a dope test on DeMont proved positive and he was disqualified and the gold awarded instead to Cooper. DeMont had taken ephedrine to prevent asthma attacks. This was one of the drugs on the Olympic "banned" list. As further disciplinary action, the distressed 16-year-old DeMont was barred from competing in the 1500 meters freestyle.

Shane Gould, a 15-year-old Australian schoolgirl, made a Spitz-style gold collection in the women's events. She collected three gold medals and three world records in the 200 meters and 400 meters freestyle and in the 200 meters individual medley. Shane finished second in the 800 meters and was a bronze medallist in the 100 meters freestyle. Both these events were won by American women, Keena Rothhammer (800 meters) and Sandra Neilson (100 meters freestyle).

Melissa Belote of the United States took the gold medals in both backstroke events (100 and 200 meters), and Catharine Carr (100 meters breaststroke) and Karen Moe (200 meters butterfly) were also in on the American golden run. The unluckiest American in the water apart from Rick DeMont was Tim McKee, who was beaten to first place in the 400 meters individual medley by just one five-hundredth of a second on the electronic timing. The winner was Sweden's powerful and versatile Gunnar Larsson, who also won the gold in the 200 meters medley.

In the diving, Micki King won the spring-board title for the United States. This was compensation for her painful experience in Mexico when she had seemed certain of a medal until fracturing a bone in her wrist during her fourth dive. Sweden's Ulrike Knape, second to Micki King in the springboard, won the highboard title. In the men's diving, Italian Klaus Dibiasi retained the highboard championship. His team-mate Franco Cagnotto was the bronze medallist and came second in the springboard to the first ever Russian Olympic diving champion, Vladimir Vasin.

There was another first for Russia when it won the water polo by holding favored Hungary to a 3–3 draw in the last match. A win for Hungary would have pushed the Russians back into second place. But this provided nothing like the shock and the drama of Russia's first-time victory in basketball. The United States had won every basketball championship since the sport had been introduced into the Olympics in 1936. They looked on their way to another gold medal success in Munich when two free throws by Kevin Collins put them into a 50–49 lead with just two seconds to go. The umpire restarted the game and two seconds later called a halt. American victory celebrations proved premature because a Russian protest that the game had finished three seconds too early was upheld. After long and bitter argument the game was restarted. Russia had possession and with the last throw of the match Alexander Belov dropped the ball into the basket to give the Russians a sensational 51–50 victory. The Americans held a team meeting and by a unanimous vote decided not to accept

Olga Korbut, a tiny, springy 88lb Russian gymnast, emerged as the darling of the millions of viewers watching the Munich Games on world-wide television. She was 17 but looked 12 and captured everybody's heart with her charm and charisma on the gymnasium floor and apparatus. Olga lacked the elegance of her team-mate Ludmilla Turischeva but won millions of new followers for the sport with her sheer bouncing enthusiasm and pure femininity. She got gold medals for the beam and floor exercises and finished seventh in the overall competition. Ludmilla Turischeva was more consistent and took the overall title with a 0.05 points lead over East German Karin Janz, who although technically close to perfection failed to generate the same excitement as the Russian girls who took the team award.

The men's events, as in Mexico, were monopolized by the Japanese, with Sawao Kato retaining his overall combined exercises gold medal and leading his country to another team championship.

Britain's best moments came in the equestrian events.

Left: Olga Korbut, charm, charisma and elfin elegance in the gymnasium.

their Olympic silver medals in protest.

There was another angry demonstration by the losers at the end of the hockey final. Pakistan, beaten 1–0 by West Germany, argued that the goal should have been disallowed and that they had scored a perfectly good goal that had been ruled out. At the presentation ceremony the Pakistanis showed a total disrespect for the entire proceedings and as a result of their poor sportsmanship were banned from the Olympics for life, with the Pakistan Hockey Federation suspended from all international competition for four years.

Highlight of the boxing finals was the powerful heavyweight performances of Cuban Teofilo Stevenson. Included among his victims on the way through to the final was highly rated American Duane Bobick, who was bombed to defeat in the third round. The superbly built Stevenson won the final without throwing a punch after his Romanian opponent, perhaps wisely, withdrew because of an injury. Stevenson retained his championship in Montreal and would have been a multi-million dollar earner had he been allowed to turn professional. America's only gold medallist in the boxing was Ray Seales at light-welterweight, who later became a world-ranked professional, as did Duane Bobick.

RICHARD MEADE
A HAPPY EVENT FOR BRITAIN'S MASTER HORSEMAN

Riding a superbly trained horse called Laurieston, Britain's master horseman Richard Meade led the United Kingdom team to a second

Richard Meade steers Laurieston towards golden glory in the three-day equestrian event.

successive victory in the equestrian three-day event. It was the first time a team had retained the title since the Netherlands won for a second time in 1928.

Meade, a lieutenant in the Hussars, was Britain's first ever individual equestrian gold medal winner and was quick to give the credit for his success to Derek Allhusen, who had won a silver medal in the same event in 1968. It was Major Allhusen who had bred and trained Meade's mount, Laurieston. This was Meade's third Olympics and his experience shone through as he guided eight-year-old Laurieston to a championship-clinching clear round in the show jumping section of the gruelling competition that is an all-round test for both rider and horse. Combining with Meade in the British team were Mary Gordon-Watson, Bridget Parker and Mark Phillips, who was later to get world attention when he married Princess Anne.

West Germany, including the great Hans Winkler on Torphy, won the grand prix, with Bill Steinkraus leading the United States into second place. Graziano Mancinelli on Ambassador won the individual gold medal after a jump off against Britain's Ann Moore on Psalm and American Neal Shapiro on Sloopy.

Archery was back on the Olympic program for the first time since 1920 and it was 18-year-old American army private John Williams who got stuck right into winning action with a world record score of 2528 points, 47 ahead of Swedish runner-up Gunnar Jervill. The most astonishing aspect of the American soldier's performance was that he accumulated his massive score despite completely missing the target with one arrow that got away. There was a double for America when Doreen Wilbur came from behind to narrowly beat her old rival from Poland, 44-year-old Irene Szydlowka.

Russian Aleksandr Medved proved himself one of the greatest wrestlers of all time when he became the first man in his sport to win gold medals at three successive Olympics. He was freestyle light-heavyweight champion in 1964, heavyweight gold medal winner in 1968 and super-heavyweight champion in Munich. Although rarely weighing more than 230lb, Medved could outmaneuver giant opponents. One of his victims in Munich, for instance, was American Chris Taylor, an immensely strong man who weighed 420lb. However, the strongest man at the Games was unquestionably Russian weightlifter Vasili Alexeev, who set an Olympic record total of $1410\frac{3}{4}$lb (640kg) in the super-heavyweight division.

Possibly the finest all-round sportsman in the Munich Games was Hungarian Andras Balczo, who won the individual gold medal in the modern pentathlon to go with the silver he had collected in Mexico. He also won team golds in 1960 and 1968 and a team silver in Munich.

Russia had an extraordinary run of success in the canoeing championships, taking six of the seven gold medals. East Germany won a medal in each of the seven rowing finals, including three golds. But the outstanding performance came from the New Zealand eight who beat the well-drilled American crew and the East Germans to take the Olympic title for the first time.

Valentin Mankin, who won a rare yachting gold for Russia in the Finn class in 1968, followed this at Munich by winning the Tempest gold. Dane Paul Elvstrom, whose four gold medals in previous Olympics made him a legend in the sport, made an unhappy exit from Munich. Competing in the Soling class, he revealed none of his usual brilliance and quit in a bad temper midway through the regatta and drove off home with his boat on a trailer behind him.

Japan won the men's title in the volleyball and was runner-up to the Russians in the women's event. Perhaps the Japanese coach was too hard on the women. A spectator in Munich started legal proceedings against him for alleged cruelty with his bawling and cajoling tactics!

OLYMPIC FUN AND GAMES

Television commentators were baffled by the identity of the leading rider in the 125 miles road cycling race. It transpired that his name was Batty Flynn, an Irishman who had joined the race with three team-mates after the start. They were making a protest at Ireland's exclusion from the cycling.

olitics and prices threatened to poison the 1976 Games in Montreal. It was politics that led to a mass withdrawal from the Games of the black African countries. Their boycott was a protest of the IOC's refusal to bar New Zealand for allowing a Rugby Union team to tour apartheid-practicing South Africa. However, it was prices that provided the biggest headache for the people of Montreal, who found themselves having to pay increased taxes and rates to help foot a colossal $1.7 billion bill, more than twice the sum originally planned for by Jean Drapeau who as Mayor of Montreal had been mainly responsible for bringing the Games to Canada.

Galloping inflation and industrial disputes had combined to push the cost of the Games to this massive amount. As far back as 1936, former IOC President Avery Brundage had been enough of a visionary to warn of the dangers of "giganticism." Now the Games were growing so big as to be almost beyond control and there was genuine concern among caring people in the Olympic movement for the future of the Games. Clearly, on such a scale, promotion of future Games would be beyond the scope of any but the very richest nations.

But despite the politics, despite the inflationary prices and despite the industrial troubles that meant the main stadium was not quite finished in time for the opening ceremony, the Montreal Games went ahead on schedule and in terms of personalities and performances were as successful and memorable as any of the preceding celebrations. There were nine world and 12 Olympic records set in the track and field, where one of the main talking points was the wipe-out of the American team, which managed

just one solitary individual gold medal on the track. Once again the nation with such a great tradition in sprinting was knocked cold in the explosive events, as had happened in Munich when they were blitzed by rushing Russian Valeri Borzov.

The insistence of the Americans on sticking rigidly to a selection policy based solely on the 1–2–3 finishing order in their Olympic trials meant they went into the 100 meters without their two best sprinters. Steve Williams and Houston McTear failed to make the team because of injury and for the first time since 1928 America did not have a man placed in the first three in the final. Hasely Crawford, a 6ft 1in, 166lb powerhouse, won the first-ever gold medal for Trinidad and Tobago when he beat Jamaican Don Quarrie to the tape by just two hundredths of a second in 10.06 sec. Defending champion Borzov was third in 10.14 sec, exactly the time in which he had won the 100 meters in Munich. American Harvey Glance was a disappointing and disappointed fourth.

Quarrie gained rich consolation for his inches defeat in the 100 meters final by winning the 200 in 20.23 sec, with Americans Millard Hampton and Dwayne Evans second and third. Crawford was just stretching into his full stride in his quest for a double in the final when he pulled up with a painful muscle injury. Borzov declined to defend his 200 meters title because he wanted to save himself for the sprint relay, in which he anchored the Russian team to a bronze medal. Harvey Glance, John Stones, Millard Hampton and Steve Riddick combined to retain the title for the United States in a fast 38.33 sec.

Both the 400 meters and 800 meters gold medals went to an astonishing athlete who became known as "White Lightning."

Instant action replays at the Montreal Olympic stadium. Truly a modern Olympics.

Hasely Crawford (left) and Don Quarrie (below), sprinting gold medallists from the West Indies.

ALBERTO JUANTORENA
A UNIQUE DOUBLE FOR THE MUSCLEMAN FROM CUBA

Born in Santiago, Cuba, on 3 December 1951, Alberto Juantorena first set his sights on becoming a basketball player but at the age of 19 was advised to switch to the track. That was in 1971. Within 18 months he was breaking 46 sec for the 400 meters and just missed qualifying for the 1972 Olympic final by five-hundredths of a second. He won the World Student Games title in 1973 and the following year led the world 400 meters rankings with a time of 44.7 sec.

Juantorena was already looking a golden prospect for Montreal but then had a set-back that knocked him out of the world ratings and also out of people's minds as a threat to the best in the 1976 Games. He went into the hospital for two delicate operations on his foot and for a time it looked doubtful whether he would even make the Cuban team for the Olympics.

The spell in a hospital inspired Juantorena to step up his training program in a search for full fitness, with the result that he was in better shape than ever for the Montreal Games. With a huge stride that meant he could keep up an almost non-stop sprint from gun to tape, the muscular 6ft 3in Cuban made the Montreal crowds gasp with his awesome speed and power.

He had barely any experience of the 800 meters before Olympic year yet he dashed to victory in the final in a world record 1 min

43.5 sec. "The man is just phenomenal," said 1948–52 800 meters champion Mal Whitfield. "You are seeing the future of athletics in Juantorena. He is the first of what will become a whole generation of middle-distance sprinters." Stylish Belgian Ivo van Damme was second to Juantorena, with American champion Rick Wohlhuter (having survived a disqualification for pushing in the preliminary rounds) finishing third.

Juantorena then put his mind and muscle to the 400 meters for a unique double that had been beyond the reach of even great Olympians like Ted Meredith, Arthur Wint and Whitfield. He made a casual, almost sluggish start and at halfway it looked as if American Fred Newhouse was going to win. Then Juantorena stepped on the gas, lengthened his stride and came streaking like "white lightning" off the final bend to win in 44.26 sec, with Newhouse second and his United States team-mate Herman Frazier third.

The giant Cuban had not yet finished astounding the spectators. He ran his eighth race of the Games in the 4 × 400 meters final and took the baton on the anchor leg in seventh place. With an impressive but suicidal burst of speed he chopped back the leaders with a 200 meters time of 20.1 sec. Even he could not maintain such blinding speed and he "died" in the last 100 meters and finally brought Cuba home in seventh place in a race won in 2 min 58.56 sec by the American squad.

Lasse Viren rivalled Juantorena as the star of the Games by becoming the first man in Olympic history to retain both the 5000 and

Lassie Viren wins the 5000 meters from Dick Quax, with Klaus Peter Hildenbrand falling after hurling himself into third place. In a heat, Brendan Foster (leading, right) had set a new Olympic record.

10,000 meters titles. It is an incredible record that some day somebody might equal but it is never likely to be beaten and it puts Viren right up alongside his countryman Paavo Nurmi as the greatest middle-distance runner of all time. What made Viren's feat all the more fantastic was that since his Munich triumph he had been in the hospital for a hamstring operation and had received minor nasal surgery to assist his breathing. His pre-Games form gave no indication that he could win one gold medal, let alone two. But like a true champion he produced his best form where and when it mattered and sprinted away from the field with just over a lap to go in the 10,000 meters to win in 27 min 40.4 sec, with Portugal's courageous Carlos Lopes second and British hope Brendan Foster third.

In the 5000 meters final, Viren fought off a brave challenge in the home stretch from New Zealander Dick Quax to win in 13 min 24.76 sec. West German Klaus Peter Hildenbrand literally threw himself across the finish line to snatch third place from another New Zealander, Rod Dixon. Brendan Foster, who had set an Olympic record of 13 min 20.34 sec in a heat, was weakened by a stomach ailment and did well to come in fifth. The next day Viren went out to try the Zatopek triple of 5000/10,000/marathon but had to be content with a creditable fifth place in the exhausting 26 miles 385 yards race, which was won by East Germany's underrated Waldemar Cierpinski in an Olympic record of 2 hr 9 min 55.0 sec. Defending champion Frank Shorter was second and his American team-mate Don Kardong fourth, three seconds behind bronze medallist Karel Lismont of Belgium.

New Zealand's fine tradition in the 1500 meters was continued by John Walker, the first man to break 3 min 50 sec for the mile. Walker felt a sense of anticlimax after his victory in Montreal in 3 min 39.17 sec. He had been preparing himself both physically and mentally for a continuation of his thrilling duel with Filbert Bayi but the black African boycott put the Tanzanian world record holder at 1500 meters out of the Games. It took the edge off Walker's win but he still looked a worthy successor to two previous New Zealand 1500 meters Olympic champions Jack Lovelock and Peter Snell. As in the 800 meters, Belgian Ivo van Damme was the silver medallist and a few months later the world of athletics mourned the death of this talented runner in a car crash.

America's only individual gold medal winner in the men's track events was a hurdler who switched to his event just four months before the Montreal Games opened.

ED MOSES
THE HURDLER WHO HURTLED TO OLYMPIC FAME

At high school, Ed Moses was a moderate performer. He had never broken 50 sec for the flat quarter and was unable to get under 15 sec in the 110 meters hurdles. But he quickly developed after leaving school, and at the age of 19 in 1975 ran 45.5 sec in a 440 yards relay leg and clocked 14.0 sec for the high hurdles. Wisely, his coach suggested his best event would be

Top: Waldemar Cierpinski has an eager companion on his gold medal-winning marathon journey.
Above: John Walker receives victory with open arms as he beats Belgian Ivo van Damme in a desperate finish to the 1500 meters.

157

400 meters hurdles.

Moses, born at Dayton, Ohio, on 31 August 1955, went to the starting blocks for his first ever competitive 400 meters hurdles race in March 1976 and won in 50.1 sec. On 25 July 1976 he went to the starting blocks in the Olympic final and became the fastest man ever over the 400 meters hurdles with a run of 47.64 sec that took him to victory by the devastating margin of eight meters.

It was the third successive time that the Olympic title in this event had been won in a world record (David Hemery in 48.1 sec in 1968 and John Akii-Bua in 47.82 sec in 1972). Moses used a 13-stride pattern throughout the Montreal final, the first time this had ever been seen in a major race. The tall, bespectacled American black finished 1.05 sec ahead of his team-mate Mike Shrine in second place. There was conjecture as to what would have happened had Akii-Bua not been forced to boycott the Games but nobody could take away the fact that Moses had proved himself fitting to wear the Olympic crown even though, in experience terms, he was still a virtual novice at the event!

As early as 1975, Frenchman Guy Drut forecast that he would win the 110 meters hurdles in a time of 13.28 sec at Montreal. He was proved not only an outstanding champion but also a remarkable prophet when he scissored over the hurdles to win the gold medal in 13.28 sec. The time was later rounded up to 13.3 sec by the timekeepers but the victory proved

Drut's uncanny skill in knowing exactly what was needed to become an Olympic champion in his event, in which he had taken the silver medal in 1972. Veteran American hurdler Willie Davenport, competing in his fourth Olympics, took the bronze medal to go with the gold he had won in 1968. Cuban Alejandro Casanas, who had handed Drut a shock defeat in a pre-Games competition, was second in 13.33 sec.

Sweden's Anders Garderud broke his own world record in the 3000 meters steeplechase after a dramatic incident at the final hurdle. He was being challenged by world junior record holder Frank Baumgartl, who was running way beyond his best performance. The young East German was exhausted as he cleared the final hurdle in pursuit of Garderud and fell flat on his face. Garderud went on to win in 8 min 8.02 sec, with Poland's Bronislaw Malinowski, the European champion, second. Baumgartl bravely pulled himself up and in a semi-conscious state crossed the finish line in the bronze medal position.

Mexico captured their first ever athletics gold medal when Daniel Bautista won the 20 kilometers walk by more than half a minute after breaking the dual challenge of East Germans Hans Reimann and Peter Frenkel, who finished second and third. Bautista dropped to his knees to pray after striding through the tape.

One of the greatest performances in the field events was Russian Viktor Saneyev's third

ling vault of 18ft 0½in (5.50m). Finland's Antti Kalliomaki and American favorite Dave Roberts cleared the same height but had more failures.

The gold medals were shared out between four countries in the throwing events. East German Udo Beyer took the shot put with 69ft 0¾in (21.05m), an effort that third-placed Alexandr Barisnikov of Russia had beaten by 10 inches in the qualifying round. For the first time since 1936 there was not an American in the first three. But Mac Wilkins regained the discus title for the United States with his sixth and final throw of 221ft 5in (67.50m). Russian Yuriy Sedyh led a 1–2–3 sweep for the USSR in the hammer with an Olympic record throw of 254ft 4in (77.52m). Sedyh was coached by 36-year-old Anatoli Bondarchuk, who took the bronze medal to add to his 1972 gold.

In the 1948 Games in London, Imre Nemeth had won the hammer for Hungary. Twenty-eight years later in Montreal his son, Miklos Nemeth, won the javelin for Hungary with a marvellous world record throw of 310ft 4in (94.58m). Nemeth, Jr, had been considered past his best at 29 and was reckoned something of a non-competitor because he had never been able to produce his best form in major tournaments. But he silenced all his critics and delighted his father with his very first throw in the final.

Nobody, however, was left in any doubt that the finest all-round athlete at the Games was Bruce Jenner, a brash, likeable American who won the decathlon with a world record points total of 8618. Jenner, born at Mt Kisco, New York, on 28 October 1949, had been the world's top ranked decathlete for two years and made no secret of the fact that he expected to win the gold medal at Montreal. He finished the first day's action in third place and then unleashed the most devastating second day display ever seen in a decathlon to finish more than 200 points ahead of his nearest rival, Guido Kratschmer of West Germany.

His individual performances in the ten events were, first day: 100 meters (10.94 sec), long jump (23ft 8¼in; 7.22m), shot put (50ft 4¼in; 15.35m), high jump (6ft 8in; 2.03m), 400 meters (47.51 sec); second day: 110 meters hurdles (14.84 sec), discus (164ft 2in; 50.03m), pole vault (15ft 9in; 4.8m), javelin (224ft 9in; 68.5m) and finally a 4 min 29.55 sec 1500 meters run. The mighty-muscled Jenner said later: "As I came off the final bend in the 1500 meters I took a mental picture of everything I could see so that the moment would last with me for a lifetime. There is nobody in the world feeling better than me right now."

successive Olympic gold medal in the triple jump. This is one of the most demanding of all events on an athlete's legs and it was amazing that Saneyev was able to compete in his third Games, let alone win the title for a third time. He won by 4½in from American James Butts with a best effort of 56ft 8¾in (17.29m). Carlos de Oliveira, the world record holder from Brazil, was third.

Arnie Robinson, bronze medallist in Munich when he struggled to get into his stride, was at peak form in the Montreal long jump final and won with a leap of 27ft 4¾in (8.35m). It was his first jump in the final and defending champion Randy Williams could not match it, finishing second with 26ft 7¾in.

High jumper Dwight Stones upset the Canadian hosts by criticizing their organization of the Games. He was booed every time he went to the mark to prepare for his jump and, troubled by the puddle-patched run-up, finally finished third, as he had as an 18-year-old competitor in Munich. In a long, tense and exciting duel, Poland's Jacek Wszola beat Canadian idol Greg Joy for the gold medal with a winning clearance of 7ft 4¾in (2.25m). It was an Olympic record for the 19-year-old Pole but pre-Games favorite Stones bounced back just four days later to increase his own world record to 7ft 7¼in (2.31m).

There was another gold medal for Poland in the perhaps aptly named pole vault. Tadeusz Slusarski won with an Olympic-record-equal-

East Germany dominated the women's track and field. Ruth Fuchs successfully defended her javelin title with an Olympic record throw of 216ft 4in (65.94m). There were eight other East German successes: Barbel Eckhert (200 meters in an Olympic record 22.37 sec), Johanna Schaller (100 meters hurdles), Rosemarie Ackermann (high jump with an Olympic record 6ft 4in/1.93m), Angela Voigt (long jump), Evelin Schlaak (discus with an Olympic record 226ft 4in/68.98m), Siegrun Siegl (pentathlon), plus the two relay titles. They won the 4 × 100 meters relay in an Olympic record 42.55 sec and the 4 × 400 meters in a world record 3 min 19.23 sec. It was the greatest all-round performance by a women's team in Olympic history. For good measure, Renate Stecher (double gold medallist in Munich) took a silver in the 100 meters behind West German Annagret Richter and a bronze in the 200 meters. But there was no question that the queen of the Games on the track was a remarkable Polish athlete.

IRENA SZEWINSKA
A WORLD RECORD FOR THE FIRST LADY OF THE TRACK

Born in Russia and brought up in Poland, Irena Szewinska first came to world notice as an inexperienced 18-year-old competitor in the 1964 Tokyo Olympics. Then competing under her maiden name of Kirszenstein, she collected silver medals in the long jump and 200 meters and a gold with the Polish world record breaking 4 × 100 meters relay squad. In the 1968 Mexico Games, she won the Olympic 200 meters title in a world record 22.5 sec and took the bronze in the 100 meters. She was a mother with a bouncing baby by the time of the 1972 Games in Munich and had to be content with just a bronze medal in the 200 meters.

Irena, born in Leningrad on 24 May 1946, saved the race of her life for Montreal. She gave 12 years and a beating to East German wonder girl Christina Brehmer, 18-year-old world record holder, in the 400 meters final. A winner by a margin of more than 10 meters, Irena went through the tape in 49.29 sec to push her East German rival into second place and also to relieve her of her world record. It was a performance that left track and field experts comparing her with Fanny Blankers-Koen as the first lady of athletics.

Small, thin and anemic-looking, Russian Tatyana Kazankina belied her appearance with two storming runs in the 800 and 1500 meters finals. She sprinted from fifth to first in

Angela Voigt lands the long jump title (right), and her East German team-mates celebrate a world record victory in the 4 × 400 meters relay (below).

the last 50 meters to shatter the world record in the 800 meters with a time of 1 min 54.94 sec. The first four to finish in a rush for the tape were all inside the old world record. Tatyana, better known for her talent over longer distances, was content to sit with the slow-moving field in the 1500 meters final and then peeled off an electrifying last lap of 56.9 sec to complete her golden double in 4 min 5.48 sec.

Bulgarian Ivanka Christova briefly interrupted the East German monopoly in the field events with an Olympic record shot put of 69ft 5in (21.16m) to add a gold medal to the bronze she collected in Munich.

East German women were in an even more dominant mood in the Olympic swimming pool, where they took no less than 11 of the 13 titles. Their leading golden girl was described by Australia's famous coach Don Talbot as "a swimmer years ahead of her time."

KORNELIA ENDER
A FOUR-GOLD SPLASH FOR THE SWIMMER SUPREME

In Munich in 1972, few people took a lot of notice of a 13-year-old East German girl who swam to two silver medals in a Games monopolized by the Spitz blitz. But four years later all eyes were drawn by the girl, Kornelia Ender, as she emerged as a supreme swimmer in the Spitz class.

Brought up in Plauen, East Germany, Kornelia first started taking an interest in swimming when going on holidays to the Baltic with her parents. Her potential was spotted by East German coaches and she was put through a scientific and strenuous training program that helped her develop from holiday splasher to the greatest woman swimmer in the world. She demonstrated her all-round technical proficiency and controlled power in Montreal where she won four gold medals, one more than any other female competitor in Olympic swimming history. Kornelia, 5ft 10in tall and weighing 154lb, set world records in winning the 100 meters freestyle (55.65 sec), 200 meters freestyle (1 min 59.26 sec) and when sharing in the East German triumph in the 4 × 100 meters medley relay. Her fourth gold came in the   meters butterfly with a world-record-equalling 1 min 0.13 sec. She revealed her full qualities when taking the butterfly title and then, just one race later, the 200 meters freestyle by the stunning margin of three meters.

Kornelia gave her East German team-mates what looked like a winning send-off in the last event, the 4 × 100 meters freestyle relay. But

she watched with growing concern as the battling American team (Kim Peyton, Wendy Boglioli, Jill Sterkel and Shirley Babashoff) combined to overhaul the East Germans and win in a world record 3 min 44.82 sec. The disappointed Kornelia threw her swimming cap down in disgust as her fifth medal turned from gold to silver. The gold medal win for the United States was some consolation for their star swimmer, the blonde and beautiful Shirley Babashoff. She collected three individual silver medals in the backwash of the East German mermaids.

Almost in the Ender class were two dual gold medallists in the East German team. Petra Thumer set world records on her way to victory in the 400 and 800 meters freestyle events and Ulrike Richter created new Olympic records when winning the 100 and 200 meters backstroke titles.

In the men's events, the Americans were every bit as dominant as the East German women. They won 12 of the 13 gold medals and

Kornelia Ender (above, right) learns she has just broken the world 100 meters freestyle record after beating her team-mate Petra Griemer into second place.

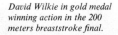

David Wilkie in gold medal winning action in the 200 meters breaststroke final.

the only one that got away was won by an American-trained swimmer in David Wilkie, a Scotsman who took the 200 meters breaststroke with a marvellous world record swim of 2 min 15.11 sec. Wilkie had driven American John Hencken to a world record in the 100 meters breaststroke (1 min 3.11 sec) and Hencken was leading in the 200 meters until Wilkie poured on the power for a finishing burst that took him to a revenge victory over his old rival.

John Naber, a third year student of psychology at the University of Southern California, led the American gold rush. He won both backstroke events, shared in the medley and freestyle relay triumphs and collected a silver medal in the 200 meters freestyle. American swimmers took 27 of the possible 35 medals and world records were set in every event apart from the 100 meters butterfly. Brian Goodell won two individual freestyle gold medals, winning both the 400 and 1500 meters events in world record times.

Jennifer Chandler and Phil Boggs won the springboard diving titles for America. Elena Vaytsekhovskaia of Russia took the women's highboard, with the men's event going to a legendary figure in the diving world.

KLAUS DIBIASI
HE DIVES INTO OLYMPIC HISTORY

When he was 17, Klaus Dibiasi won the highboard silver medal in the Tokyo Olympics of 1964. The inhabitants of his hometown in Bolzano, Italy, encouraged him by building an indoor tank so that he could train all year round. Dibiasi, born in Austria on 6 October 1947, of Italian parents, paid them back by winning the gold medal in the 1968 highboard diving championship and the silver in the springboard event. Four years later in Munich he retained his highboard title.

In Montreal he achieved the first ever diving triple by winning his third successive highboard crown. To do it, the 28-year-old veteran had to overcome the handicap of tendonitis of both heels. He was in danger of being beaten by Californian Greg Louganis until his fifth of six dives, when he produced a stunning triple twist with one and a half somersaults. It was the dive of a great fighting champion and put him into the lead and on the way to his unique hat-trick.

There was sheer perfection in the gymnasium where Nadia Comaneci, a 14-year-old Romanian schoolgirl, took over from Olga Korbut as the darling of millions of television viewers. She lacked the elf-like charm of Olga but was a more stylish and composed gymnast, as she proved when receiving maximum points for her performances on the beam and uneven parallel bars. They were the first perfect scores in Olympic history and overshadowed Russia's victory in the team event.

Nadia was the all-round women's champion as well as collecting two individual golds and a team silver. Nelli Kim was the most successful of the Russians, with golds for the horse and floor exercises, a silver in the all-round competition and a team gold.

The nerveless Nikolai Andrianov, a contender for the title of the greatest male gymnast of all time, took gold medals in the floor exercises, on the rings and in the vault as well as for being the all-round champion, but he could not lift the Russian team past the Japanese for the team gold.

There was a revival by the American boxers who had their most successful Olympics since 1952, with five champions: Leo Randolph (flyweight), Howard Davis (lightweight), Ray Leonard (light-welterweight), Mike Spinks (middleweight) and his brother Leon Spinks (light-heavyweight), who later went on to become brief holder of the world professional heavyweight title after a shock points win over

Nadia Comaneci – sheer perfection on the uneven parallel bars.

through Edmund Coffin and John Plumb. Richard Meade rode his fourth clear cross-country round in four Olympics for Great Britain but his team colleagues were overtaken by a succession of accidents including a fall by Princess Anne on Goodwill. Winners of the gold medal in the previous two Olympics, the British were this time eliminated.

Alwin Shockemoehle rode a succession of clear rounds, including one during a thunderstorm, for a magnificent individual victory in the grand prix on Warwick. But he could not quite repeat his untouchable form in the team grand prix when a clear round would have won the championship for West Germany and a sixth gold medal for the incredible Hans Winkler. Warwick failed to clear the final double and the title went to France, with West Germany in second place.

East Germany, winners of a medal in every event in the rowing championships in Munich,

Left: Jim Fox riding for the British team that won the modern pentathlon.
Below: Endo Sumio proved he was not short on judo talent when beating the giant North Korean Jong Gil Pak (No 114) in this heavyweight bout.

Muhammad Ali.

As at Munich, the most intimidating sight in the boxing ring was that of Cuban heavyweight Teofilo Stevenson knocking opponents over with his mighty right hand. On his way to retaining the championship, Stevenson destroyed American challenger John Tate in one round and won an untidy final by suddenly exploding his right on the chin of Romanian Mircea Simon in the last minute after the referee had called for more action. After he had won in Munich, Stevenson – then 20 – was said to be worth two million dollars as a professional. By the time he won in Montreal, those estimates had gone up to ten million. But Stevenson, no doubt with the persuasion of the Castro government to help him in his decision making, elected to stay in the amateur ranks and looked forward to completing a hat-trick of wins in Moscow.

The modern pentathlon, usually one of the lesser publicized Olympic events, made world headlines when Russian Boris Onischenko was disqualified for "bugging" his épée so that it registered a hit in the fencing duels even when he failed to connect. Great Britain's unrated team pulled off a shock gold medal victory. It was a great and well-deserved triumph for 34-year-old Jim Fox, who was competing in his fourth and final Olympics. Adrian Parker and Danny Nightingale were his young teammates, who are expected to make Great Britain a force again in the Moscow Games.

In the three-day event in the equestrian sports, the United States team was in magnificent form and took the team title and also the gold and silver medals in the individual section

Roman Dmitriev, Russian silver medallist in the freestyle wrestling, topples American Willie Rosado with a leg lock as he defends the light-flyweight title he won in Munich.

were again well in control in Montreal, where they took five gold medals in eight finals. For the first time there were women's events and again it was the East Germans who had a monopoly, taking five of the seven golds.

Japan was, as expected, the most successful nation in the judo, winning three gold medals, a silver and a bronze. But its supremacy was far from total and the Russians showed they were an emerging power in the sport by taking three golds.

The massive Russian weightlifter Vasili Alexeev, who had been unbeaten since 1970, retained his Olympic superheavyweight title with a record lift of 444.0kg. Few people would care to argue with the claim that the 350lb Alexeev is the strongest man in the world.

Russia was the dominant nation in both the freestyle and Greco-Roman wrestling, cap-

turing 12 of the 20 gold medals. John Peterson was America's only successful wrestler, winning the freestyle middleweight title. His brother, Ben, was runner-up in the light-heavyweight category.

The United States wiped away the memory of its disputed defeat in the 1972 Munich basketball final when it regained the championship in Montreal with a convincing 95–74 victory over Yugoslavia in the final. Superbly coached by Dean Smith, the Americans swamped the Yugoslavs with fine team play and great individual shooting, particularly by Adrian Dantley, who was top scorer in the final with 30 points. The Yugoslavs had been shock semi-final winners against Russia, so robbing America of the revenge chance they had been waiting for since 1972.

There was some consolation for Russia when their women, including seven-footer Iuliyaka Semenova, took the first women's Olympic basketball title. They won all five of their matches in a competition decided on a league basis. The United States was runner-up.

New Zealand beat Australia 1–0 in the most unexpected final of all in the hockey, where for the first time neither India nor Pakistan was involved. Pakistan was bronze medallist.

Luann Ryon, a 23-year-old student who took a year off from college to prepare for the Montreal archery tournament, retained the women's title for the United States. Darell Pace, a computer expert, made it a golden double by winning the men's championship. Both won with Olympic record scores.

OLYMPIC FUN AND GAMES

Two British yachtsmen Alan Warren and David Hunt – noted for their zany and sometimes eccentric humor – went overboard with their jokes. They posed as naval officers working on behalf of the Queen and "screened" the Canadian police who had been appointed as Her Majesty's bodyguards. But they saved their biggest laugh for the actual competition. They were so disillusioned after their Tempest class yacht, Gift 'Orse, had broken down for the third time that they set light to it and sat in a dinghy watching it burn until a coastguard cutter rammed it and sent it to the bottom of Lake Ontario. Hunt, crewman to Warren, told astonished pressmen: "My skipper is lacking in style. I told him his place as captain was with the ship but he refused to go down with it."

Opposite: John Akii-Bua conveys the feeling every Olympic champion has for that gold medal winning moment. He was the 400 meters hurdles winner in Munich.

OLYMPIC RESULTS

The following tables list all the Olympic champions in the events that are still part of the Games program.

ARCHERY — MEN

Event not held until 1972		
1972	John Williams *US*	2,528pts
1976	Darrell Pace *US*	2,571pts
1980		

Hasely Crawford, 1976 100 meters champion.

ARCHERY — WOMEN

Event not held until 1972		
1972	Doreen Wilber *US*	2,424pts
1976	Luann Ryon *US*	2,499pts
1980		

ATHLETICS 100 Meters — MEN

1896	Thomas Burke *US*	12.0 s
1900	Frank Jarvis *US*	11.0 s
1904	Archie Hahn *US*	11.0 s
1908	Reginald Walker *SAF*	10.8 s
1912	Ralph Craig *US*	10.8 s
1920	Charles Paddock *US*	10.8 s
1924	Harold Abrahams *GB*	10.6 s
1928	Percy Williams *CAN*	10.8 s
1932	Eddie Tolan *US*	10.3 s
1936	Jesse Owens *US*	10.3 s
1948	W. Harrison Dillard *US*	10.3 s
1952	Lindy Remigino *US*	10.4 s
1956	Bobby Morrow *US*	10.5 s
1960	Armin Hary *GER*	10.2 s
1964	Robert Hayes *US*	10.0 s
1968	James Hines *US*	*09.9 s
1972	Valeri Borzov *USSR*	10.14s
1976	Hasely Crawford *TRI*	10.06s
1980		

ATHLETICS 200 Meters	MEN
1896 Event not held	
1900 J. Walter Tewksbury *US*	22.2 s
1904 Archie Hahn *US*	21.6 s
1908 Robert Kerr *CAN*	22.6 s
1912 Ralph Craig *US*	21.7 s
1920 Allen Woodring *US*	22.0 s
1924 Jackson Scholz *US*	21.6 s
1928 Percy Williams *CAN*	21.8 s
1932 Eddie Tolan *US*	21.2 s
1936 Jesse Owens *US*	20.7 s
1948 Melvin Patton *US*	21.1 s
1952 Andy Stanfield *US*	20.7 s
1956 Bobby Morrow *US*	20.6 s
1960 Livio Berutti *ITA*	20.5 s
1964 Henry Carr *US*	20.3 s
1968 Tommie Smith *US*	*19.8 s
1972 Valeri Borzov *USSR*	20.0 s
1976 Don Quarrie *JAM*	20.23s
1980	

ATHLETICS 400 Meters	MEN
1896 Thomas Burke *US*	54.2 s
1900 Maxwell Long *US*	49.4 s
1904 Harry Hillman *US*	49.2 s
1908 Wyndham Halswelle *GB*	50.0 s
1912 Charles Reidpath *US*	48.2 s
1920 Bevil Rudd *SAF*	49.6 s
1924 Eric Liddell *GB*	47.6 s
1928 Raymond Barbuti *US*	47.8 s
1932 William Carr *US*	46.2 s
1936 Archie Williams *US*	46.5 s
1948 Arthur Wint *JAM*	46.2 s
1952 George Rhoden *JAM*	45.9 s
1956 Charles Jenkins *US*	46.7 s
1960 Otis Davis *US*	44.9 s
1964 Michael Larrabee *US*	45.1 s

1968 Lee Evans *US*	*43.8 s
1972 Vincent Matthews *US*	44.66s
1976 Alberto Juantorena *CUB*	44.26s
1980	

ATHLETICS 800 Meters	MEN
1896 Edwin Flack *AUS*	2min 11.0s
1900 Alfred Tysoe *GB*	2min 01.2s
1904 James Lightbody *US*	1min 56.0s
1908 Melvin Sheppard *US*	1min 52.8s
1912 James Meredith *US*	1min 51.9s
1920 Albert Hill *GB*	1min 53.4s
1924 Douglas Lowe *GB*	1min 52.4s
1928 Douglas Lowe *GB*	1min 51.8s
1932 Thomas Hampson *GB*	1min 49.8s
1936 John Woodruff *US*	1min 52.9s
1948 Malvin Whitfield *US*	1min 49.2s
1952 Malvin Whitfield *US*	1min 49.2s
1956 Thomas Courtney *US*	1min 47.7s
1960 Peter Snell *NZ*	1min 46.3s
1964 Peter Snell *NZ*	1min 45.1s
1968 Ralph Doubell *AUS*	1min 44.3s
1972 David Wottle *US*	1min 45.9s
1976 Alberto Juantorena *CUB*	*1min 43.5s
1980	

ATHLETICS 1500 Meters	MEN
1896 Edwin Flack *AUS*	4min 33.2 s
1900 Charles Bennett *GB*	4min 6.2 s
1904 James Lightbody *US*	4min 5.4 s
1908 Melvin Sheppard *US*	4min 3.4 s
1912 Arnold Jackson *GB*	3min 56.8 s
1920 Albert Hill *GB*	4min 01.8 s
1924 Paavo Nurmi *FIN*	3min 53.6 s
1928 Harri Larva *FIN*	3min 53.2 s
1932 Luigi Beccali *ITA*	3min 51.2 s
1936 John Lovelock *NZ*	3min 47.8 s

167

1948 Henry Eriksson *SWE*	3min 49.8 s
1952 Josef Barthel *LUX*	3min 45.1 s
1956 Ron Delany *EIR*	3min 41.2 s
1960 Herbert Elliot *AUS*	3min 35.6 s
1964 Peter Snell *NZ*	3min 38.1 s
1968 Kipchoge Keino *KEN*	*3min 34.9 s
1972 Pekka Vasala *FIN*	3min 36.3 s
1976 John Walker *NZ*	3min 39.17s
1980	

1948 Emil Zatopek *CZECH*	29min 59.6 s
1952 Emil Zatopek *CZECH*	29min 17.0 s
1956 Vladmir Kuts *USSR*	28min 45.6 s
1960 Pytor Bolotnikov *USSR*	28min 32.2 s
1964 William Mills *US*	28min 24.4 s
1968 Naftali Temu *KEN*	29min 27.4 s
1972 Lasse Viren *FIN*	*27min 38.4 s
1976 Lasse Viren *FIN*	27min 40.38s
1980	

ATHLETICS 5000 Meters   MEN

Event not held until 1912	
1912 Hannes Kolehmainen *FIN*	14min 36.6 s
1920 Joseph Guillemot *FR*	14min 55.6 s
1924 Paavo Nurmi *FIN*	14min 31.2 s
1928 Ville Ritola *FIN*	14min 38.0 s
1932 Lauri Lehtinen *FIN*	14min 30.0 s
1936 Gunnar Hockert *FIN*	14min 22.2 s
1948 Gaston Reiff *BEL*	14min 17.6 s
1952 Emil Zatopek *CZECH*	14min 06.6 s
1956 Vladmir Kuts *USSR*	13min 39.6 s
1960 Murray Halberg *NZ*	13min 43.4 s
1964 Robert Schul *US*	13min 48.8 s
1968 Mohamed Gammoudi *TUN*	14min 05.0 s
1972 Lasse Viren *FIN*	13min 26.4 s
1976 Lasse Viren *FIN*	†13min 24.76s
1980	

Lee Calhoun, 1956 and 1960 110 meters hurdles champion.

† Brendan Foster (*GB*) achieved Olympic record of 13min 20.34s in heat.

ATHLETICS 10,000 Meters   MEN

Event not held until 1912	
1912 Hannes Kolehmainen *FIN*	31min 20.8 s
1920 Paavo Nurmi *FIN*	31min 45.8 s
1924 Ville Ritola *FIN*	30min 23.2 s
1928 Paavo Nurmi *FIN*	30min 18.8 s
1932 Janusz Kusocinski *POL*	30min 11.4 s
1936 Ilmari Salminen *FIN*	30min 15.4 s

ATHLETICS 110 Meters Hurdles†   MEN

1896 Thomas Curtis *US*	17.6 s
1900 Alvin Kraenzlein *US*	15.4 s
1904 Fred Schule *US*	16.0 s
1908 Forrest Smithson *US*	15.0 s
1912 Fred Kelly *US*	15.1 s
1920 Earl Thomson *CAN*	14.8 s
1924 Daniel Kinsey *US*	15.0 s
1928 Sydney Atkinson *SAF*	14.8 s
1932 George Saling *US*	14.6 s
1936 Forrest Towns *US*	14.2 s
1948 William Porter *US*	13.9 s
1952 W. Harrison Dillard *US*	13.7 s
1956 Lee Calhoun *US*	13.5 s
1960 Lee Calhoun *US*	13.8 s
1964 Hayes Jones *US*	13.6 s
1968 Willie Davenport *US*	13.3 s
1972 Rodney Milburn *US*	*13.24s
1976 Guy Drut *FR*	13.3 s
1980	

†The distance was 100m in 1896.

ATHLETICS 400 Meters Hurdles   MEN

1896 Event not held	
1900 J. Walter Tewksbury *US*	57.6 s
1904 Harry Hillman *US*	53.0 s
1908 Charles Bacon *US*	55.0 s
1912 Event not held	

1920	Frank Loomis	US	54.0 s
1924	F. Morgan Taylor	US	52.6 s
1928	Lord Burghley	GB	53.4 s
1932	Robert Tisdall	EIR	51.7 s
1936	Glenn Hardin	US	52.4 s
1948	Roy Cochran	US	51.1 s
1952	Charles Moore	US	50.8 s
1956	Glenn Davis	US	50.1 s
1960	Glenn Davis	US	49.3 s
1964	R. Warren Cawley	US	49.6 s
1968	David Hemery	GB	48.1 s
1972	John Akii-Bua	UGA	47.82s
1976	Edwin Moses	US	*47.64s
1980			

ATHLETICS 3000 Meters Steeplechase†   MEN

1896	Event not held		
1900	George Orton	US	7min 34.4 s
1904	James Lightbody	US	7min 39.6 s
1908	Arthur Russell	GB	10min 47.8 s
1912	Event not held		
1920	Percy Hodge	GB	10min 00.4 s
1924	Ville Ritola	FIN	9min 33.6 s
1928	Toivo Loukola	FIN	9min 21.8 s
1932	Volmari Iso-Hollo	FIN	10min 33.4 s
1936	Volmari Iso-Hollo	FIN	9min 3.8 s
1948	Tore Sjostrand	SWE	9min 4.6 s
1952	Horace Ashenfelter	US	8min 45.4 s
1956	Christopher Brasher	GB	8min 41.2 s
1960	Zdzislaw Krzyszkowiak	POL	8min 34.2 s
1964	Gaston Roelants	BEL	8min 30.8 s
1968	Amos Biwott	KEN	8min 51.0 s
1972	Kipchoge Keino	KEN	8min 23.6 s
1976	Anders Garderud	SWE	*8min 08.02s
1980			

†The distance was 2500m in 1900 and 1904, 3200m in 1908, and 3460m in 1932, when an extra lap was run due to an official's error.

ATHLETICS Marathon (42,195 Meters)†   MEN

1896	Spyridon Louis	GR	2h 58min 50.0s
1900	Michel Theato	FR	2h 59min 45.0s
1904	Thomas Hicks	US	3h 28min 53.0s
1908	John Hayes	US	2h 55min 18.4s
1912	Kenneth McArthur	SAF	2h 36min 54.8s
1920	Hannes Kolehmainen	FIN	2h 32min 35.8s
1924	Albin Stenroos	FIN	2h 41min 22.6s
1928	M. El Ouafi	FR	2h 32min 57.0s
1932	Juan Carlos Zabala	ARG	2h 31min 36.0s
1936	Kitei Son	JAP	2h 29min 19.2s
1948	Delfo Cabrera	ARG	2h 34min 51.6s
1952	Emil Zatopek	CZECH	2h 23min 03.2s
1956	Alain Mimoun	FR	2h 25min
1960	Abebe Bikila	ETH	2h 15min 16.2s
1964	Abebe Bikila	ETH	2h 12min 11.2s
1968	Mamo Wolde	ETH	2h 20min 26.4s
1972	Frank Shorter	US	2h 12min 19.8s
1976	Waldemar Cierpinski	GDR	*2h 9min 55.0s
1980			

†The distance of 42,195m was established in 1908 and retained since 1924. In other years the distance has varied.

ATHLETICS 4 × 100 Meters Relay   MEN

	Event not held until 1912	
1912	Great Britain	42.4 s
1920	United States of America	42.2 s
1924	United States of America	41.0 s
1928	United States of America	41.0 s
1932	United States of America	40.0 s
1936	United States of America	39.8 s
1948	United States of America	40.6 s
1952	United States of America	40.1 s
1956	United States of America	39.5 s
1960	Germany	39.5 s
1964	United States of America	39.0 s
1968	United States of America	38.2 s
1972	United States of America	*38.19s
1976	United States of America	38.33s

Jacek Wszola, 1976 high jump champion.

1980		

ATHLETICS 4 × 400 Meters Relay		MEN
	Event not held until 1912	
1912	United States of America	3min 16.6 s
1920	Great Britain	3min 22.2 s
1924	United States of America	3min 16.0 s
1928	United States of America	3min 14.2 s
1932	United States of America	3min 08.2 s
1936	Great Britain	3min 09.0 s
1948	United States of America	3min 10.4 s
1952	Jamaica	3min 03.9 s
1956	United States of America	3min 04.8 s
1960	United States of America	3min 02.2 s
1964	United States of America	3min 00.7 s
1968	United States of America	*2min 56.1 s
1972	Kenya	2min 59.8 s
1976	United States of America	2min 58.56s
1980		

ATHLETICS 20 Kilometers Walk		MEN
	Event not held until 1956	
1956	Leonid Spirin *USSR*	1h 31min 27.4s
1960	Vladimir Golubnichi *USSR*	1h 34min 07.2s
1964	Kenneth Matthews *GB*	1h 29min 34.0s
1968	Vladimir Golubnichi *USSR*	1h 33min 58.4s
1972	Peter Frenkel *GDR*	1h 26min 42.4s
1976	Daniel Bautista *MEX*	*1h 24min 40.6s
1980		

ATHLETICS 50 Kilometers Walk		MEN
	Event not held until 1932	
1932	Thomas Green *GB*	4h 50min 10.0s
1936	Harold Whitlock *GB*	4h 30min 41.1s
1948	John Ljunggren *SWE*	4h 41min 52.0s
1952	Giuseppe Bordoni *ITA*	4h 28min 07.8s
1956	Norman Read *NZ*	4h 30min 42.8s
1960	Don Thompson *GB*	4h 25min 30.0s
1964	Abdon Pamich *ITA*	4h 11min 12.4s
1968	Christoph Hohne *GDR*	4h 20min 13.6s
1972	Bern Kannenberg *GER*	*3h 56min 11.6s
1976	Event not held	
1980		

ATHLETICS High Jump		MEN
1896	Ellery Clark *US*	1.81m 5ft 11¼in
1900	Irving Baxter *US*	1.90m 6ft 2¾in
1904	Samuel Jones *US*	1.80m 5ft 11 in
1908	Harry Porter *US*	1.90m 6ft 3 in
1912	Alma Richards *US*	1.93m 6ft 4 in
1920	Richmond Landon *US*	1.94m 6ft 4⅜in
1924	Harold Osborn *US*	1.98m 6ft 6 in
1928	Robert King *US*	1.94m 6ft 4⅜in
1932	Duncan McNaughton *CAN*	1.97m 6ft 5½in
1936	Cornelius Johnson *US*	2.03m 6ft 7⅞in
1948	John Winter *AUS*	1.98m 6ft 6 in
1952	Walter Davis *US*	2.04m 6ft 8⅜in
1956	Charles Dumas *US*	2.12m 6ft 11½in
1960	Robert Shavlakadze *USSR*	2.16m 7ft 1⅛in
1964	Valeri Brumel *USSR*	2.18m 7ft 1¾in
1968	Richard Fosbury *US*	2.24m 7ft 4¼in
1972	Yuri Tarmak *USSR*	2.23m 7ft 3¾in
1976	Jacek Wszola *POL*	2.25m *7ft 4¾in
1980		

ATHLETICS Long Jump		MEN
1896	Ellery Clark *US*	6.35m 20ft 10 in
1900	Alvin Kraenzlein *US*	7.185m 23ft. 6¾in
1904	Myer Prinstein *US*	7.34m 24ft 1 in
1908	Frank Irons *US*	7.48m 24ft 6½in
1912	Albert Gutterson *US*	7.60m 24ft 11¼in
1920	William Pettersson *SWE*	7.15m 23ft 5½in
1924	William De Hart Hubbard *US*	7.44m 24ft 5 in
1928	Edward Hamm *US*	7.73m 25ft 4½in

1932 Edward Gordon *US*	7.64m 25ft 0¾in	
1936 Jesse Owens *US*	8.06m 26ft 5¼in	
1948 Willie Steele *US*	7.82m 25ft 8 in	
1952 Jerome Biffle *US*	7.57m 24ft 10 in	
1956 Gregory Bell *US*	7.83m 25ft 8¼in	
1960 Ralph Boston *US*	8.12m 26ft 7¾in	
1964 Lynn Davies *GB*	8.07m 26ft 5¾in	
1968 Robert Beamon *US*	8.90m *29ft 2½in	
1972 Randy Williams *US*	8.24m 27ft 0½in	
1976 Arnie Robinson *US*	8.35m 27ft 4¾in	
1980		

ATHLETICS Triple Jump   MEN

1896 James Connolly *US*	13.71m 44ft 11¾in
1900 Myer Prinstein *US*	14.47m 47ft 5¾in
1904 Myer Prinstein *US*	14.35m 47ft 1 in
1908 Timothy Ahearne *GB*	14.91m 48ft 11¼in
1912 Gustaf Lindblom *SWE*	14.76m 48ft 5 in
1920 Vilho Tuulos *FIN*	14.50m 47ft 7 in
1924 Anthony Winter *AUS*	15.52m 50ft 11¼in
1928 Mikio Oda *JAP*	15.21m 49ft 10¾in
1932 Chuhei Nambu *JAP*	15.72m 51ft 7 in
1936 Naoto Tajima *JAP*	16.00m 52ft 6 in
1948 Arne Ahman *SWE*	15.40m 50ft 6¼in
1952 Adhemar Ferreira da Silva *BRA*	16.22m 53ft 2½in
1956 Adhemar Ferreira da Silva *BRA*	16.35m 53ft 7¾in
1960 Jozef Szmidt *POL*	16.81m 55ft 1¾in
1964 Jozef Szmidt *POL*	16.85m 55ft 3½in
1968 Viktor Saneyev *USSR*	17.39m *57ft 0¾in
1972 Viktor Saneyev *USSR*	17.35m 56ft 11¼in
1976 Viktor Saneyev *USSR*	17.29m 56ft 8¾in
1980	

ATHLETICS Pole Vault   MEN

1896 William Hoyt *US*	3.30m 10ft 10 in
1900 Irving Baxter *US*	3.30m 10ft 10 in
1904 Charles Dvorak *US*	3.50m 11ft 6 in

1908 A. Gilbert and E. Cooke *US*	3.71m 12ft 2 in
1912 Henry Babcock *US*	3.95m 12ft 11½in
1920 Frank Foss *US*	4.09m 13ft 5 in
1924 Lee Barnes *US*	3.95m 12ft 11½in
1928 Sabin Carr *US*	4.20m 13ft 9¼in
1932 William Miller *US*	4.32m 14ft 1⅞in
1936 Earle Meadows *US*	4.35m 14ft 3¼in
1948 O. Guinn Smith *US*	4.30m 14ft 1¼in
1952 Robert Richards *US*	4.55m 14ft 11¼in
1956 Robert Richards *US*	4.56m 14ft 11½in
1960 Donald Bragg *US*	4.70m 15ft 5 in
1964 Fred Hansen *US*	5.10m 16ft 8¾in
1968 Robert Seagren *US*	5.40m 17ft 8½in
1972 Wolfgang Nordwig *GDR*	5.50m *18ft 0½in
1976 Tadeusz Slusarski *POL*	5.50m *18ft 0½in
1980	

ATHLETICS Shot Put   MEN

1896 Robert Garrett *US*	11.22m 36ft 9¾in
1900 Richard Sheldon *US*	14.10m 46ft 3 in
1904 Ralph Rose *US*	14.81m 48ft 7 in
1908 Ralph Rose *US*	14.21m 46ft 7½in
1912 Patrick McDonald *US*	15.34m 50ft 4 in
1920 Ville Porhola *FIN*	14.81m 48ft 7 in
1924 L. Clarence Houser *US*	14.99m 49ft 2½in
1928 John Kuck *US*	15.87m 52ft 0¾in
1932 Leo Sexton *US*	16.01m 52ft 6⅛in
1936 Hans Wollke *GER*	16.20m 53ft 1¾in
1948 Wilbur Thompson *US*	17.12m 56ft 2 in
1952 W. Parry O'Brien *US*	17.41m 57ft 1½in
1956 W. Parry O'Brien *US*	18.57m 60ft 11¼in
1960 William Nieder *US*	19.68m 64ft 6¾in
1964 Dallas Long *US*	20.33m 66ft 8½in
1968 Randy Matson *US*	20.54m 67ft 4¾in
1972 Wladyslaw Komar *POL*	21.18m *69ft 6 in
1976 Udo Beyer *GDR*	21.05m 69ft 0¾in
1980	

171

John Flanagan, 1900, 1904 and 1908 hammer-throwing champion.

ATHLETICS Discus Throw	MEN
1896 Robert Garrett *US*	29.15m 95ft 7¾in
1900 Rudolph Bauer *HUN*	36.04m 118ft 3 in
1904 Martin Sheridan *US*	39.28m 128ft 10½in
1908 Martin Sheridan *US*	40.89m 134ft 2 in
1912 Armas Taipale *FIN*	45.21m 148ft 4 in
1920 Elmer Niklander *FIN*	44.69m 146ft 7½in
1924 L. Clarence Houser *US*	46.16m 151ft 5 in
1928 L. Clarence Houser *US*	47.32m 155ft 3 in
1932 John Anderson *US*	49.49m 162ft 4½in
1936 Kenneth Carpenter *US*	50.48m 165ft 7½in
1948 Adolfo Consolini *ITA*	52.78m 172ft 2 in
1952 Sim Iness *US*	55.03m 180ft 6½in
1956 Alfred Oerter *US*	56.36m 184ft 11 in
1960 Alfred Oerter *US*	59.18m 194ft 1¾in
1964 Alfred Oerter *US*	61.00m 200ft 1½in
1968 Alfred Oerter *US*	64.78m 212ft 6½in
1972 Ludvik Danek *CZECH*	64.40m 211ft 3 in
1976 Mac Wilkins *US*	67.50m *221ft 5 in
1980	

ATHLETICS Hammer Throw	MEN
1896 Event not held	
1900 John Flanagan *US*	49.73m 163ft 2 in
1904 John Flanagan *US*	51.23m 168ft 1 in
1908 John Flanagan *US*	51.92m 170ft 4½in
1912 Matthew McGrath *US*	54.74m 179ft 7 in
1920 Patrick Ryan *US*	52.88m 173ft 5½in
1924 Fred Tootell *US*	53.30m 174ft 10 in
1928 Patrick O'Callaghan *EIR*	51.39m 168ft 7 in
1932 Patrick O'Callaghan *EIR*	53.92m 176ft 11 in
1936 Karl Hein *GER*	56.49m 185ft 4 in
1948 Imre Nemeth *HUN*	56.07m 183ft 11½in
1952 Jozsef Csermak *HUN*	60.34m 197ft 11½in
1956 Harold Connolly *US*	63.19m 207ft 3½in
1960 Vasili Rudenkov *USSR*	67.10m 220ft 1¾in
1964 Romuald Klim *USSR*	69.74m 228ft 10 in
1968 Gyula Zsivotzky *HUN*	73.36m 240ft 8 in
1972 Anatoli Bondarchuk *USSR*	75.50m 247ft 8 in
1976 Yuri Sedyh *USSR*	77.52m *254ft 4 in
1980	

ATHLETICS Javelin Throw	MEN
Event not held until 1908	
1908 Erik Lemming *SWE*	54.83m 179ft 10½in
1912 Erik Lemming *SWE*	60.64m 198ft 11½in
1920 Jonni Myyra *FIN*	65.78m 215ft 9½in
1924 Jonni Myyra *FIN*	62.96m 206ft 6½in
1928 Erik Lundkvist *SWE*	66.60m 218ft 6 in
1932 Matti Jaervinen *FIN*	72.71m 238ft 6½in
1936 Gerhard Stock *GER*	71.84m 235ft 8½in
1948 Tapio Rautavaara *FIN*	69.77m 228ft 11 in
1952 Cyrus Young *US*	73.78m 242ft 0½in
1956 Egil Danielsen	85.71m 281ft 2½in
1960 Viktor Tsibulenko *USSR*	84.64m 277ft 8¼in
1964 Pauli Nevala *FIN*	82.66m 271ft 2 in
1968 Janis Lusis *USSR*	90.10m 295ft 7 in
1972 Klaus Wolfermann *GER*	90.48m 296ft 10 in
1976 Miklos Nemeth *HUN*	94.58m *310ft 4 in
1980	

ATHLETICS Decathlon	MEN
Event not held until 1912	
1912 Hugo Wieslander *SWE*	6,162pts
1920 Helge Lovland *NOR*	5,970pts
1924 Harold Osborn *US*	6,668pts
1928 Paavo Yrjola *FIN*	6,770pts
1932 James Bausch *US*	6,896pts
1936 Glenn Morris *US*	7,421pts
1948 Robert Mathias *US*	6,326pts
1952 Robert Mathias *US*	7,731pts
1956 Milton Campbell *US*	7,708pts
1960 Rafer Johnson *US*	8,001pts
1964 Willi Holdorf *GER*	7,887pts

1968 William Toomey *US*	8,193pts	
1972 Nikolai Avilov *USSR*	8,454pts	
1976 Bruce Jenner *US*	*8,618pts	
1980		

ATHLETICS 100 Meters   WOMEN

Event not held until 1928	
1928 Elizabeth Robinson *US*	12.2 s
1932 Stanislawa Walasiewicz *POL*	11.9 s
1936 Helen Stephens *US*	11.5 s
1948 Francina Blankers-Koen *NETH*	11.9 s
1952 Marjorie Jackson *AUS*	11.5 s
1956 Betty Cuthbert *AUS*	11.5 s
1960 Wilma Rudolph *US*	†11.0 s
1964 Wyomia Tyus *US*	11.4 s
1968 Wyomia Tyus *US*	11.0 s
1972 Renate Stecher *GDR*	11.07s
1976 Annagret Richter *GER*	‡11.08s
1980	

† Final wind assisted
‡ Set world record of 11.01s in semi-finals

ATHLETICS 200 Meters   WOMEN

Event not held until 1948	
1948 Francina Blankers-Koen *NETH*	24.4 s
1952 Marjorie Jackson *AUS*	23.7 s
1956 Betty Cuthbert *AUS*	23.4 s
1960 Wilma Rudolph *US*	24.0 s
1964 Edith Maguire *US*	23.0 s
1968 Irena Szewinska *POL*	22.5 s
1972 Renate Stecher *GDR*	22.4 s
1976 Barbel Eckhert *GDR*	*22.37s
1980	

ATHLETICS 400 Meters   WOMEN

Event not held until 1964	
1964 Betty Cuthbert *AUS*	52.0 s
1968 Colette Besson *FR*	52.0 s

1972 Monika Zehrt *GDR*	51.08s
1976 Irena Szewinska *POL*	*49.29s
1980	

ATHLETICS 800 Meters   WOMEN

Event not held until 1928	
1928 Lina Radke *GER*	2min 16.8 s
1932–1956 Event not held	
1960 Ludmilla Shevtsova *USSR*	2min 04.3 s
1964 Ann Packer *GB*	2min 01.1 s
1968 Madeline Manning *US*	2min 00.9 s
1972 Hildergard Falck *GER*	1min 58.6 s
1976 Tatiana Kazankina *USSR*	*1min 54.94s
1980	

ATHLETICS 1500 Meters   WOMEN

Event not held until 1972	
1972 Ludmila Bragina *USSR*	*4min 01.4 s
1976 Tatiana Kazankina *USSR*	4min 05.48s
1980	

ATHLETICS 100 Meters Hurdles   WOMEN

Event not held until 1972	
1972 Annelie Ehrhardt *GDR*	*12.59s
1976 Johanna Schaller *GDR*	12.77s
1980	

ATHLETICS 4 × 100 Meters   WOMEN

Event not held until 1928	
1928 Canada	48.4 s
1932 United States of America	47.0 s
1936 United States of America	46.9 s
1948 Netherlands	47.5 s
1952 United States of America	45.9 s
1956 Australia	44.5 s
1960 United States of America	44.5 s
1964 Poland	43.6 s

Bruce Jenner, 1976 decathlon champion.

1968	United States of America	42.8 s
1972	West Germany	42.81s
1976	East Germany	*42.55s
1980		

ATHLETICS 4 × 400 Meters Relay — WOMEN

	Event not held until 1972	
1972	East Germany	3min 23.0 s
1976	East Germany	*3min 19.23s
1980		

ATHLETICS High Jump — WOMEN

	Event not held until 1928	
1928	Ethel Catherwood *CAN*	1.59m 5ft 2⅝in
1932	Jean Shiley *US*	1.65m 5ft 5¼in
1936	Ibolya Csak *HUN*	1.60m 5ft 3 in
1948	Alice Coachman *US*	1.68m 5ft 6¼in
1952	Esther Brand *SAF*	1.67m 5ft 5¾in
1956	Mildred McDaniel *US*	1.76m 5ft 9¼in
1960	Iolanda Balas *ROM*	1.85m 6ft 0⅞in
1964	Iolanda Balas *ROM*	1.90m 6ft 2¾in
1968	Milena Rezkova *CZECH*	1.82m 5ft 11¾in
1972	Ulrike Meyfarth *GER*	1.92m 6ft 3¾in
1976	Rosemarie Ackermann *GDR*	1.93m *6ft 4 in
1980		

ATHLETICS Long Jump — WOMEN

	Event not held until 1948	
1948	Olga Gyarmati *HUN*	5.70m 18ft 8¼in
1952	Yvette Williams *NZ*	6.24m 20ft 5⅝in
1956	Elzbieta Krzesinska *POL*	6.35m 20ft 10 in
1960	Vyera Krepkina *USSR*	6.37m 20ft 10¾in
1964	Mary Rand *GB*	6.76m 22ft 2¼in
1968	Viorica Viscopoleanu *ROM*	6.82m *22ft 4½in
1972	Heide Rosendahl *GER*	6.78m 22ft 3 in
1976	Angela Voight *GDR*	6.72m 22ft 0½in
1980		

Emil and Dana Zatopek, husband and wife gold medallists from Czechoslovakia.

ATHLETICS Shot Put — WOMEN

	Event not held until 1948	
1948	Micheline Ostermeyer *FR*	13.75m 45ft 1½in
1952	Galina Zybina *USSR*	15.28m 50ft 1½in
1956	Tamara Tyshkyevich *USSR*	16.59m 54ft 5 in
1960	Tamara Press *USSR*	17.32m 56ft 10 in
1964	Tamara Press *USSR*	18.14m 59ft 6 in
1968	Margarita Gummel *GDR*	19.61m 64ft 4 in
1972	Nadezha Chizhova *USSR*	21.03m 69ft
1976	Ivanka Christova *BUL*	21.16m *69ft 5 in
1980		

ATHLETICS Discus Throw — WOMEN

	Event not held until 1928	
1928	Helena Konopacka *POL*	39.62m 129ft 11¾in
1932	Lilian Copeland *US*	40.58m 133ft 1¾in
1936	Gisela Mauermayer *GER*	47.63m 156ft 3¼in
1948	Micheline Ostermeyer *FR*	41.92m 137ft 6⅛in
1952	Nina Romashkova *USSR*	51.42m 168ft 8½in
1956	Olga Fikotova *CZECH*	53.69m 176ft 1½in
1960	Nina Ponomaryeva *USSR*	55.10m 180ft 9¼in
1964	Tamara Press *USSR*	57.27m 187ft 10½in
1968	Lia Manoliu *ROM*	58.28m 191ft 2½in
1972	Faina Melnik *USSR*	66.62m 218ft 7 in
1976	Evelin Schlaak *GDR*	'68.98m *226ft 4 in
1980		

ATHLETICS Javelin Throw — WOMEN

	Event not held until 1932	
1932	Mildred Didrikson *US*	43.68m 143ft 4 in
1936	Tilly Fleischer *GER*	45.18m 148ft 2¾in
1948	Hermine Bauma *AUST*	45.57m 149ft 6 in
1952	Dana Zatopkova *CZECH*	50.47m 165ft 7 in
1956	Inese Jaunzeme *USSR*	53.86m 176ft 8½in
1960	Elvira Ozolina *USSR*	55.98m 183ft 8 in
1964	Mihaela Penes *ROM*	60.54m 198ft 7½in
1968	Angela Nemeth *HUN*	60.36m 198ft 0½in

1972 Ruth Fuchs *GDR*	63.88m 209ft 7 in	
1976 Ruth Fuchs *GDR*	65.94m *216ft 4 in	
1980		

ATHLETICS Pentathlon — WOMEN

Event not held until 1964	
1964 Irina Press *USSR*	5,246pts
1968 Ingrid Becker *GER*	5,098pts
1972 Mary Peters *GB*	4,801pts
1976 Siegrun Siegl *GDR*	4,745pts
1980	

BASKETBALL — MEN

Event not held until 1936

1936 United States of America

1948 United States of America

1952 United States of America

1956 United States of America

1960 United States of America

1964 United States of America

1968 United States of America

1972 USSR

1976 United States of America

1980

BOXING Light Flyweight — MEN

Event not held until 1968

1968 Francisco Rodriguez *VEN*

1972 Gyeorgy Gedo *HUN*

1976 Jorge Hernandez *CUB*

1980

BOXING Flyweight — MEN

Event not held until 1904

1904 George Finnegan *US*

1908–1912 Event not held

1920 Frank De Genaro *US*

1924 Fidel LaBarba *US*

1928 Antal Kocsis *HUN*

1932 Istvann Enekes *HUN*

1936 Willi Kaiser *GER*

1948 Pascual Perez *ARG*

1952 Nathan Brooks *US*

1956 Terence Spinks *GB*

1960 Gyula Torok *HUN*

1964 Fernando Atzori *ITA*

1968 Ricardo Delgado *MEX*

1972 Gheorghi Kostadinov *BUL*

1976 Leo Randolph *US*

1980

BOXING Bantamweight — MEN

Event not held until 1904

1904 O. L. Kirk *US*

1908 H. Thomas *GB*

1912 Event not held

1920 Clarence Walker *SAF*

1924 William Smith *SAF*

1928 Vittorio Tamagnini *ITA*

1932 Horace Gwynne *CAN*

1936 Ulderico Sergo *ITA*

1948 Tibor Csik *HUN*

1952 Pentti Hamalainen *FIN*

1956 Wolfgang Behrendt *GER*

1960 Olyeg Grigoryev *USSR*

1964 Takao Sakurai *JAP*

1968 Valeri Sokolov *USSR*

1972 Orlando Martinez *CUB*

1976 Yong Jo Gu *PRK*

1980

BOXING Featherweight — MEN

Event not held until 1904

1904 O. L. Kirk *US*

1908 Richard Gunn *GB*	**BOXING** Light Welterweight MEN
1912 Event not held	Event not held until 1952
1920 Paul Fritsch *FR*	1952 Charles Adkins *US*
1924 John Fields *US*	1956 Vladimir Jengibarian *USSR*
1928 Bep van Klaveren *NETH*	1960 Bohumil Nemecek *CZECH*
1932 Carmelo Robledo *ARG*	1964 Jerzy Kulej *POL*
1936 Oscar Casanovas *ARG*	1968 Jerzy Kulej *POL*
1948 Ernesto Formenti *ITA*	1972 Ray Seales *US*
1952 Jan Zachara *CZECH*	1976 Ray Leonard *US*
1956 Vladimir Safronov *USSR*	1980
1960 Francesco Musso *ITA*	
1964 Stanislav Stepashkin *USSR*	**BOXING** Welterweight MEN
1968 Antonio Roldan *MEX*	Event not held until 1904
1972 Boris Kousnetsov *USSR*	1904 Albert Young *US*
1976 Angel Herrara *CUB*	1908–1912 Event not held
1980	1920 T. Schneider *CAN*
	1924 Jean Delarge *BEL*
BOXING Lightweight MEN	1928 Edward Morgan *NZ*
Event not held until 1904	1932 Edward Flynn *US*
1904 H. J. Spanger *US*	1936 Sten Suvio *FIN*
1908 Frederick Grace *GB*	1948 Julius Torma *CZECH*
1912 Event not held	1952 Zyugmunt Chychla *POL*
1920 Samuel Mosberg *US*	1956 Nicolae Linca *ROM*
1924 Hans Nielsen *DEN*	1960 Giovanni Benvenuti *ITA*
1928 Carlo Orlandi *ITA*	1964 Marian Kasprzyk *POL*
1932 Lawrence Stevens *SAF*	1968 Manfred Wolke *GDR*
1936 Imre Harangi *HUN*	1972 Emilo Correa *CUB*
1948 Gerald Dreyer *SAF*	1976 Jochen Bachfeld *GDR*
1952 Aureliano Bolognesi *ITA*	1980
1956 Richard McTaggart *GB*	
1960 Kazimierz Pazdzior *POL*	**BOXING** Light Middleweight MEN
1964 Jozef Grudzien *POL*	Event not held until 1952
1968 Ronnie Harris *US*	1952 Laszlo Papp *HUN*
1972 Jan Szczepanski *POL*	1956 Laszlo Papp *HUN*
1976 Howard Davis *US*	1960 Wilbert McClure *US*
1980	1964 Boris Lagutin *USSR*
	1968 Boris Lagutin *USSR*

1972 Dieter Kottysch *GER*	1972 Mate Parlov *YUG*
1976 Jerzy Rybicki *POL*	1976 Leon Spinks *US*
1980	1980

BOXING Middleweight MEN	**BOXING** Heavyweight MEN
Event not held until 1904	Event not held until 1904
1904 Charles Mayer *US*	1904 Samuel Berger *US*
1908 John Douglas *GB*	1908 A. L. Oldham *GB*
1912 Event not held	1912 Event not held
1920 Harry Mallin *GB*	1920 Ronald Rawson *GB*
1924 Harry Mallin *GB*	1924 Otto von Porath *NOR*
1928 Piero Toscani *ITA*	1928 Arturo Rodriguez Jurado *ARG*
1932 Carmen Barth *US*	1932 Alberto Lovell *ARG*
1936 Jean Despeaux *FR*	1936 Herbert Runge *GER*
1948 Laszlo Papp *HUN*	1948 Rafael Iglesias *ARG*
1952 Floyd Patterson *US*	1952 Edward Sanders *US*
1956 Genadiy Schatkov *USSR*	1956 T. Peter Rademacher *US*
1960 Edward Crook *US*	1960 Franco de Piccoli *ITA*
1964 Valeri Popenchenko *USSR*	1964 Joe Frazier *US*
1968 Christopher Finnegan *GB*	1968 George Foreman *US*
1972 Veitchesiav Lemechev *USSR*	1972 Teofilo Stevenson *CUB*
1976 Michael Spinks *US*	1976 Teofilo Stevenson *CUB*
1980	1980

BOXING Light Heavyweight MEN	**CANOEING** Canadian Singles MEN	
Event not held until 1920	Event not held until 1936	
1920 Edward Eagan *US*	1936 Francis Amyot *CAN*	5min 32.1 s
1924 Harry Mitchell *GB*	1948 Josef Holecek *CZECH*	5min 42.0 s
1928 Victorio Avendano *ARG*	1952 Josef Holecek *CZECH*	4min 56.3 s
1932 David Carstens *SAF*	1956 Leon Rottman *ROM*	5min 05.3 s
1936 Roger Michelot *FR*	1960 Janos Parti *HUN*	4min 33.9 s
1948 George Hunter *SAF*	1964 J. Eschert *GER*	4min 35.14s
1952 Norvel Lee *US*	1968 Tibor Tatai *HUN*	4min 36.14s
1956 James Boyd *US*	1972 I. Patzaichin *ROM*	4min 08.94s
1960 Cassius Clay *US*	1976 Ljubek Matija *YUG*	4min 09.51s
1964 Cosimo Pinto *ITA*	1980	
1968 Dan Pozniak *USSR*		

CANOEING Canadian Pairs   MEN

Event not held until 1936		
1936	Czechoslovakia	4min 50.1 s
1948	Czechoslovakia	5min 07.1 s
1952	Denmark	4min 38.3 s
1956	Romania	4min 47.4 s
1960	USSR	4min 17.9 s
1964	USSR	4min 04.64s
1968	Romania	4min 07.18s
1972	USSR	3min 52.60s
1976	USSR	3min 52.76s
1980		

CANOEING Kayak Singles– 1000 Meters   MEN

Event not held until 1936		
1936 Gregor Hradetzky	*AUST*	4min 22.9 s
1948 Gert Fredriksson	*SWE*	4min 33.2 s
1952 Gert Fredriksson	*SWE*	4min 07.9 s
1956 Gert Fredriksson	*SWE*	4min 12.8 s
1960 Erik Hansen	*DEN*	3min 53.0 s
1964 Rolf Peterson	*SWE*	3min 57.13s
1968 Mihaly Hesz	*HUN*	4min 02.63s
1972 A. Shaparenko	*USSR*	3min 48.06s
1976 Rudiger Helm	*GDR*	3min 48.20s
1980		

CANOEING Kayak Pairs– 1000 Meters   MEN

Event not held until 1936		
1936	Austria	4min 03.8 s
1948	Sweden	4min 07.3 s
1952	Finland	3min 51.1 s
1956	Germany	3min 49.6 s
1960	Sweden	3min 34.7 s
1964	Sweden	3min 38.54s
1968	USSR	3min 37.54s
1972	USSR	2min 31.23s
1976	USSR	3min 29.01s

1980

CANOEING Kayak Fours   MEN

Event not held until 1964		
1964	USSR	3min 14.67s
1968	Norway	3min 14.38s
1972	USSR	3min 14.02s
1976	USSR	3min 08.69s
1980		

CANOEING 4 × 500 Meters   MEN

Event not held until 1960		
1960	Germany	7min 39.4s
1964–1976 Event not held		
1980		

CANOEING Kayak Singles – 500 Meters   MEN

Event not held until 1976		
1976 Vasile Diba	*ROM*	1min 46.41s
1980		

CANOEING Kayak Pairs – 500 Meters   MEN

Event not held until 1976		
1976	East Germany	1min 35.87s
1980		

CANOEING Slalom – Canadian Singles   MEN

Event not held until 1972		
1972 Reinhard Eiben	*GDR*	315.84pts
1976 Event not held		
1980		

CANOEING Slalom – Canadian Pairs   MEN

Event not held until 1972		
1972	East Germany	310.68pts
1976 Event not held		
1980		

CANOEING Slalom – Kayak Singles	MEN
Event not held until 1972	
1972 Siegbert Horn *GDR*	268.56pts
1976 Event not held	
1980	

CANOEING Kayak Singles	WOMEN
Event not held until 1948	
1948 Karen Hoff *DEN*	2min 31.9 s
1952 Sylvi Saimo *FIN*	2min 18.4 s
1956 Elisaveta Dementyeva *USSR*	2min 18.9 s
1960 Antonina Seredina *USSR*	2min 08.08s
1964 Ludmila Khvedosiuk *USSR*	2min 12.87s
1968 Ludmila Pinayeva *USSR*	2min 11.09s
1972 Y. Ryabchinskaya *USSR*	2min 03.17s
1976 Carola Zirzow *GDR*	2min 01.05s
1980	

CANOEING Kayak Pairs	WOMEN
Event not held until 1960	
1960 USSR	1min 54.7 s
1964 Germany	1min 56.95s
1968 West Germany	1min 56.44s
1972 USSR	1min 53.50s
1976 USSR	1min 51.15s
1980	

CANOEING Slalom – Kayak Singles	WOMEN
Event not held until 1972	
1972 Angelika Bahmann *GDR*	364.50pts
1976 Event not held	
1980	

CYCLING 1000 Meters Scratch Sprint†	MEN
1896 P. Masson *FR*	4min 56.0 s
1900 G. Taillandier *FR*	2min 16.0 s
1904 Event not held	

1908 Final declared void	
1912 Event not held	
1920 Mauritius Peeters *NETH*	1min 38.3 s
1924 Lucien Michard *FR*	12.8 s
1928 R. Beaufrand *FR*	13.2 s
1932 Jacobus van Egmond *NETH*	12.6 s
1936 Toni Merkens *GER*	11.8 s
1948 Mario Ghella *ITA*	12.0 s
1952 Enzo Sacchi *ITA*	12.0 s
1956 Michel Rousseau *FR*	11.4 s
1960 Sante Gaiardoni *ITA*	11.1 s
1964 Giovanni Pettenella *ITA*	13.69s
1968 Daniel Morelon *FR*	10.68s
1972 Daniel Morelon *FR*	11.69s
1976 Anton Tkac *CZECH*	
1980	

†The distance was 2000m in 1896 and 1900. From 1924 only times over the last 200m have been recorded.

CYCLING 1000 Meters Time Trial	MEN
Event not held until 1928	
1928 Willy Falck-Hansen *DEN*	1min 14.4 s
1932 Edgar Gray *AUS*	1min 13.0 s
1936 Arie van Vliet *NETH*	1min 12.0 s
1948 Jacques Dupont *FR*	1min 13.5 s
1952 Russell Mockridge *AUS*	1min 11.1 s
1956 Leandro Faggin *ITA*	1min 09.8 s
1960 Sante Gaiardoni *ITA*	1min 7.27 s
1964 Patrick Sercu *BEL*	1min 09.59 s
1968 Pierre Trentin *FR*	*1min 03.91 s
1972 Niels Fredborg *DEN*	1min 06.44 s
1976 Klaus Jurgen Grunke *GDR*	1min 05.297s
1980	

CYCLING 2000 Meters Tandem	MEN
Event not held until 1908	
1908 France	3min 07.6 s
1912 Event not held	
1920 Great Britain	2min 49.4 s

Sylvi Saimo, 1952 kayak singles champion.

1924 France	2min 40.0 s
1928 Netherlands	†11.8 s
1932 France	12.0 s
1936 Germany	11.8 s
1948 Italy	11.3 s
1952 Australia	11.0 s
1956 Australia	10.8 s
1960 Italy	10.7 s
1964 Italy	10.75s
1968 France	9.83s
1972 USSR	10.52s
1976 Event not held	
1980	

† From 1928 only times over the last 200m have been recorded.

Jiri Daler, 1964 4000 meters pursuit cycling champion.

CYCLING 4000 Meters Pursuit (Individual)　MEN

Event not held until 1964	
1964 Jiri Daler *CZECH*	5min 04.75s
1968 Daniel Rebillard *FR*	4min 41.71s
1972 Knut Knudsen *NOR*	4min 45.74s
1976 Gregor Braun *GER*	4min 47.61s
1980	

CYCLING 4000 Meters Pursuit (Team)　MEN

Event not held until 1920	
1920 Italy	5min 20.0 s
1924 Italy	5min 15.0 s
1928 Italy	5min 01.8 s
1932 Italy	4min 53.0 s
1936 France	4min 45.0 s
1948 France	4min 57.8 s
1952 Italy	4min 46.1 s
1956 Italy	4min 37.4 s
1960 Italy	4min 30.90s
1964 Germany	4min 35.67s
1968 Denmark	4min 22.44s
1972 West Germany	4min 22.14s

1976 West Germany	4 min 21.06s
1980	

CYCLING Road Race (Individual)†　MEN

1896 A. Konstantinidis *GR*	3h 22min 31.0s
1900–1908 Event not held	
1912 Rudolph Lewis *SAF*	10h 42min 39.0 s
1920 Harry Stenquist *SWE*	4h 40min 01.8 s
1924 Armand Blanchonnet *FR*	6h 20min 48.0 s
1928 Henry Hansen *DEN*	4h 47min 18.0 s
1932 Attilio Pavesi *ITA*	2h 28min 05.6 s
1936 Robert Charpentier *FR*	2h 33min 05.0 s
1948 Jose Beyaert *FR*	5h 18min 12.6 s
1952 Andre Noyelle *BEL*	5h 06min 03.4 s
1956 Ercole Baldini *ITA*	5h 21min 17.0 s
1960 Viktor Kapitonov *USSR*	4h 20min 37.0 s
1964 Mario Zanin *ITA*	4h 39min 51.63s
1968 Pierfranco Vianelli *ITA*	4h 41min 25.24s
1972 Hennie Kuiper *NETH*	4h 14min 37.0 s
1976 Bernt Johansson *SWE*	4h 46min 52.0 s
1980	

†The distance has varied widely from year to year, the longest being 320km in 1912.

CYCLING Road Race (Team)†　MEN

Event not held until 1912	
1912 Sweden	44h 35min 33.6 s
1920 France	19h 16min 43.2 s
1924 France	19h 30min 14.0 s
1928 Denmark	15h 09min 14.0 s
1932 Italy	7h 27min 15.2 s
1936 France	7h 39min 16.2 s
1948 Belgium	15h 58min 17.4 s
1952 Belgium	15h 20min 46.6 s
1956 France	16h 10min 36s
1960 Italy	2h 14min 33.53s
1964 Netherlands	2h 26min 31.19s
1968 Netherlands	2h 07min 49.06s

1972 USSR	2h 11min 17.8 s	
1976 USSR	2h 08min 53.0 s	
1980		

† From 1960 this race has been a 100-km time trial.
  Before then the distance varied.

EQUESTRIAN Jumping Grand Prix (Individual)

Event not held until 1912

1912 Jean Cariou *FR*	186	pts
1920 Tommaso Leqiuo *ITA*	0	flts
1924 Alphons Gemuseus *SWI*	6	flts
1928 Frantisek Ventura *CZECH*	0	flts
1932 Takeichi Nishi *JAP*	8	flts
1936 Kurt Hasse *GER*	4	flts
1948 Humberto Mariles *MEX*	6.25	flts
1952 Pierre Jonqueres d'Oriola *FR*	8	flts
1956 Hans Gunter Winkler *GER*	4	flts
1960 Raimondo d'Inzeo *ITA*	12	flts
1964 Pierre Jonqueres d'Oriola *FR*	9	flts
1968 William Steinkraus *US*	4	flts
1972 Graziano Mancinelli *ITA*	8	flts
1976 Alwin Schockemoehle *GER*	0	flts
1980		

EQUESTRIAN Jumping Grand Prix (Team)

Event not held until 1912

1912 Sweden	545	pts
1920 Sweden	14	flts
1924 Sweden	42.5	flts
1928 Spain	4	flts
1932 Medal not awarded		
1936 Germany	44	flts
1948 Mexico	34.25	flts
1952 Great Britain	40.75	flts
1956 Germany	40	flts
1960 Germany	46.50	flts
1964 Germany	68.50	flts
1968 Canada	102.75	flts

EQUESTRIAN Dressage (Individual)

Event not held until 1912

1912 Carl Bonde *SWE*	15	flts
1920 Janne Lundblad *SWE*	27.936	pts
1924 Ernst von Linder *SWE*	276.4	pts
1928 Carl von Langen *GER*	237.42	pts
1932 Xavier Lesage *FR*	1031.25	pts
1936 Heinrich Pollay *GER*	1760	pts
1948 Hans Moser *SWI*	492.5	pts
1952 Henri St Cyr *SWE*	561	pts
1956 Henri St Cyr *SWE*	860	pts
1960 Sergey Filatov *USSR*	2144	pts
1964 Henri Chammartin *SWI*	1504	pts
1968 Ivan Kizimov *USSR*	1572	pts
1972 Liselott Linsenhoff *GER*	1229	pts
1976 Christine Stueckelberger *SWI*	1486	pts
1980		

EQUESTRIAN Dressage (Team)

Event not held until 1928

1928 Germany	669.72	pts
1932 France	2818.75	pts
1936 Germany	5074	pts
1948 France	1269	pts
1952 Sweden	1597.5	pts
1956 Sweden	2475	pts
1960 Event not held		
1964 Germany	2558	pts
1968 West Germany	2699	pts
1972 USSR	5095	pts
1976 West Germany	5155	pts
1980		

181

Jean-Jacques Guyon, 1968 three-day event individual champion.

EQUESTRIAN Three-Day Event (Individual)

Event not held until 1912		
1912 Axel Nordlander *SWE*		46.59pts
1920 Helmer Morner *SWE*	1775	pts
1924 Adolph van Zjip *NETH*	1976	pts
1928 Ferdinand de Mortanges *NETH*		1969.82pts
1932 Ferdinand de Mortanges *NETH*		1813.83pts
1936 Ludwig Stubbendorff *GER*		37.7flts
1948 Bernard Chevalier *FR*	plus 4	pts
1952 Hans von Blixen-Finecke *SWE*		28.33flts
1956 Petrus Kastenman *SWE*		66.53flts
1960 Laurence Morgan *AUS*		plus 7.15pts
1964 Mauro Checcoli *ITA*		64.40pts
1968 Jean-Jacques Guyon *FR*		38.86flts
1972 Richard Meade *GB*		57.73pts
1976 Edmund Coffin *US*		114.99pts
1980		

EQUESTRIAN Three-Day Event (Team)

Event not held until 1912	
1912 Sweden	139.06pts
1920 Sweden	5057.5 pts
1924 Netherlands	5294.5 pts
1928 Netherlands	5865.68pts
1932 United States of America	5038.08pts
1936 Germany	676.75flts
1948 United States of America	161.50flts
1952 Sweden	221.94flts
1956 Great Britain	355.48flts
1960 Australia	128.18flts
1964 Italy	85.80pts
1968 Great Britain	175.93flts
1972 Great Britain	95.53pts
1976 United States of America	441.00pts
1980	

FENCING Foil (Individual)   MEN

1896 E. Gravelotte *FR*	4 wins
1900 C. Coste *FR*	6 wins
1904 Ramon Fonst *CUB*	nda
1908 Event not held	
1912 Nedo Nadi *ITA*	7 wins
1920 Nedo Nadi *ITA*	10 wins
1924 Roger Ducret *FR*	6 wins
1928 Lucien Gaudin *FR*	9 wins
1932 Gustavo Marzi *ITA*	9 wins
1936 Giulio Gaudini *ITA*	7 wins
1948 Jean Buhan *FR*	7 wins
1952 Christian d'Oriola *FR*	8 wins
1956 Christian d'Oriola *FR*	6 wins
1960 Viktor Zhdanovich *USSR*	7 wins
1964 Egon Franke *POL*	3 wins
1968 Ileana Drimba *ROM*	4 wins
1972 Witold Woyda *POL*	5 wins
1976 Fabio dal Zotto *ITA*	4 wins
1980	

FENCING Foil (Team)   MEN

Event not held until 1920
1920 Italy
1924 France
1928 Italy
1932 France
1936 Italy
1948 France
1952 France
1956 Italy
1960 USSR
1964 USSR
1968 France
1972 Poland
1976 West Germany
1980

FENCING Epée (Individual)		MEN
1896. Event not held		
1900 Ramon Fonst	*CUB*	nda
1904 Ramon Fonst	*CUB*	nda
1908 Gaston Alibert	*FR*	5 wins
1912 Paul Anspach	*BEL*	6 wins
1920 Armand Massard	*FR*	9 wins
1924 Charles Delporte	*BEL*	8 wins
1928 Lucien Gaudin	*FR*	8 wins
1932 Giancarlo Medici	*ITA*	8 wins
1936 Franco Riccardi	*ITA*	5 wins
1948 Luigi Cantone	*ITA*	7 wins
1952 Edoardo Mangiarotti	*ITA*	7 wins
1956 Carlo Pavesi	*ITA*	5 wins
1960 Guiseppe Delfino	*ITA*	5 wins
1964 Grigory Kriss	*USSR*	2 wins
1968 Gyozo Kulcsar	*HUN*	4 wins
1972 Csaba Fenyvesi	*HUN*	4 wins
1976 Alexander Pusch	*GER*	3 wins
1980		

FENCING Epée (Team)	MEN
Event not held until 1908	
1908 France	
1912 Belgium	
1920 Italy	
1924 France	
1928 Italy	
1932 France	
1936 Italy	
1948 France	
1952 Italy	
1956 Italy	
1960 Italy	
1964 Hungary	
1968 Hungary	
1972 Hungary	

1976 Sweden
1980

FENCING Saber (Individual)		MEN
1896 Jean Georgiadis	*GR*	4 wins
1900 G. de la Falaise	*FR*	nda
1904 Manuel Diaz	*CUB*	nda
1908 Jeno Fuchs	*HUN*	6 wins
1912 Jeno Fuchs	*HUN*	6 wins
1920 Nedo Nadi	*ITA*	11 wins
1924 Sando Posta	*HUN*	5 wins
1928 Odon Tersztyanszky	*HUN*	9 wins
1932 Gyorgy Piller	*HUN*	8 wins
1936 Endre Kabos	*HUN*	7 wins
1948 Aladar Gerevich	*HUN*	7 wins
1952 Pal Kovacs	*HUN*	8 wins
1956 Rudolf Karpati	*HUN*	6 wins
1960 Rudolf Karpati	*HUN*	5 wins
1964 Tibor Pezsa	*HUN*	2 wins
1968 Jerzy Pawlowski	*POL*	4 wins
1972 Viktor Sidiak	*USSR*	4 wins
1976 Viktor Krovonouskov	*USSR*	5 wins
1980		

Witold Woyda (right), 1972 foil champion.

FENCING Saber (Team)	MEN
Event not held until 1908	
1908 Hungary	
1912 Hungary	
1920 Italy	
1924 Italy	
1928 Hungary	
1932 Hungary	
1936 Hungary	
1948 Hungary	
1952 Hungary	
1956 Hungary	
1960 Hungary	

1964	USSR
1968	USSR
1972	Italy
1976	USSR
1980	

FENCING Foil (Individual) WOMEN

Event not held until 1924

1924	Ellen Osiier *DEN*	5 wins
1928	Helene Mayer *GER*	7 wins
1932	Ellen Preis *AUST*	8 wins
1936	Ilona Elek *HUN*	6 wins
1948	Ilona Elek *HUN*	6 wins
1952	Irene Camber *ITA*	5 wins
1956	Gillian Sheen *GB*	6 wins
1960	Heidi Schmid *GER*	6 wins
1964	Ildiko Rejto *HUN*	2 wins
1968	Elena Novikova *USSR*	4 wins
1972	Antonell Ragno Lonzi *ITA*	4 wins
1976	Ildiko Schwarczenbereer *HUN*	8 wins
1980	

FENCING Foil (Team) WOMEN

Event not held until 1960

1960	USSR
1964	Hungary
1968	USSR
1972	USSR
1976	USSR
1980	

FIELD HOCKEY MEN

Event not held until 1908

1908	England
1912	Event not held
1920	England
1924	Event not held

1928	India
1932	India
1936	India
1948	India
1952	India
1956	India
1960	Pakistan
1964	India
1968	Pakistan
1972	West Germany
1976	New Zealand
1980	

GYMNASTICS Combined Exercises (Individual) MEN

1896	Event not held		
1900	Gustave Sandras *FR*	302	pts
1904	J. Lenhart *AUST*	69.80	pts
1908	Alberto Braglia *ITA*	317	pts
1912	Alberto Braglia *ITA*	135	pts
1920	Giorgio Zampori *ITA*	88.35	pts
1924	Leon Skukelj *YUG*	110.340pts	
1928	Georges Miez *SWI*	247.500pts	
1932	Romero Neri *ITA*	140.625pts	
1936	Karl Schwarzmann *GER*	133.100pts	
1948	Veikko Huhtanen *FIN*	229.7	pts
1952	Viktor Chukarin *USSR*	115.70	pts
1956	Viktor Chukarin *USSR*	114.25	pts
1960	Boris Shakhlin *USSR*	115.95	pts
1964	Yukio Endo *JAP*	115.95	pts
1968	Sawao Kato *JAP*	115.90	pts
1972	Sawao Kato *JAP*	114.650pts	
1976	Nikolai Andrianov *USSR*	116.650pts	
1980			

GYMNASTICS Combined Exercises (Team) MEN

Event not held until 1904

| 1904 | United States of America | 374.43 pts |

1908	Sweden	438	pts
1912	Italy	265.75	pts
1920	Italy	359.85	pts
1924	Italy	839.058	pts
1928	Switzerland	1718.625	pts
1932	Italy	541.850	pts
1936	Germany	657.430	pts
1948	Finland	1358.3	pts
1952	USSR	574.4	pts
1956	USSR	568.25	pts
1960	Japan	575.20	pts
1964	Japan	577.95	pts
1968	Japan	575.90	pts
1972	Japan	571.25	pts
1976	Japan	576.85	pts
1980			

GYMNASTICS Floor Exercises   MEN

Event not held until 1932

1932	Istvan Pelle *HUN*	9.6	pts
1936	Georges Miez *SWI*	18.666	pts
1948	Ferenc Pataki *HUN*	38.7	pts
1952	Karl Thoresson *SWE*	19.25	pts
1956	Valentin Muratov *USSR*	19.20	pts
1960	Nobuyuki Aihara *JAP*	19.45	pts
1964	Franco Menicelli *ITA*	19.45	pts
1968	Sawao Kato *JAP*	19.475	pts
1972	Nikolai Andrianov *USSR*	19.175	pts
1976	Nikolai Andrianov *USSR*	19.450	pts
1980			

GYMNASTICS Horizontal Bar   MEN

1896	Hermann Weingartner *GER*		nda
1900	Event not held		
1904	Anton Heida and Edward Hennig *US*	40	pts
1908–1920	Event not held		
1924	Leon Stukelj *YUG*	19.73	pts

1928	Georges Miez *SWI*	19.17	pts
1932	Dallas Bixler *US*	18.33	pts
1936	Aleksanteri Saarvala *FIN*	19.367	pts
1948	Josef Stadler *SWI*	39.7	pts
1952	Jack Gunthard *SWI*	19.55	pts
1956	Takashi Ono *JAP*	19.60	pts
1960	Takashi Ono *JAP*	19.60	pts
1964	Boris Shakhlin *USSR*	19.625	pts
1968	Mikhail Voronin *USSR* and Akinori Nakayama *JAP*	19.550	pts
1972	Mitsuo Tsukahara *JAP*	19.725	pts
1976	Mitsuo Tsukahara *JAP*	19.675	pts
1980			

GYMNASTICS Parallel Bars   MEN

1896	Alfred Flatow *GER*		nda
1900	Event not held		
1904	George Eyser *US*	44	pts
1908–1920	Event not held		
1924	August Guttinger *SWI*	21.63	pts
1928	Ladislav Vacha *CZECH*	18.83	pts
1932	Romero Neri *ITA*	18.97	pts
1936	Konrad Frey *GER*	19.067	pts
1948	Michael Reusch *SWI*	39.5	pts
1952	Hans Eugster *SWI*	19.65	pts
1956	Viktor Chukarin *USSR*	19.20	pts
1960	Boris Shakhlin *USSR*	19.40	pts
1964	Yukio Endo *JAP*	19.675	pts
1968	Akinori Nakayama *JAP*	19.475	pts
1972	Sawao Kato *JAP*	19.475	pts
1976	Sawao Kato *JAP*	19.675	pts
1980			

GYMNASTICS Pommelled Horse   MEN

1896	Louis Zutter *SWI*		nda
1900	Event not held		
1904	Anton Heida *US*	42	pts
1908–1920	Event not held		

Georges Miez, 1936 floor exercises champion.

185

Alois Hudec, 1936 champion on the rings.

1924	Josef Wilhelm	SWI	21.23 pts
1928	Hermann Hanggi	SWI	19.75 pts
1932	Istvan Pelle	HUN	19.07 pts
1936	Konrad Frey	GER	19.333pts
1948	Paavo Aaltonen, Veikko Huhtanen and Heikki Savolainen	FIN	38.7 pts
1952	Viktor Chukarin	USSR	19.50 pts
1956	Boris Shakhlin	USSR	19.25 pts
1960	Eugen Ekman FIN and Boris Shakhlin	USSR	19.375pts
1964	Miroslav Cerar	YUG	19.525pts
1968	Miroslav Cerar	YUG	19.325pts
1972	Viktor Klimenko	USSR	19.125pts
1976	Zoltan Magyar	HUN	19.700pts
1980			

GYMNASTICS Long Horse Vault — MEN

1896	Karl Schumann	GER	nda
1900	Event not held		
1904	Anton Heida and George Eyser	US	36 pts
1908–1920	Event not held		
1924	Frank Kriz	US	9.98 pts
1928	Eugen Mack	SWI	9.58 pts
1932	Savino Guglielmetti	ITA	18.03 pts
1936	Karl Schwarzmann	GER	19.20 pts
1948	Paavo Aaltonen	FIN	39.1 pts
1952	Viktor Chukarin	USSR	19.20 pts
1956	Helmuth Bantz GER and Valentin Muratov	USSR	18.85 pts
1960	Takashi Ono JAP and Boris Shakhlin	USSR	19.35 pts
1964	Haruhiro Yamashita	JAP	19.660pts
1968	Mikhail Veronin	USSR	19.00 pts
1972	Klaus Koeste	GDR	18.850pts
1976	Nikolai Andrianov	USSR	19.450pts
1980			

GYMNASTICS Rings — MEN

1896	Jean Mitropoulos	GR	nda
1900	Event not held		
1904	Herman Glass	US	45 pts
1908–1920	Event not held		
1924	Francesco Martino	ITA	21.553pts
1928	Leon Stukelj	YUG	19.25 pts
1932	George Gulack	US	18.97 pts
1936	Alois Hudec	CZECH	19.433pts
1948	Karl Frei	SWI	39.6 pts
1952	Grant Shaginyan	USSR	19.75 pts
1956	Albert Azaryan	USSR	19.35 pts
1960	Albert Azaryan	USSR	19.72 pts
1964	Takuji Hayata	JAP	19.475pts
1968	Akinori Nakayama	JAP	19.450pts
1972	Akinori Nakayama	JAP	19.350pts
1976	Nikolai Andrianov	USSR	19.650pts
1980			

GYMNASTICS Combined Exercises (Individual) WOMEN

	Event not held until 1952		
1952	Maria Gorokhovskaya	USSR	76.78 pts
1956	Larisa Latynina	USSR	74.93 pts
1960	Larisa Latynina	USSR	77.03 pts
1964	Vera Caslavska	CZECH	77.564pts
1968	Vera Caslavska	CZECH	78.25 pts
1972	Ludmilla Turischeva	USSR	77.025pts
1976	Nadia Comaneci	ROM	79.275pts
1980			

GYMNASTICS Combined Exercises (Team) WOMEN

	Event not held until 1928	
1928	Netherlands	316.75pts
1932	Event not held	
1936	Germany	506.50pts
1948	Czechoslovakia	445.45pts
1952	USSR	527.03pts
1956	USSR	444.80pts
1960	USSR	382.32pts

1964	USSR	380.89pts
1968	USSR	382.85pts
1972	USSR	380.50pts
1976	USSR	390.35pts
1980		

GYMNASTICS Beam   WOMEN

	Event not held until 1952	
1952	Nina Bocharyova USSR	19.22 pts
1956	Agnes Keleti HUN	18.80 pts
1960	Eva Bosakova CZECH	19.28 pts
1964	Vera Caslavska CZECH	19.449pts
1968	Natalya Kuchinskaya USSR	19.650pts
1972	Olga Korbut USSR	19.400pts
1976	Nadia Comaneci ROM	19.950pts
1980		

GYMNASTICS Uneven Parallel Bars   WOMEN

	Event not held until 1952	
1952	Margit Korondi HUN	19.40 pts
1956	Agnes Keleti HUN	18.96 pts
1960	Polina Astakhova USSR	19.61 pts
1964	Polina Astakhova USSR	19.332pts
1968	Vera Caslavska CZECH	19.650pts
1972	Karin Janz GDR	19.675pts
1976	Nadia Comaneci ROM	20.000pts
1980		

GYMNASTICS Horse Vault   WOMEN

	Event not held until 1952	
1952	Yekaterina Kalinchuk USSR	19.20 pts
1956	Larisa Latynina USSR	18.83 pts
1960	Margarita Nikolayeva USSR	19.31 pts
1964	Vera Caslavska CZECH	19.483pts
1968	Vera Caslavska CZECH	19.775pts
1972	Karin Janz GDR	19.525pts
1976	Nelli Kim USSR	19.800pts

1980	

GYMNASTICS Floor Exercises   WOMEN

	Event not held until 1952	
1952	Agnes Keleti HUN	19.36 pts
1956	Larisa Latynina USSR and Agnes Keleti HUN	18.73 pts
1960	Larisa Latynina USSR	19.58 pts
1964	Larisa Latynina USSR	19.599pts
1968	Larissa Petrik USSR and Vera Caslavska CZECH	19.675pts
1972	Olga Korbut USSR	19.575pts
1976	Nelli Kim USSR	19.850pts
1980		

HANDBALL   MEN

	Event not held until 1936
1936	Germany
1948–1968	Event not held
1972	Yugoslavia
1976	USSR
1980	

JUDO Open (any body weight)   MEN

	Event not held until 1964
1964	Anton Geesink NETH
1968	Event not held
1972	Wim Ruska NETH
1976	Haruki Uemura JAP
1980	

JUDO Heavyweight   MEN

	Event not held until 1964
1964	Isao Inokuma JAP
1968	Event not held
1972	Willem Ruska NETH
1976	Sergei Novikov USSR
1980	

187

Lars Hall, 1952 and 1956 modern pentathlon champion.

JUDO Light Heavyweight	MEN
Event not held until 1972	
1972 Shota Khokhoshvili *USSR*	
1976 Kazuhiro Ninomiya *JAP*	
1980	

JUDO Middleweight	MEN
Event not held until 1964	
1964 Isao Okano *JAP*	
1968 Event not held	
1972 Shinobu Sekine *JAP*	
1976 Isamu Sonoda *JAP*	
1980	

JUDO Welterweight	MEN
Event not held until 1972	
1972 Toyokazu Nomura *JAP*	
1976 Vladimir Nevzorov *USSR*	
1980	

JUDO Lightweight	MEN
Event not held until 1964	
1964 Takehide Nakatani *JAP*	
1968 Event not held	
1972 Takeo Kawaguchi *JAP*	
1976 Hector Rodriguez *CUB*	
1980	

MODERN PENTATHLON Individual	MEN
Event not held until 1912	
1912 Gustaf Lilliehook *SWE*	27 pts
1920 Gustaf Dryssen *SWE*	18 pts
1924 Bo Lindman *SWE*	18 pts
1928 Sven Thofelt *SWE*	47 pts
1932 Johan Gabriel Oxenstierna *SWE*	32 pts
1936 Gotthardt Hendrick *GER*	31.5 pts
1948 William Grut *SWE*	16 pts

1952 Lars Hall *SWE*	32	pts
1956 Lars Hall *SWE*	4833	pts
1960 Ferenc Nemeth *HUN*	5024	pts
1964 Ferenc Torok *HUN*	5116	pts
1968 Bjorn Ferm *SWE*	4964	pts
1972 Andras Balczo *HUN*	5412	pts
1976 Janusz Pyciak-Peciak *POL*	5520	pts
1980		

MODERN PENTATHLON Team	MEN
Event not held until 1952	
1952 Hungary	166 pts
1956 USSR	13,609.5 pts
1960 Hungary	14,863 pts
1964 USSR	14,961 pts
1968 Hungary	14,325 pts
1972 USSR	15,968 pts
1976 Great Britain	15,559 pts
1980	

ROWING† Single Sculls	MEN
1896 Event not held	
1900 Henri Barrelet *FR*	7min 35.6 s
1904 Frank Greer *US*	10min 08.5 s
1908 Harry Blackstaffe *GB*	9min 26.0 s
1912 William Kinnear *GB*	7min 47.6 s
1920 John Kelly *US*	7min 35.0 s
1924 Jack Beresford *GB*	7min 49.2 s
1928 Henry Pearce *AUS*	7min 11.0 s
1932 Henry Pearce *AUS*	7min 44.4 s
1936 Gustav Schafer *GER*	8min 21.5 s
1948 Mervyn Wood *AUS*	7min 24.4 s
1952 Yuri Tyukalov *USSR*	8min 12.8 s
1956 Vyacheslav Ivanov *USSR*	8min 02.5 s
1960 Vyacheslav Ivanov *USSR*	7min 13.9 s
1964 Vyacheslav Ivanov *USSR*	8min 22.5 s
1968 Henri Jan Wienese *NETH*	7min 47.80 s

1972 Yuri Malyshev *USSR*	*7min 10.12s	
1976 Pertti Karppinen *FIN*	7min 29.03s	
1980		

†In 1904 the course was 3219m, in 1908 2414m and in 1948 1880m. Since 1952 the course for all events has been 2000m.

ROWING Double Sculls	MEN
Event not held until 1904	
1904 United States of America	10min 03.2 s
1908–1912 Event not held	
1920 United States of America	7min 09.0 s
1924 United States of America	7min 45.0 s
1928 United States of America	6min 41.4 s
1932 United States of America	7min 17.4 s
1936 Great Britain	7min 20.8 s
1948 Great Britain	6min 51.3 s
1952 Argentina	7min 32.2 s
1956 USSR	7min 24.0 s
1960 Czechoslovakia	6min 47.50s
1964 USSR	7min 10.66s
1968 USSR	6min 51.82s
1972 USSR	7min 01.77s
1976 Norway	7min 13.20s
1980	

ROWING Coxless Pairs	MEN
1896 Event not held	
1900 Belgium	7min 49.6 s
1904 United States of America	10min 57.0 s
1908 Great Britain	9min 41.0 s
1912 Event not held	
1920 Italy	7min 56.0 s
1924 Netherlands	8min 19.4 s
1928 Germany	7min 06.4 s
1932 Great Britain	8min 00.0 s
1936 Germany	8min 16.1 s
1948 Great Britain	7min 21.1 s

1952 United States of America	8min 20.7 s	
1956 United States of America	7min 55.4 s	
1960 USSR	7min 02.00s	
1964 Canada	7min 32.94s	
1968 East Germany	7min 26.56s	
1972 East Germany	6min 53.16s	
1976 East Germany	7min 23.31s	
1980		

ROWING Coxed Pairs	MEN
1896 Event not held	
1900 Netherlands	7min 34.2 s
1904–1920 Event not held	
1924 Switzerland	8min 39.0 s
1928 Switzerland	7min 42.6 s
1932 United States of America	8min 25.8 s
1936 Germany	8min 36.9 s
1948 Denmark	8min 05.0 s
1952 France	8min 28.6 s
1956 United States of America	8min 26.1 s
1960 Germany	7min 29.14s
1964 United States of America	8min 21.33s
1968 Italy	8min 04.81s
1972 East Germany	7min 17.25s
1976 East Germany	7min 58.99s
1980	

ROWING Coxless Fours	MEN
1896 Event not held	
1900 France	7min 11.0 s
1904 United States of America	9min 53.8 s
1908 Great Britain	8min 34.0 s
1912–1920 Event not held	
1924 Great Britain	7min 08.6 s
1928 Great Britain	6min 36.0 s
1932 Great Britain	6min 58.2 s
1936 Germany	7min 01.8 s

1948 Italy	6min 39.0 s
1952 Yugoslavia	7min 16.0 s
1956 Canada	7min 08.8 s
1960 United States of America	6min 26.26s
1964 Denmark	6min 59.30s
1968 East Germany	6min 39.18s
1972 East Germany	6min 24.27s
1976 East Germany	6min 37.42s
1980	

ROWING Coxed Fours — MEN

1896 Event not held	
1900 Germany	5min 59.0 s
1904–1908 Event not held	
1912 Germany	6min 59.4 s
1920 Switzerland	6min 54.0 s
1924 Switzerland	7min 18.4 s
1928 Italy	6min 47.8 s
1932 Germany	7min 19.0 s
1936 Germany	7min 16.2 s
1948 United States of America	6min 50.3 s
1952 Czechoslovakia	7min 33.4 s
1956 Italy	7min 19.4 s
1960 Germany	6min 39.12s
1964 Germany	7min 00.44s
1968 New Zealand	6min 45.62s
1972 West Germany	6min 31.85s
1976 USSR	6min 40.22s
1980	

ROWING Quadruple Sculls — MEN

Event not held until 1976	
1976 East Germany	6min 18.25s
1980	

ROWING Eights — MEN

1896 Event not held	

1900 United States of America	6min 09.8 s
1904 United States of America	7min 50.0 s
1908 Great Britain	7min 52.0 s
1912 Great Britain	6min 15.0 s
1920 United States of America	6min 02.6 s
1924 United States of America	6min 33.4 s
1928 United States of America	6min 03.2 s
1932 United States of America	6min 37.6 s
1936 United States of America	6min 25.4 s
1948 United States of America	5min 56.7 s
1952 United States of America	6min 25.9 s
1956 United States of America	6min 35.2 s
1960 Germany	5min 57.18s
1964 United States of America	6min 18.23s
1968 West Germany	6min 07.00s
1972 New Zealand	6min 8.94s
1976 East Germany	5min 58.29s
1980	

ROWING Singles Sculls — WOMEN

Event not held until 1976	
1976 Christine Scheiblich *GDR*	4min 05.56s
1980	

ROWING Double Sculls — WOMEN

Event not held until 1976	
1976 Bulgaria	3min 44.36s
1980	

ROWING Coxless Pairs — WOMEN

Event not held until 1976	
1976 Bulgaria	4min 01.22s
1980	

ROWING Coxed Fours — WOMEN

Event not held until 1976	
1976 East Germany	3min 29.99s

1980

ROWING Coxless Fours   WOMEN

	Event not held until 1976	
1976	East Germany	3min 45.08s
1980		

ROWING Eights   WOMEN

	Event not held until 1976	
1976	East Germany	3min 33.32s
1980		

SHOOTING Free Pistol   MEN

1896	Sommer Paine *US*	442pts
1900	Karl Roderer *SWI*	503pts
1904–1908	Event not held	
1912	Alfred Lane *US*	499pts
1920	Carl Frederick *US*	496pts
1924–1932	Event not held	
1936	Thorsten Ullmann *SWE*	559pts
1948	Edwin Vazquez *PER*	545pts
1952	Huelet Benner *US*	553pts
1956	Pentti Linnosvuo *FIN*	556pts
1960	Aleksey Gushchin *USSR*	560pts
1964	Vaino Markkanen *FIN*	560pts
1968	Grigory Kosykh *USSR*	562pts
1972	Ragner Skanaker *SWE*	567pts
1976	Uwe Potteck *GDR*	*573pts
1980		

SHOOTING Rapid-Fire Pistol   MEN

	Event not held until 1924	
1924	H. N. Bailey *US*	18pts
1928	Event not held	
1932	Renzo Morigi *ITA*	36pts
1936	Cornelius van Oyen *GER*	36pts
1948	Karoly Takacs *HUN*	580pts

1952	Karoly Takacs *HUN*	579pts
1956	Stefan Petrescu *ROM*	587pts
1960	William McMillan *US*	587pts
1964	Pentti Linnosvuo *FIN*	592pts
1968	Jozef Zapedzki *POL*	593pts
1972	Jozef Zapedzki *POL*	595pts
1976	Norbert Glaar *GDR*	*597pts
1980		

SHOOTING Free Rifle   MEN

	Event not held until 1908	
1908	Albert Helgerud *NOR*	909pts
1912	Paul Colas *FR*	987pts
1920	Morris Fisher *US*	997pts
1924	Morris Fisher *US*	95pts
1928–1936	Event not held	
1948	Emil Grunig *SWI*	1120pts
1952	Anatoli Bogdanov *USSR*	1123pts
1956	Vasili Borisov *USSR*	1138pts
1960	Hubert Hammerer *AUST*	1129pts
1964	Gary Anderson *US*	1153pts
1968	Gary Anderson *US*	1157pts
1972	Lones Wigger *US*	1155pts
1976	Event not held	
1980		

SHOOTING Smallbore Rifle – Prone   MEN

	Event not held until 1908	
1908	A. A. Carnell *GB*	387pts
1912	Frederick Hird *US*	194pts
1920	Lawrence Nuesslein *US*	391pts
1924	Charles Coquelin de Lisle *FR*	398pts
1928	Event not held	
1932	Bartil Ronmark *SWE*	294pts
1936	Willy Rogeberg *NOR*	300pts
1948	Arthur Cook *US*	599pts
1952	Iosif Sarbu *ROM*	400pts

191

Evgeny Petrov, 1968 skeet shooting champion.

1956	Gerald Quelette *CAN*	600pts
1960	Peter Kohnke *GER*	590pts
1964	Laszlo Hammerl *HUN*	597pts
1968	Jan Kurka *CZECH*	598pts
1972	Ho Jun Li *PRK*	*599pts
1976	Karl Heinz Smieszek *GER*	599pts
1980		

SHOOTING Smallbore Rifle – Three Positions   MEN

	Event not held until 1952	
1952	Erling Kongshaug *NOR*	1164pts
1956	Anatoli Bogdanov *USSR*	1172pts
1960	Viktor Shamburkin *USSR*	1149pts
1964	Lones Wigger *US*	1164pts
1968	Bernd Klingner *GER*	1157pts
1972	John Writer *US*	*1166pts
1976	Lanny Bassham *US*	1162pts
1980		

SHOOTING Clay Pigeon (Trap)   MEN

1896	Event not held	
1900	R. de Barbarin *FR*	17pts
1904	Event not held	
1908	W. H. Ewing *CAN*	72pts
1912	James Graham *US*	96pts
1920	Mark Arie *US*	95pts
1924	Gyula Halasy *HUN*	98pts
1928–1948	Event not held	
1952	George Généreux *CAN*	192pts
1956	Galliano Rossini *ITA*	195pts
1960	Ion Dumitrescu *ROM*	192pts
1964	Ennio Mattarelli *ITA*	198pts
1968	Bob Braithwaite *GB*	198pts
1972	Angelo Scalzone *ITA*	*199pts
1976	Donald Halderman *US*	190pts
1980		

SHOOTING Skeet   MEN

	Event not held until 1968	
1968	Evgeny Petrov *USSR*	*198pts
1972	Konrad Wirnhier *GER*	195pts
1976	Josef Panacek *CZECH*	198pts
1980		

SHOOTING Moving Target   MEN

	Event not held until 1972	
1972	Lako Zhelezniak *USSR*	569pts
1976	Alexandr Gazov *USSR*	*579pts
1980		

SOCCER   MEN

	Event not held until 1908
1908	Great Britain
1912	Great Britain
1920	Belgium
1924	Uruguay
1928	Uruguay
1932	Event not held
1936	Italy
1948	Sweden
1952	Hungary
1956	USSR
1960	Yugoslavia
1964	Hungary
1968	Hungary
1972	Poland
1976	East Germany
1980	

SWIMMING 100 Meters Freestyle   MEN

1896	Alfred Hajos *HUN†*	1min 22.2 s
1900	Event not held	
1904	Zoltan Halmay *HUN*	1min 02.8 s
1908	Charles Daniels *US*	1min 05.6 s

1912 Duke Kahanamoku *US*	1min 03.4 s	1936 Jack Medica *US*	4min 44.5 s
1920 Duke Kahanamoku *US*	1min 01.4 s	1948 William Smith *US*	4min 41.0 s
1924 Johnny Weissmuller *US*	59.0 s	1952 Jean Boiteux *FR*	4min 30.7 s
1928 Johnny Weissmuller *US*	58.6 s	1956 Murray Rose *AUS*	4min 27.3 s
1932 Yasmuji Miyazaki *JAP*	58.2 s	1960 Murray Rose *AUS*	4min 18.3 s
1936 Ferenc Csik *HUN*	57.6 s	1964 Donald Schollander *US*	4min 12.2 s
1948 Walter Ris *US*	57.3 s	1968 Michael Burton *US*	4min 09.0 s
1952 C. Clarke Scholes *US*	57.4 s	1972 Bradford Cooper *AUS*	4min 00.27s
1956 Jon Henricks *AUS*	55.4 s	1976 Brian Goodell *US*	*3min 51.93s
1960 John Devitt *AUS*	55.2 s	1980	
1964 Donald Schollander *US*	53.4 s	†The distance was 402.3m in 1904.	
1968 Michael Wenden *AUS*	52.2 s		

1972 Mark Spitz *US* — 51.22s

1976 Jim Montgomery *US* — *49.99s

1980

†The distance was 91.44m in 1904.

SWIMMING 200 Meters Freestyle† — MEN

1896 Event not held

1900 Frederick Lane *AUS* — 2min 25.2 s

1904 Charles Daniels *US* — 2min 44.2 s

1908–1964 Event not held

1968 Michael Wenden *AUS* — 1min 55.2 s

1972 Mark Spitz *US* — 1min 52.78s

1976 Bruce Furniss *US* — *1min 50.29s

1980

†The distance was 201.17m in 1904.

SWIMMING 400 Meters Freestyle† — MEN

1896–1900 Event not held

1904 Charles Daniels *US* — 6min 16.2 s

1908 Henry Taylor *GB* — 5min 36.8 s

1912 George Hodgson *CAN* — 5min 24.4 s

1920 Norman Ross *US* — 5min 26.8 s

1924 Johnny Weissmuller *US* — 5min 04.2 s

1928 Alberto Zorilla *ARG* — 5min 01.6 s

1932 Clarence Crabbe *US* — 4min 48.4 s

SWIMMING 1500 Meters Freestyle† — MEN

Event not held until 1904

1904 Emil Rausch *GER* — 27min 18.2 s

1908 Henry Taylor *GB* — 22min 48.4 s

1912 George Hodgson *CAN* — 22min 00.0 s

1920 Norman Ross *US* — 22min 23.2 s

1924 Andrew Charlton *AUS* — 20min 06.6 s

1928 Arne Borg *SWE* — 19min 51.8 s

1932 Kusuo Kitamura *JAP* — 19min 12.4 s

1936 Noboru Terada *JAP* — 19min 13.7 s

1948 James McLane *US* — 19min 18.5 s

1952 Ford Konno *US* — 18min 30.0 s

1956 Murray Rose *AUS* — 17min 58.9 s

1960 Jon Konrads *AUS* — 17min 19.6 s

1964 Robert Windle *AUS* — 17min 01.7 s

1968 Michael Burton *US* — 16min 38.9 s

1972 Michael Burton *US* — 15min 52.58s

1976 Brian Goodell *US* — *15min 02.40s

1980

†The distance was 1200m in 1896, 1000m in 1900 and 1609.34m in 1904.

SWIMMING 100 Meters Breaststroke — MEN

Event not held until 1968

1968 Donald McKenzie *US* — 1min 07.7 s

193

1972	Nobutaka Taguchi	JAP	1min 04.94s
1976	John Hencken	US	*1min 03.11s
1980			

SWIMMING 200 Meters Breaststroke   MEN

Event not held until 1908

1908	Frederick Holman	GB	3min 09.2 s
1912	Walter Bathe	GER	3min 01.8 s
1920	Hakan Malmroth	SWE	3min 04.4 s
1924	Robert Skelton	US	2min 56.6 s
1928	Yoshiyuki Tsuruta	JAP	2min 48.8 s
1932	Yoshiyuki Tsuruta	JAP	2min 45.4 s
1936	Tetsuo Hamuro	JAP	2min 41.5 s
1948	Joseph Verdeur	US	2min 39.3 s
1952	John Davies	AUS	2min 34.4 s
1956	Masura Furukawa	JAP	2min 34.7 s
1960	William Mulliken	US	2min 37.4 s
1964	Ian O'Brien	AUS	2min 27.8 s
1968	Felipe Munox	MEX	2min 28.7 s
1972	John Hencken	US	2min 21.55s
1976	David Wilkie	GB	*2min 15.11s
1980			

Mark Spitz, winner of seven swimming gold medals in Munich.

SWIMMING 100 Meters Backstroke   MEN

Event not held until 1908

1908	Arno Bieberstein	GER	1min 24.6 s
1912	Harry Hebner	US	1min 21.2 s
1920	Warren Kealoha	US	1min 15.2 s
1924	Warren Kealoha	US	1min 13.2 s
1928	George Kojac	US	1min 08.2 s
1932	Masaji Kiyokawa	JAP	1min 08.6 s
1936	Adolf Kiefer	US	1min 05.9 s
1948	Allen Stack	US	1min 06.4 s
1952	Yoshio Oyakawa	JAP	1min 05.4 s
1956	David Thiele	AUS	1min 02.2 s
1960	David Thiele	AUS	1min 01.9 s
1964	Event not held		

1968	Roland Matthes	GDR	58.7 s
1972	Roland Matthes	GDR	56.58s
1976	John Naber	US	*55.49s
1980			

SWIMMING 200 Meters Backstroke   MEN

1896	Event not held		
1900	Ernest Hoppenberg	GER	2min 47.0 s
1904–1960	Event not held		
1964	Jed Graef	US	2min 10.3 s
1968	Roland Matthes	GDR	2min 09.6 s
1972	Roland Matthes	GDR	2min 02.82s
1976	John Naber	US	*1min 59.19s
1980			

SWIMMING 100 Meters Butterfly   MEN

Event not held until 1968

1968	Douglas Russell	US	55.9 s
1972	Mark Spitz	US	*54.27s
1976	Matt Vogel	US	54.35s
1980			

SWIMMING 200 Meters Butterfly   MEN

Event not held until 1956

1956	William Yorzyk	US	2min 19.3 s
1960	Michael Troy	US	2min 12.8 s
1964	Kevin Berry	AUS	2min 06.6 s
1968	Carl Robie	US	2min 08.7 s
1972	Mark Spitz	US	2min 00.70s
1976	Mike Bruner	US	*1min 59.23s
1980			

SWIMMING 200 Meters Individual Medley   MEN

Event not held until 1968

1968	Charles Hickcox	US	2min 12.0 s
1972	Gunnar Larsson	SWE	2min 07.17s
1976	Event not held		

1980

SWIMMING 400 Meters Individual Medley   MEN

Event not held until 1964		
1964	Richard Roth *US*	4min 45.4 s
1968	Charles Hickcox *US*	4min 48.4 s
1972	Gunnar Larsson *SWE*	4min 31.98s
1976	Rod Strachan *US*	*4min 23.68s
1980		

SWIMMING 4 × 100 Meters Freestyle Relay   MEN

Event not held until 1964		
1964	United States of America	3min 33.2 s
1968	United States of America	3min 31.7 s
1972	United States of America	3min 26.42s
1976	Event not held	
1980		

SWIMMING 4 × 200 Meters Freestyle Relay   MEN

Event not held until 1908		
1908	Great Britain	10min 55.6 s
1912	Australasia	10min 11.6 s
1920	United States of America	10min 04.4 s
1924	United States of America	9min 53.4 s
1928	United States of America	9min 36.2 s
1932	Japan	8min 58.4 s
1936	Japan	8min 51.5 s
1948	United States of America	8min 46.0 s
1952	United States of America	8min 31.1 s
1956	Australia	8min 23.6 s
1960	United States of America	8min 10.2 s
1964	United States of America	7min 52.1 s
1968	United States of America	7min 52.3 s
1972	United States of America	7min 35.78s
1976	United States of America	*7min 23.22s
1980		

SWIMMING 4 × 100 Meters Medley Relay   MEN

Event not held until 1960		
1960	United States of America	4min 05.4 s
1964	United States of America	3min 58.4 s
1968	United States of America	3min 54.9 s
1972	United States of America	3min 48.16s
1976	United States of America	*3min 42.22s
1980		

DIVING Highboard Diving   MEN

1896	Event not held	
1904	G. Sheldon *USS*	12.66pts
1908	Hjalmar Johansson *SWE*	83.75pts
1912	Erik Adlerz *SWE*	73.94pts
1920	Clarence Pinkston *US*	100.67pts
1924	Albert White *US*	97.46pts
1928	Peter Desjardins *US*	98.74pts
1932	Harold Smith *US*	124.80pts
1936	Marshall Wayne *US*	113.58pts
1948	Samuel Lee *US*	130.05pts
1952	Samuel Lee *US*	156.28pts
1956	Joaquin Capilla *MEX*	152.44pts
1960	Robert Webster *US*	165.56pts
1964	Robert Webster *US*	148.58pts
1968	Klaus Dibiasi *ITA*	164.18pts
1972	Klaus Dibiasi *ITA*	504.12pts
1976	Klaus Dibiasi *ITA*	600.51pts
1980		

DIVING Springboard Diving   MEN

Event not held until 1908		
1908	Albert Zurner *GER*	85.5 pts
1912	Paul Gunther *GER*	79.23pts
1920	Louis Kuehn *US*	675.40pts
1924	Albert White *US*	696.40pts
1928	Peter Desjardins *US*	185.04pts
1932	Michael Galitzen *US*	161.38pts

Phil Boggs, 1976 springboard diving champion.

1936 Richard Degener *US*		163.57pts
1948 Bruce Harlan *US*		163.64pts
1952 David Browning *US*		205.29pts
1956 Robert Clotworthy *US*		159.56pts
1960 Gary Tobian *US*		170.00pts
1964 Ken Sitzberger *US*		159.90pts
1968 Bernard Wrightson *US*		170.15pts
1972 Vladimir Vasin *USSR*		594.09pts
1976 Philip Boggs *US*		619.05pts
1980		

SWIMMING 100 Meters Freestyle	WOMEN
Event not held until 1912	
1912 Fanny Durack *AUS*	1min 22.2 s
1920 Ethelda Bleibtrey *US*	1min 13.6 s
1924 Ethel Lackie *US*	1min 12.4 s
1928 Albina Osipowich *US*	1min 11.0 s
1932 Helene Madison *US*	1min 06.8 s
1936 Hendrika Mastenbroek *NETH*	1min 05.9 s
1948 Greta Andersen *DEN*	1min 06.3 s
1952 Katalin Szoke *HUN*	1min 06.8 s
1956 Dawn Fraser *AUS*	1min 02.0 s
1960 Dawn Fraser *AUS*	1min 01.2 s
1964 Dawn Fraser *AUS*	59.5 s
1968 Jan Henne *US*	1min 00.0 s
1972 Sandra Neilson *US*	58.59s
1976 Kornelia Ender *GDR*	*55.65s
1980	

SWIMMING 200 Meters Freestyle	WOMEN
Event not held until 1968	
1968 Debbie Meyer *US*	2min 10.5 s
1972 Shane Gould *AUS*	2min 03.56s
1976 Kornelia Ender *GDR*	*1min 59.26s
1980	

SWIMMING 400 Meters Freestyle	WOMEN
Event not held until 1924	
1924 Martha Norelius *US*	6min 02.2 s
1928 Martha Norelius *US*	5min 42.8 s
1932 Helene Madison *US*	5min 28.5 s
1936 Hendrika Mastenbroek *NETH*	5min 26.4 s
1948 Ann Curtis *US*	5min 17.8 s
1952 Valeria Gyenge *HUN*	5min 12.1 s
1956 Lorraine Crapp *AUS*	4min 54.6 s
1960 Christine von Saltza *US*	4min 50.6 s
1964 Virginia Duenkel *US*	4min 43.3 s
1968 Debbie Meyer *US*	4min 31.8 s
1972 Shane Gould *AUS*	4min 19.04s
1976 Petra Thurmer *GDR*	*4min 08.89s
1980	

SWIMMING 800 Meters Freestyle	WOMEN
Event not held until 1968	
1968 Debbie Meyer *US*	9min 24.0 s
1972 Keen Rothhammer *US*	8min 53.68s
1976 Petra Thumer *GDR*	*8min 20.59s
1980	

SWIMMING 100 Meters Breaststroke	WOMEN
Event not held until 1968	
1968 Djurdjica Bjedov *YUG*	1min 15.8 s
1972 Catherine Carr *US*	1min 13.58s
1976 Hannelore Anke *GDR*	*1min 11.16s
1980	

SWIMMING 200 Meters Breaststroke	WOMEN
Event not held until 1924	
1924 Lucy Morton *GB*	3min 33.2 s
1928 Hilde Schrader *GER*	3min 12.6 s
1932 Clare Dennis *AUS*	3min 06.3 s
1936 Hideko Maehata *JAP*	3min 03.6 s
1948 Petronella van Vliet *NETH*	2min 57.2 s

1952 Eva Szekely	*HUN*	2min 51.7 s
1956 Ursula Happe	*GER*	2min 53.1 s
1960 Anita Lonsbrough	*GB*	2min 49.5 s
1964 Galina Prosumenshchikova	*USSR*	2min 46.4 s
1968 Sharon Wichman	*US*	2min 44.4 s
1972 Beverley Whitfield	*AUS*	2min 41.71s
1976 Marina Koshevaia	*USSR*	*2min 33.35s
1980		

SWIMMING 100 Meters Butterfly — WOMEN

Event not held until 1956

1956 Shelley Mann	*US*	1min 11.0 s
1960 Carolyn Schuler	*US*	1min 09.5 s
1964 Sharon Stouder	*US*	1min 04.7 s
1968 Lynette McClements	*AUS*	1min 05.5 s
1972 Mayumi Aoki	*JAP*	1min 03.34s
1976 Kornelia Ender	*GDR*	*1min 00.13s
1980		

SWIMMING 200 Meters Butterfly — WOMEN

Event not held until 1968

1968 Aagje Kok	*NETH*	2min 24.7 s
1972 Karen Moe	*US*	2min 15.57s
1976 Andrea Pollack	*GDR*	*2min 11.41s
1980		

SWIMMING 100 Meters Backstroke — WOMEN

Event not held until 1924

1924 Sybil Bauer	*US*	1min 23.2 s
1928 Marie Braun	*NETH*	1min 22.0 s
1932 Eleanor Holm	*US*	1min 19.4 s
1936 Dina Senff	*NETH*	1min 18.9 s
1948 Karen Harup	*DEN*	1min 14.4 s
1952 Joan Harrison	*SAF*	1min 14.3 s
1956 Judy Grinham	*GB*	1min 12.9 s
1960 Lynn Burke	*US*	1min 09.3 s
1964 Cathy Ferguson	*US*	1min 07.7 s

1968 Kaye Hall	*US*	1min 06.2 s
1972 Melissa Belote	*US*	1min 05.78s
1976 Ulrike Richter	*GDR*	*1min 01.83s
1980		

SWIMMING 200 Meters Backstroke — WOMEN

Event not held until 1968

1968 Lillian Watson	*US*	2min 24.8 s
1972 Melissa Belote	*US*	2min 19.19s
1976 Ulrike Richter	*GDR*	*2min 13.43s
1980		

SWIMMING 200 Meters Individual Medley — WOMEN

Event not held until 1968

1968 Claudia Kolb	*US*	2min 24.7 s
1972 Shane Gould	*AUS*	*2min 23.07s
1976 Event not held		
1980		

SWIMMING 400 Meters Individual Medley — WOMEN

Event not held until 1964

1964 Donna de Varona	*US*	5min 18.7 s
1968 Claudia Kolb	*US*	5min 08.5 s
1972 Gail Neall	*AUS*	5min 02.97s
1976 Ulrike Tauber	*GDR*	*4min 42.77s
1980		

SWIMMING 4 × 100 Meters Freestyle Relay — WOMEN

Event not held until 1912

1912 Great Britain	5min 52.8 s
1920 United States of America	5min 11.6 s
1924 United States of America	4min 58.8 s
1928 United States of America	4min 47.6 s
1932 United States of America	4min 38.0 s
1936 Netherlands	4min 36.0 s
1948 United States of America	4min 29.2 s
1952 Hungary	4min 24.4 s

The United States freestyle relay team, champions in 1960: (from top) Chris von Saltza, Joan Spillane, Carolyn Jones and Shirley Ann Jones.

1956 Australia	4min 17.1 s
1960 United States of America	4min 08.9 s
1964 United States of America	4min 03.8 s
1968 United States of America	4min 02.5 s
1972 United States of America	3min 55.19s
1976 United States of America	*3min 44.82s
1980	

SWIMMING 4 × 100 Meters Medley Relay	WOMEN
Event not held until 1960	
1960 United States of America	4min 41.1 s
1964 United States of America	4min 33.9 s
1968 United States of America	4min 28.3 s
1972 United States of America	4min 20.75s
1976 East Germany	*4min 07.95s
1980	

DIVING Highboard Diving	WOMEN
Event not held until 1912	
1912 Greta Johansson SWE	39.9 pts
1920 Stefani Fryland-Clausen DEN	34.6 pts
1924 Caroline Smith US	33.2 pts
1928 Elizabeth Pinkston US	31.6 pts
1932 Dorothy Poynton US	40.26pts
1936 Dorothy (Poynton) Hill US	33.93pts
1948 Victoria Draves US	68.87pts
1952 Patricia McCormick US	79.37pts
1956 Patricia McCormick US	84.85pts
1960 Ingrid Kramer GER	91.28pts
1964 Lesley Bush US	99.80pts
1968 Milena Duchkova CZECH	109.59pts
1972 Ulrika Knape SWE	390.00pts
1976 Elena Vaytsekhovskaia USSR	406.59pts
1980	

DIVING Springboard Diving	WOMEN
Event not held until 1920	

1920 Aileen Riggin US	539.9 pts
1924 Elizabeth Becker US	474.5 pts
1928 Helen Meany US	78.62pts
1932 Georgia Coleman US	87.52pts
1936 Marjorie Gestring US	89.27pts
1948 Victoria Draves US	108.74pts
1952 Patricia McCormick US	147.30pts
1956 Patricia McCormick US	142.36pts
1960 Ingrid Kramer GER	155.81pts
1964 Ingrid Engel (Kramer) GER	145.00pts
1968 Sue Gossick US	150.77pts
1972 Micki King US	450.03pts
1976 Jennifer Chandler US	506.19pts
1980	

VOLLEYBALL	MEN
Event not held until 1964	
1964 USSR	
1968 USSR	
1972 Japan	
1976 Poland	
1980	

VOLLEYBALL	WOMEN
Event not held until 1964	
1964 Japan	
1968 USSR	
1972 USSR	
1976 Japan	
1980	

WATER POLO	MEN
1896 Event not held	
1900 Great Britain	
1904 United States of America	
1908 Great Britain	
1912 Great Britain	

1920 Great Britain	
1924 France	
1928 Germany	
1932 Hungary	
1936 Hungary	
1948 Italy	
1952 Hungary	
1956 Hungary	
1960 Italy	
1964 Hungary	
1968 Yugoslavia	
1972 USSR	
1976 Hungary	
1980	

WEIGHTLIFTING Flyweight — MEN

Event not held until 1972

1972 Zygmunt Smalcerz *POL*	337.5kg 744lb
1976 Alexandr Voronin *USSR*	242.5kg 535lb
1980	

WEIGHTLIFTING Bantamweight

Event not held until 1948

1948 Joseph de Pietro *US*	307.5kg 678lb
1952 Ivan Udodov *USSR*	315.0kg 694$\frac{1}{2}$lb
1956 Charles Vinci *US*	342.5kg 754$\frac{1}{2}$lb
1960 Charles Vinci *US*	345.0kg 760$\frac{1}{2}$lb
1964 Alexey Vakhonin *USSR*	357.5kg 787$\frac{3}{4}$lb
1968 Mohammad Nasiri Seresht *IRAN*	367.5kg 810 lb
1972 Imre Foeldi *HUN*	377.5kg 832 lb
1976 Norai Nurikyan *BUL*	262.5kg 579 lb
1980	

WEIGHTLIFTING Featherweight — MEN

Event not held until 1920

1920 F. de Haes *BEL*	220.0kg 485 lb
1924 Pierino Gabetti *ITA*	402.5kg 887$\frac{1}{4}$lb
1928 Franz Andrysek *AUST*	287.5kg 633$\frac{3}{4}$lb
1932 Raymond Suvigny *FR*	287.5kg 633$\frac{3}{4}$lb
1936 Anthony Terlazzo *US*	312.5kg 688$\frac{3}{4}$lb
1948 Mahmoud Fayad *EGY*	332.5kg 733 lb
1952 Rafael Chimishkyan *USSR*	337.5kg 744 lb
1956 Issac Berger *US*	352.5kg 777 lb
1960 Evgeniy Minayev *USSR*	372.5kg 821 lb
1964 Yoshinobu Miyake *JAP*	397.5kg 876$\frac{1}{4}$lb
1968 Yoshinobu Miyake *JAP*	392.5kg 865 lb
1972 Norai Nurikyan *BUL*	402.5kg 887$\frac{1}{4}$lb
1976 Nikolai Koleshikov *USSR*	285.0kg 628 lb
1980	

WEIGHTLIFTING Lightweight — MEN

Event not held until 1920

1920 Alfred Neuland *EST*	257.5kg 567$\frac{1}{4}$lb
1924 Edmond Decottignies *FR*	440.0kg 970 lb
1928 Kurt Helbig *GER* and Hans Hass *AUST*	332.5kg 711 lb
1932 Rene Duverger *FR*	325.0kg 716$\frac{1}{2}$lb
1936 Mohammed Mesbah *EGY* and Robert Fein *AUST*	342.5kg 755 lb
1948 Ibrahim Shams *EGY*	360.0kg 793$\frac{1}{2}$lb
1952 Thomas Kono *US*	362.5kg 799 lb
1956 Igor Rybak *USSR*	380.0kg 837$\frac{1}{2}$lb
1960 Viktor Bushuyev *USSR*	397.5kg 876 lb
1964 Waldemar Baszanowski *POL*	432.5kg 953$\frac{1}{4}$lb
1968 Waldemar Baszanowski *POL*	437.5kg 963$\frac{1}{2}$lb
1972 Mukharbi Kirzhinov *USSR*	460.0kg 1014lb
1976 Zbigniew Kaczmarek *POL*	307.5kg 678 lb
1980	

WEIGHTLIFTING Middleweight — MEN

Event not held until 1920

1920 Henri Gance *FR*	245.0kg 540 lb
1924 Carlo Galimberti *ITA*	492.5kg 1085$\frac{3}{4}$lb
1928 Roger Francois *FR*	335.0kg 738$\frac{1}{2}$lb
1932 Rudolf Ismayr *GER*	345.0kg 760$\frac{1}{2}$lb
1936 Khadr El Touni *EGY*	387.5kg 854$\frac{1}{4}$lb

Leonid Zhabotinsky, 1964 and 1968 super-heavyweight weightlifting champion.

1948 Frank Spellman *US*	390.0kg 860 lb
1952 Peter George *US*	400.0kg 882 lb
1956 Fyeodor Bogdanovski *USSR*	420.0kg 925¾lb
1960 Aleksandr Kurynov *USSR*	437.5kg 964¼lb
1964 Hans Zdrazila *CZECH*	445.0kg 981 lb
1968 Viktor Kurentsov *USSR*	475.0kg 1047 lb
1972 Jordan Mikov *BUL*	485.0kg 1069 lb
1976 Jordan Mikov *BUL*	335.0kg 738½lb
1980	

WEIGHTLIFTING Light-Heavyweight	MEN
Event not held until 1920	
1920 Ernest Cadine *FR*	290.0kg 131½lb
1924 Charles Rigoulot *FR*	502.5kg 1107¾lb
1928 Said Nosseir *EGY*	355.0kg 782½lb
1932 Louis Hostin *FR*	365.0kg 804½lb
1936 Louis Hostin *FR*	372.5kg 821 lb
1948 Stanley Stanczyk *US*	417.5kg 920¼lb
1952 Trofim Lomakin *USSR*	417.5kg 920½lb
1956 Thomas Kono *US*	447.5kg 986½lb
1960 Ireneusz Palinski *POL*	442.5kg 975½lb
1964 Rudolf Plyukeider *USSR*	475.0kg 1047 lb
1968 Boris Selitsky *USSR*	485.0kg 1069 lb
1972 Leif Jenssen *NOR*	507.5kg 1118¾lb
1976 Valeri Shary *USSR*	365.0kg 805 lb
1980	

WEIGHTLIFTING Middle-Heavyweight	MEN
Event not held until 1952	
1952 Norbert Schemansky *US*	445.0kg 981 lb
1956 Arkhadiy Vorobyev *USSR*	462.5kg 1019¼lb
1960 Arkhadiy Vorobyev *USSR*	472.5kg 1041¼lb
1964 Vladimir Golovanov *USSR*	487.5kg 1074 lb
1968 Kaarlo Kangasniemi *FIN*	517.5kg 1140½lb
1972 Andon Nikolov *BUL*	525.0kg 1157¼lb
1976 David Rigert *USSR*	382.5kg 843 lb
1980	

WEIGHTLIFTING Heavyweight	MEN
See Super Heavyweight for results before 1972	
1972 Yan Talts *USSR*	580.0kg 1278½lb
1976 Valentin Khristov *BUL*	400.0kg 882 lb
1980	

WEIGHTLIFTING Super-Heavyweight	MEN
Until 1972 this class was called Heavyweight	
1896 Viggo Jensen *DEN*	111.5kg 245¾lb
1900 Event not held	
1904 Perikles Kakousis *GR*	111.58kg 246 lb
1908–1912 Event not held	
1920 Filipo Bottino *ITA*	270.0kg 595 lb
1924 Giuseppe Tonani *ITA*	517.5kg 1104¾lb
1928 Josef Strassberger *GER*	372.5kg 821 lb
1932 Jaroslav Skobla *CZECH*	380.0kg 837¾lb
1936 Jozef Manger *AUST*	410.0kg 902¾lb
1948 John Davis *US*	452.5kg 997½lb
1952 John Davis *US*	460.0kg 1014 lb
1956 Paul Anderson *US*	500.0kg 1102 lb
1960 Yuri Vlasov *USSR*	537.5kg 1184½lb
1964 Leonid Zhabotinsky *USSR*	572.5kg 1262 lb
1968 Leonid Zhabotinsky *USSR*	572.5kg 1261¾lb
1972 Vasili Alexeev *USSR*	640.0kg 1410¾lb
1976 Vasili Alexeev *YSSR*	440.0kg 970 lb
1980	

WRESTLING Freestyle – Light-Flyweight	MEN
Event not held until 1972	
1972 Roman Dmitriev *USSR*	
1976 Khassan Issaev *BUL*	
1980	

WRESTLING Freestyle – Flyweight	MEN
Event not held until 1904	
1904 Robert Curry *US*	
1908–1936 Event not held	

1948 Lennart Vitala *FIN*	1932 Hermanni Pihlajamaki *FIN*
1952 Hasan Gemici *TUR*	1936 Kustaa Pihlajamaki *FIN*
1956 Mirian Tsalkalamanidze *USSR*	1948 Gazanfer Bilge *TUR*
1960 Ahmet Bilek *TUR*	1952 Bayram Sit *TUR*
1964 Yoshikatsu Yoshida *JAP*	1956 Shoze Sasahara *JAP*
1968 Shigeo Nakata *JAP*	1960 Mustafa Dagistanli *TUR*
1972 Kiyomi Kato *JAP*	1964 Osamu Watanabe *JAP*
1976 Yuji Takada *JAP*	1968 Masaaki Kaneko *JAP*
1980	1972 Zagalav Abdulbekov *USSR*
	1976 Jung-Mo Yang *PKR*
	1980

WRESTLING Freestyle – Bantamweight   MEN

Event not held until 1904

1904 I. Niflot *US*
1908 George Mehnert *US*
1912–1920 Event not held
1924 Kustaa Pihlajamaki *FIN*
1928 Kalle Makinen *FIN*
1932 Robert Pearce *US*
1936 Odon Zombori *HUN*
1948 Nasuk Akkar *TUR*
1952 Shohaci Ishii *JAP*
1956 Mustapha Dagistanli *TUR*
1960 Terence McCann *US*
1964 Yojiro Uetake *JAP*
1968 Yojiro Uetake *JAP*
1972 Hideaki Yanagida *JAP*
1976 Vladimir Umin *USSR*
1980

WRESTLING Lightweight   MEN

Event not held until 1904

1904 O. Roehm *US*
1908 G. de Relwyskow *GB*
1912 Event not held
1920 Kalle Anttila *FIN*
1924 Russell Vis *US*
1928 Osvald Kapp *EST*
1932 Charles Pacome *FR*
1936 Karoly Karpati *HUN*
1948 Selal Atik *TUR*
1952 Olle Anderberg *SWE*
1956 Emamali Habibi *IRAN*
1960 Shelby Wilson *US*
1964 Enio Valchev *BUL*
1968 Abdollah Mohaved *IRAN*
1972 Dan Gable *US*
1976 Pavel Pinigin *USSR*
1980

WRESTLING Freestyle – Featherweight   MEN

Event not held until 1904

1904 B. Bradshaw *US*
1908 George Dole *US*
1912 Event not held
1920 Charles Ackerley *US*
1924 Robin Reed *US*
1928 Allie Morrison *US*

WRESTLING Freestyle – Welterweight   MEN

Event not held until 1904

1904 Charles Erickson *US*
1908–1920 Event not held
1924 Hermann Gehri *SWI*

1928 Arve Haavisto *FIN*

1932 Jack van Bebber *US*

1936 Frank Lewis *US*

1948 Yasar Dogu *TUR*

1952 William Smith *US*

1956 Mitsuo Ikeda *JAP*

1960 Douglas Blubaugh *US*

1964 Ismail Ogan *TUR*

1968 Mahmut Atalay *TUR*

1972 Wayne Wells *US*

1976 Jiichiro Date *JAP*

1980

WRESTLING Freestyle – Middleweight MEN

Event not held until 1908

1908 Stanley Bacon *GB*

1912 Event not held

1920 Eino Leino *FIN*

1924 Fritz Haggmann *SWI*

1928 Ernst Kyburz *SWI*

1932 Ivar Johansson *SWE*

1936 Emile Poilve *FR*

1948 Glen Brand *US*

1952 David Tsimakuridze *USSR*

1956 Nikola Nikolov *BUL*

1960 Hassan Gungor *TUR*

1964 Prodan Gardshev *BUL*

1968 Boris Gurevitch *USSR*

1972 Levan Tediashvili *USSR*

1976 John Peterson *US*

1980

WRESTLING Freestyle – Light-Heavyweight MEN

Event not held until 1920

1920 Anders Larsson *SWE*

1924 John Spellman *US*

1928 Thure Sjostedt *SWE*

1932 Peter Mehringer *US*

1936 Knut Fridell *SWE*

1948 Henry Wittenberg *US*

1952 Wiking Palm *SWE*

1956 Gholamreza Tahkti *IRAN*

1960 Ismet Atli *TUR*

1964 Alexandr Medved *USSR*

1968 Ahmet Ayik *TUR*

1972 Ben Peterson *US*

1976 Levan Tediashvili *USSR*

1980

WRESTLING Freestyle – Heavyweight MEN

1896 Karl Schumann *GER*

1900 Event not held

1904 B. Hansen *US*

1908 G. C. O'Kelly *GB*

1912 Event not held

1920 Robert Rothe *SWI*

1924 Harry Steele *US*

1928 Johan Richtoff *SWE*

1932 Johan Richtoff *SWE*

1936 Kristjan Palusalu *EST*

1948 Gyula Bobis *HUN*

1952 Arsen Makokishvili *USSR*

1956 Hamit Kaplan *TUR*

1960 Wilfried Dietrich *GER*

1964 Alexandr Wanitsky *USSR*

1968 Alexandr Medved *USSR*

1972 Ivan Yarygin *USSR*

1976 Ivan Yarygin *USSR*

1980

WRESTLING Freestyle – Super-Heavyweight MEN

Event not held until 1972

1972 Alexandr Medved *USSR*

1976 Soslan Andiev *USSR*

1980

WRESTLING Greco-Roman – Light-Flyweight   MEN

Event not held until 1972

1972 Gheorghe Berceanu *ROM*

1976 Alexey Schumakov *USSR*

1980

WRESTLING Greco-Roman – Flyweight   MEN

Event not held until 1948

1948 Pietro Lombardi *ITA*

1952 Boris Gurevich *USSR*

1956 Nikolay Solovyev *USSR*

1960 Dumitru Pirvulescu *ROM*

1964 Tsutomu Hanahara *JAP*

1968 Petar Kirov *BUL*

1972 Petar Kirov *BUL*

1976 Vitaly Konstantinov *USSR*

1980

WRESTLING Greco-Roman – Bantamweight   MEN

Event not held until 1924

1924 Edvard Putsep *EST*

1928 Kurt Leucht *GER*

1932 Jakob Brendel *GER*

1936 Marton Lorinc *HUN*

1948 Kurt Petterssen *SWE*

1952 Imre Hodes *HUN*

1956 Konstantin Vyrupayev *USSR*

1960 Olyeg Karavayev *USSR*

1964 Masamitsu Ichiguchi *JAP*

1968 Janos Varga *HUN*

1972 Rustem Kazakov *USSR*

1976 Petti Ukkola *FIN*

1980

WRESTLING Greco-Roman – Featherweight   MEN

Event not held until 1912

1912 Kalle Koskelo *FIN*

1920 Oskari Friman *FIN*

1924 Kalle Anttila *FIN*

1928 Voldemar Vali *EST*

1932 Giovanni Gozzi *ITA*

1936 Yasar Erkan *TUR*

1948 Mohammed Oktav *TUR*

1952 Yakov Punkin *USSR*

1956 Rauno Makinen *FIN*

1960 Muzahir Sille *TUR*

1964 Imre Polyak *HUN*

1968 Roman Rurua *USSR*

1972 Gheorghi Markov *BUL*

1976 Kazikierz Lipien *POL*

1980

WRESTLING Greco-Roman – Lightweight   MEN

Event not held until 1908

1908 Enrico Porro *ITA*

1912 Eemil Vare *FIN*

1920 Eemil Vare *FIN*

1924 Oskari Friman *FIN*

1928 Lajos Keresztes *HUN*

1932 Erik Malmberg *SWE*

1936 Lauri Koskela *FIN*

1948 Karl Freij *SWE*

1952 Shazam Safin *USSR*

1956 Kyosti Lehtonen *FIN*

1960 Avtandil Koridze *USSR*

1964 Kazim Ayvaz *TUR*

1968 Muneji Munemura *JAP*

1972 Shamil Khisamutdinov *USSR*

1976 Suren Nalbandyan *USSR*

1980

WRESTLING Greco-Roman – Welterweight   MEN

	Event not held until 1932	
1932	Ivar Johansson	SWE
1936	Rudolf Svedberg	SWE
1948	Gosta Andersson	SWE
1952	Miklos Szilvasi	HUN
1956	Mithat Bayrak	TUR
1960	Mithat Bayrak	TUR
1964	Anatoly Koleslov	USSR
1968	Rudolf Vesper	GDR
1972	Vitezlav Macha	CZECH
1976	Anatoli Bykov	USSR
1980		

WRESTLING Greco-Roman – Middleweight   MEN

	Event not held until 1908	
1908	Fritjof Martensson	SWE
1912	Claes Johansson	SWE
1920	Carl Westergren	SWE
1924	Edvard Westerlund	FIN
1928	Vaino Kokkinen	FIN
1932	Vaino Kokkinen	FIN
1936	Ivar Johansson	SWE
1948	Axel Gronberg	SWE
1952	Axel Gronberg	SWE
1956	Guivi Kartozia	USSR
1960	Dimitar Dobrev	BUL
1964	Branislav Simic	YUG
1968	Lothar Metz	GDR
1972	Csaba Hegedus	HUN
1976	Momir Petkovic	YUG
1980		

Alexandr Kolchinski (right), 1976 super-heavyweight Greco-Roman wrestling champion.

WRESTLING Greco-Roman – Light-Heavyweight   MEN

	Event not held until 1908	
1908	Verner Weckman	FIN
1912	gold medal not awarded	

1920	Claes Johansson	SWE
1924	Carl Westergren	SWE
1928	Ibrahim Moustafa	EGY
1932	Rudolf Svensson	SWE
1936	Axel Cadier	SWE
1948	Karl Nilsson	SWE
1952	Kaelpo Grondahl	FIN
1956	Valentin Nikolayev	USSR
1960	Terfik Kis	TUR
1964	Boyan Alexandrov	BUL
1968	Boyan Radev	BUL
1972	Valeri Rezantsev	USSR
1976	Valeri Rezantsev	USSR
1980		

WRESTLING Greco-Roman – Heavyweight

	Event not held until 1908	
1908	Richard Weisz	HUN
1912	Yrjo Saarela	FIN
1920	Adolf Lindfors	FIN
1924	Henry Deglane	FR
1928	Rudolf Svensson	SWE
1932	Carl Westergren	SWE
1936	Kristjan Palusalu	EST
1948	Ahmed Kirecci	TUR
1952	Johannes Kotkas	USSR
1956	Anatoli Parfenyov	USSR
1960	Ivan Bogdan	USSR
1964	Istvan Kozma	HUN
1968	Istvan Kozma	HUN
1972	Nikolai Martinescu	ROM
1976	Nikolai Bolboshin	USSR
1980		

WRESTLING Greco-Roman – Super-Heavyweight   MEN

	Event not held until 1972	
1972	Antoly Roschin	USSR

1976	Alexandr Kolchinski *USSR*	
1980		

YACHTING Soling

	Event not held until 1972	
1972	United States of America	8.7 pts
1976	Denmark	46.70pts
1980		

YACHTING Tempest

	Event not held until 1972	
1972	USSR	28.1 pts
1976	Sweden	14.00pts
1980		

YACHTING Dragon

	Event not held until 1948	
1948	Norway	4746 pts
1952	Norway	6130 pts
1956	Sweden	5723 pts
1960	Greece	6733 pts
1964	Denmark	5854 pts
1968	United States of America	6.0pts
1972	Australia	13.7pts
1976	Event not held	
1980		

YACHTING Star

	Event not held until 1932	
1932	United States of America	46 pts
1936	Germany	80 pts
1948	United States of America	5828 pts
1952	Italy	7635 pts
1956	United States of America	5876 pts
1960	USSR	7619 pts
1964	Bahamas	5664 pts
1968	United States of America	14.4pts

1972	Australia	28.1pts
1976	Event not held	
1980		

YACHTING Flying Dutchman

	Event not held until 1960	
1960	Norway	6774 pts
1965	New Zealand	6255 pts
1968	Great Britain	3 pts
1972	Great Britain	22.7pts
1976	West Germany	34.7pts
1980		

YACHTING Finn

	Event not held until 1956	
1956	Paul Elvstrom *DEN*	7509 pts
1960	Paul Elvstrom *DEN*	8171 pts
1964	Willi Kuhweide *GER*	7638 pts
1968	Valentin Mankin *USSR*	11.7pts
1972	Serge Maury *FR*	58.0pts
1976	Jochen Schumann *GDR*	35.4pts
1980		

YACHTING Tornado

	Event not held until 1976	
1976	Great Britain	18.00pts
1980		

YACHTING 470

	Event not held until 1976	
1976	West Germany	42.40pts
1980		

Pictures are supplied by
kind permission of the
following:
All-Sport: 66; Associated
Press Ltd: 102, 104, 109,
110, 112 (both), 113, 114,
120 (below), 137 (both),
140, 141 (both), 144
(both), 148 (above), 151,
174; Central Press Photos
Ltd: 118 (above), 122, 127
(below), 131; Colorsport:
2–3, 6, 8 (above and below
left), 9 (above left), *17,
18–19* (both), *20, 21* (both),
23, 25 (all three), *26–7*
(both), *28, 29* (both), *30,
31, 32* (both), *33* (right),
41 (both), 148 (below),
161 (below), 162, 163
(above), 194; Press
Association Ltd: 64, 69
(above), 71, 73, 87, 95
(right); Radio Times
Hulton Picture Library:
42–3, 44, 46, 47, 53, 55, 56
(both), 57, 58 (both), 59,
60, 61, 62, 75, 83, 94, 96
(both), 97 (above left), 98
(above right), 172;
Syndication International:
22, 24, 95 (above), 152
(above), 155 (above), 156
(below left); Weidenfeld
archive: 85. All other
illustrations are from
Popperfoto Limited.

INDEX